THE NEW LEVIATHAN

ALSO BY DAVID HOROWITZ

ONE-PARTY CLASSROOM
*How Radical Professors
at America's Top Colleges
Indoctrinate Students and
Undermine Our Democracy*
(with Jacob Laksin)

PARTY OF DEFEAT
*How Democrats and Radicals
Undermined America's War on
Terror Before and After 9/11*
(with Ben Johnson)

INDOCTRINATION U
*The Left's War Against
Academic Freedom*

THE SHADOW PARTY
*How George Soros, Hillary
Clinton, and Sixties Radicals
Seized Control of the
Democratic Party*

THE PROFESSORS
*The 101 Most Dangerous
Academics in America*

THE END OF TIME

UNHOLY ALLIANCE
*Radical Islam and the
American Left*

LEFT ILLUSIONS
An Intellectual Odyssey

UNCIVIL WARS
*The Controversy Over
Reparations for Slavery*

HOW TO BEAT THE
DEMOCRATS AND
OTHER SUBVERSIVE
IDEAS

THE ART OF POLITICAL
WAR AND OTHER
RADICAL PURSUITS

THE POLITICS OF
BAD FAITH
*The Radical Assault on
America's Future*

HATING WHITEY AND
OTHER PROGRESSIVE
CAUSES

RADICAL SON
A Generational Odyssey

DESTRUCTIVE
GENERATION
*Second Thoughts About
the '60s*
(with Peter Collier)

THE NEW LEVIATHAN

HOW THE LEFT-WING MONEY MACHINE
SHAPES AMERICAN POLITICS
AND THREATENS AMERICA'S FUTURE

David Horowitz

AND

Jacob Laksin

CROWN
FORUM
NEW YORK

Library of Congress Cataloging-in-Publication Data
Horowitz, David, 1939–
    The new Leviathan : how the left-wing money machine shapes American
politics and threatens America's future / by David Horowitz and Jacob Laksin.
—1st ed.
        p. cm.
    1. Pressure groups—United States—History. 2. Pressure groups—United
States—Finance. 3. Campaign funds—United States—History. I. Laksin, Jacob.
II. Title.
    JK1118.H67 2012
    322.4'30973—dc23   2011049536

ISBN 978-0-307-71645-3
eISBN 978-0-307-71647-7

Printed in the United States of America

Jacket design by Nupoor Gordon

10 9 8 7 6 5 4 3 2

First Edition

This book is dedicated with love and affection to
my parents, Mikhail and Olga, for their friendship and
their steadfast and generous support.

—Jacob Laksin

And to mine, Phil and Blanche Horowitz, for their
efforts to set me on the right path.

—David Horowitz

CONTENTS

THE NEW LEVIATHAN

1.

THE NEW LEVIATHAN

This book is about a political force of unprecedented magnitude in American life. The "New Leviathan" is a network of billion-dollar tax-exempt foundations and advocacy think tanks that work in concert with government unions and grassroots radical groups to make up the organizational core of the political left. The New Leviathan is not only a political force in the narrow sense of directly influencing electoral outcomes through the support of candidates and parties. Because its power derives from institutions whose mandates are educational and philanthropic, its influence extends into every aspect of the nation's life. This influence is exerted through a tax-exempt universe of policy think tanks, grassroots campaign organizations, and public-interest groups, created and supported by its donations. The components of the New Leviathan operate within the framework of a "progressive" ideology that promotes an ever-expanding state, along with policies that undermine America's sovereignty and weaken her defenses. The New Leviathan's ever-growing power has already tipped the scales of the national political debate and, as we will show in this volume, transformed its very nature.

Conventional wisdom would dismiss the very possibility of such dominance in the political arena by a money machine of the Left. In the conventional view, it is Republicans and the political right with their corporate sponsors and big-money donors who make up the "party of the rich," while progressives speak for the powerless and the poor. In this perspective, conservatives are agents of an economic "ruling class," organized to defend its social privileges. In the exercise of financial power in politics, conservatives are assumed to enjoy an overweening advantage, utilizing unrivaled resources to orchestrate "vast right-wing conspiracies," which are designed to thwart progressive efforts in behalf of equality and "social justice."

While casting conservatives as mouthpieces for the rich, the same perspective portrays Democrats as the party of "working Americans and their families," providing a voice for the voiceless and a shield for the disadvantaged. Accepting the Democratic Party's presidential nomination in 2000, Al Gore summed up this outlook in a slogan: "They're for the powerful; we're for the people!"[1]

The political melodrama in which Democrats and progressives posture as paladins of enlightenment has a long and unpretty history. It was forged during the moderately populist and immoderately corrupt presidency of Andrew Jackson, spokesman for the "common man," who entered the White House as a self-proposed champion of the people battling the "moneyed elite." Both the image and the aura were transparent manipulations to seduce a willing public. Despite humble beginnings, Jackson was a man of means who basked in the privileges of an aristocratic life. The same comfortable circumstances did not discourage him from plundering the property of his political rivals, or justifying his avarice as a "sharing" of the wealth, or from exploiting the morality play he had created to expand his personal power. Nor did Jackson's "everyman" enthusiasms keep him from owning and selling slaves throughout his life or from presiding over the forced removal of American Indian tribes from their native lands on the "Trail of Tears."

Politics being a market in which fictions are currency, the Jacksonian myth established the enduring template of the two-party system. As a Republican newspaper in Tennessee complained, "The rank and file of the democratic party honestly believes . . . the democratic party is the poor man's party, that the republican party is the party of boodle and corruption and that they obtain and maintain their supremacy in all the states by the undue use of money."[2]

Franklin Roosevelt entered the White House a hundred years after Jackson, and despite being a born aristocrat, a "son of privilege who never depended on a pay check," he was also able to frame his presidential tenure as "the Era of the Common Man."[3] In the 1970s, Jimmy Carter took up the folksy mantle, touting himself as a simple peanut farmer from Georgia and promising to be the "people's president." Yet Carter was the son of a wealthy plantation owner, inherited his own business, and spurned a lucrative job in the private sector in order to sow the seeds of a political career with a tale of humble beginnings.[4] Carter's claim to be a progressive was particularly dubious since he won his 1970 gubernatorial campaign by courting the support of southern segregationists and projecting what one biographer has called a "not-so-subtle racism" away from public view.[5]

In the election of 2000, Al Gore, another scion of an elite segregationist family, took up the populist theme with the campaign slogan, "The People vs. the Powerful." As part of a White House that set records fund-raising from "special interests," Gore's claim was hardly credible, although a politically sympathetic media helped to make it seem so. After losing the presidency, Gore launched a new career posing himself as the people's champion against global polluters, even winning an Academy Award and a Nobel Prize from fellow progressives for these efforts while trampling on the environment and making himself a wealthy man in the process. Today, Gore travels the world on private carbon-gorging jets and spends an estimated $30,000 a year to heat just one of his luxury mansions, which include a recently purchased $9 million villa in Montecito, California, with six bedrooms, nine bathrooms, a large pool house, and six fireplaces.[6] His stake in a "green" energy company that profits from lucrative environmentally correct government contracts has positioned him to become the world's first "carbon billionaire."[7]

Populist hypocrisy was on display again and in a particularly sordid fashion during the next national election when Democratic vice-presidential candidate John Edwards cast America as a benighted home of the oppressed. According to Edwards, there were "two Americas"—on the one hand, the rich Republican America with its boot heel on the necks of the hapless and helpless; on the other, the Democrat America of the poor and voiceless (if not for noble crusaders like Edwards). Back on earth this selfless servant of the workingman had accumulated a personal net worth of $188 million, while his running mate, John Kerry, had married into two fortunes three times the size of Edwards's own, making him the richest lawmaker in the country.[8] Kerry's opulence was not untypical of the balance between the parties: among the twelve richest lawmakers, Democrats outnumber Republicans three to one.[9]

The ability to see itself as a perennial underdog in a class war it regards as integral to capitalism is an abiding strength of the political left. But the image is unsupported by the facts. Far from being the party of the people, Democrats and their progressive core represent America's social and cultural elites and constitute the richest, the most organized, and most economically powerful political force in American history. As Christopher Caldwell observed in a *New York Times* essay, "the Democratic Party is the party to which elites *belong*. It is the party of Harvard (and most of the Ivy League), of Microsoft and Apple (and most of Silicon Valley), of Hollywood and Manhattan (and most of the media) and, although there is some evidence that numbers are evening out in this election cycle, of Goldman Sachs (and most of the investment banking profession). . . . The Democrats have the support of more, and more active, billionaires [than the Republicans]. Of the twenty richest ZIP codes in America, according to the Center for Responsive Politics, 19 gave the bulk of their money to the Democrats in the last election, in most cases the vast bulk—86 percent in 10024 on the Upper West Side."[10]

Wall Street—the very symbol of capitalist excess and wealth—was a key player in Barack Obama's successful presidential election run in 2008. Counterintuitive at first, this fact becomes immediately intelligible once one realizes that big government works for Wall Street bankers who float all the bonds that underwrite government spending programs and take their percentage on every dollar of big government debt. Award-winning business reporter Charles Gasparino observes: ". . . the assumption made by most Americans, . . . [is] that because investment bankers are rich they must favor Republicans because, by definition, Republicans favor lower taxes on the wealthy and on big business. And while, of course, no one *likes* high taxes, what's more important than the tax rate is how much income you make in the first place: paying 30 percent of your money in taxes if you make a million dollars is better than paying a 20 percent tax rate on an income of only half a million."[11]

In light of these facts it is hardly surprising that the top financial backers of Barack Obama's presidential campaign included Wall Street leaders Jamie Dimon (CEO, JPMorgan Chase), Lloyd Blankfein (CEO, Goldman Sachs), Dick Fuld (CEO, Lehman Brothers), Warren Spector (CEO, Bear Stearns), Larry Fink (CEO, Black-Rock—the world's largest money management firm), Greg Fleming (number two at Merrill Lynch), and Mark Gallogly (number two at the private equity firm Blackstone). Collectively, these Wall Street titans raised more than $100 million for the Obama campaign.[12]

It is a reflection on human vanity that the Left actually believes it is the people's David to the Right's Goliath. A recent display of this misplaced self-esteem was the now-famous PowerPoint presentation that former White House official Rob Stein screened for George Soros, Clinton political operatives, and Democratic funders as the 2004 election approached. The PowerPoint was called "The Conservative Message Machine's Money Matrix," and Stein's goal was to persuade Democratic funders that they had to match the unfairly oversized conservative war chest in order to help the little people out.

Stein's presentation began with the false premise that conservatives enjoyed an overwhelming advantage in the resources they were able to funnel into American politics. In Stein's view, this advantage enabled conservatives not only to influence politics but to move the boundaries of the entire national debate to the right. Using charts and graphs, Stein purported to show that with just $300 million from two hundred "anchor donors" the conservative "message machine" was nonetheless able to fundamentally reshape the country's politics.[13] "This is perhaps the most potent, independent, institutionalized apparatus ever assembled in a democracy to promote one belief system," Stein told *New York Times* journalist Matt Bai, who didn't bother to check.[14]

In fact, Stein's figure was a modest sum in an age when one gubernatorial campaign can cost $170 million. But his portrait of an overweening and unanswered conservative message machine proved decisive in recruiting the left-wing billionaires in the room to underwrite a network of newly minted progressive organizations. The most prominent example was the Democracy Alliance, which was established in 2005 by Soros and a coalition of eighty leftist donors, each of whom contributed $1 million toward its creation.

The immediate goal of the Democracy Alliance was to lead the resurgence of the Left in the 2006 midterm elections. Almost half the groups the alliance funded hadn't existed only a few years before.[15] In its inaugural year of operations, the Democracy Alliance distributed

$50 million to assorted left-wing, tax-exempt think tanks and quasi political associations, a sum that increased to $80 million the following year. The alliance quickly became the most visible presence of the Left's immense and unappreciated financial power in shaping the political landscape.[16]

Long before Stein's presentation, the claim that the Right was massively funded compared to the Left was a standard piece of progressive folklore, supported by a bookshelf of left-wing tracts and pseudoscientific studies. In *Moving a Public Policy Agenda: The Strategic Philanthropy of Conservative Foundations* (1997), author Sally Covington charged that the conservative movement had relied on "a substantial and interconnected institutional apparatus" unrivaled by the Left in order to win the war of ideas and push the country rightward. Like Stein, Covington singled out a core of conservative foundations—Scaife, Bradley, Koch, and Olin—as the financial engine driving this ostensibly dramatic shift in the national ideology to the right. Yet, the Olin Foundation was so dedicated to this concerted effort that in 2005 it deliberately went out of business in accord with the wishes of its founder.[17]

A 1999 report by a progressive advocacy group, the National Committee for Responsive Philanthropy, made essentially the same argument. The report claimed that conservative foundations had contributed approximately $1 billion in the ten years between 1990 and 2000 to twenty leading conservative think tanks and were thereby able to produce a "rightward shift in American politics."[18] So powerful were these foundations, according to the report, that they could prevail despite opposition to their political agenda from the majority of the country. In short, conservative money trumped the democratic will of the people. The identical thesis with nearly identical supporting evidence was argued in *No Mercy: How Conservative Think Tanks and Foundations Changed America's Social Agenda*. Its left-wing authors, academics Richard Delgado and Jean Stefancic, claimed that by relying on the financial wealth of conservative funders like Bradley, Scaife, and Olin, the Right had been able to get federal policies enacted that the American people did not support.

The twin premises of all these narratives, including Stein's Power-Point, was that conservatives could draw on far superior and unrivaled tax-exempt resources to change the nation's political discourse and move it to the right. Both premises were demonstrably false. As of 2009, the financial assets of the 115 major tax-exempt foundations of the Left identified by our researchers added up to $104.56 billion. Not only is this total not *less* than the financial assets of the 75 foundations of the Right, it was more than *ten times* greater.[19]

Of the "Big Three" conservative foundations that every one of the left-wing analyses cited (Bradley, Olin, Scaife), not one has (or had) assets exceeding a billion dollars. By way of contrast, fourteen progressive foundations do, including Gates, Ford, Robert Wood Johnson, Hewlett, Kellogg, Packard, MacArthur, Mellon, Rockefeller, Casey, Carnegie, Simons, Heinz, and the Open Society Institute.[20] As already noted, the John M. Olin Foundation, which figures in each of the left-wing foundation narratives and has so alarmed the Left over the years as one of the conservative "Big Three," actually terminated itself in 2005 and has been defunct ever since. No comparable progressive foundation has so far voluntarily put itself out of business.

The conservative Scaife Foundation has assets totaling only $244 million, according to 2009 tax records,[21] or less than one-twentieth the assets of MacArthur to take one progressive example (and not the largest). The Bradley Foundation had assets of $623 million in 2009,[22] or about one-sixteenth the assets of the progressive Ford Foundation (also not the largest) and only slightly more than half of George Soros's Open Society Institute. Conservative resources may sound imposing, but only when looked at in isolation. When put in context, they are dwarfed by the financial behemoths of the Left. In 2009, the leading progressive philanthropy, the Bill and Melinda Gates Foundation, had an endowment of more than $33 billion—over three times the total of all seventy-five conservative foundations *combined*.[23]

Progressive funders have created several organizations to coordinate their efforts, including a very large foundation that was set up specifically for this purpose. The $175 million Tides Foundation was created in 1976 by activist Drummond Pike and sees itself as an engine of progressive advocacy: "We strengthen community-based organizations and the progressive movement by providing an innovative and cost-effective framework for your philanthropy."[24] Pike set up the foundation as a public charity that receives money from donors and then funnels it to the recipients of their choice. Because many of these recipient groups are quite radical, the donors often prefer not to have their names publicly linked with the donees. By letting the Tides Foundation, in effect, launder the money for them and pass it along to the intended beneficiaries, donors can avoid leaving a paper trail.[25] Such contributions are called "donor-advised," or "donor-directed," funds.

Through this legal loophole, nonprofit entities can also create for-profit organizations and then funnel money to them through Tides, thereby circumventing the laws that bar nonprofits from directly funding their own for-profit enterprises. Pew Charitable Trusts, for instance, set up three for-profit media companies and then proceeded to fund them via donor-advised contributions to Tides, which (for an 8 percent management fee) in turn sent the money to the media companies. If a donor wishes to give money to a particular cause but finds that there is no organization in existence dedicated specifically to that issue, the Tides Foundation will, for a fee, create a group to meet that perceived need.[26]

In 1996, with a $9 million seed grant, the Tides Foundation created a separate but closely related entity called the Tides Center, also headed by Drummond Pike. While the foundation's activities focus on fund-raising and grant-making, the center—in its role as fiscal sponsor—offers newly created organizations the shelter of Tides's own charitable tax-exempt status, as well as the benefits of Tides's health and liability insurance coverage. The Capital Research Center, which studies philanthropies like Tides, explains: "Under the Tides Center umbrella, the new group can then accept tax deductible contributions without needing to apply immediately to the IRS for tax-exempt 501(c)(3) public charity tax status. . . . Besides giving a new project its seal of approval, the Tides Center performs a notable service in showing new groups how to run an office, apply for grants, conduct effective public relations, and handle the many personnel, payroll, and budget problems that might baffle a novice group."[27]

Between 1996 and 2010, the Tides Center served as a fiscal sponsor to some 677 separate projects with combined revenues of $552 million. According to the Tides website: "To date, Tides has managed project and grantmaking activities totaling more than $2 billion. We have fiscally sponsored more than 800 nonprofit projects." Between 1993 and 2003, at least ninety-one foundations made grants to the Tides Foundation.[28]

As an indication of the way in which the philanthropic world itself has moved dramatically to the left, foundations that funneled money to the left-wing Tides operations included the richest and most venerable philanthropies, onetime symbols of American capitalism. These included the Rockefeller Foundation; the Rockefeller Family Fund; the Ford Foundation; the Carnegie Corporation; the Andrew W. Mellon Foundation; the Bill and Melinda Gates Foundation; the David and Lucile Packard Foundation; the W. K. Kellogg Foundation; the William and Flora Hewlett Foundation; the Heinz Family Foundation; the Howard Heinz Endowment; the Geraldine R. Dodge Foundation; the John D. and Catherine T. MacArthur Foundation; the Fannie Mae Foundation; the ChevronTexaco Foundation; the Annie E. Casey Foundation; the AT&T Foundation; the Barbra Streisand Foundation; the Bauman Family Foundation; Ben and Jerry's Foundation; Changemakers; the Columbia Foundation; the Energy

Foundation; the Foundation for Deep Ecology; the Hoffman Foundation; the Homeland Foundation; the J. M. Kaplan Fund; the James Irvine Foundation; the JEHT Foundation; the Jenifer Altman Foundation; the Jessie Smith Noyes Foundation; the Joyce Foundation; the Lear Family Foundation; the Liberty Hill Foundation; the Robert Wood Johnson Foundation; the Roberts Foundation; the Schumann Center for Media and Democracy; the Stern Family Fund; the Stewart R. Mott Charitable Trust; Vira I. Heinz Endowment; and the Woods Fund of Chicago.[29]

With over $100 billion in tax-exempt assets at their disposal, left-wing foundations have been able to invest massively greater amounts of cash in their beneficiary groups than have their conservative counterparts. The *Washington Post* observed that the Ford Foundation alone had given away more money in one year than conservative donor Richard Mellon Scaife—whom liberal journalists refer to as the "Daddy Warbucks" of the right—gave in forty years.[30]

The foundations of the Left also support an organizational universe of policy and advocacy organizations whose galaxies are far more numerous than those of the Right. Their collective investment has turned local radical organizations into a permanent national infrastructure of socialist activism as the chapters in this book will demonstrate. This universe is made up of tax-exempt 501(c)3 nonprofits and 527 political groups that shape federal and local policy agendas, help Democrats get elected, and shape the nation's "nonpartisan" cultural and social issues debates.[31]

Tax-exempt 501(c)3s receive their privileged status because they agree not to engage in partisan political activity such as the support of candidates or electoral parties. But in practice they are often political in virtually every other sense of the term. In fact, most of the public battles that take place over the issues that eventually decide elections—taxes, health care, immigration, national security, and the environment—are first waged in the media and other venues by tax-exempt 501(c)3s. The entire so-called rights coalition—including the ACLU, NARAL, the NAACP, MALDEF, and a hundred similar groups—is made up of organizations that are tax exempt under the 501(c)3 IRS code. Among such groups created to focus on areas and issues considered strategic by the Left, the resources available outweigh those of the Right by margins that are even more dramatic than the disparity between the assets of progressive and conservative funders would indicate.

In researching organizations that focus on immigration issues, for example, we were able to identify 117 progressive 501(c)3s that devote more than 50 percent of their program activities to supporting open borders or citizen rights for illegal aliens but only 9 conservative 501(c)3s that oppose these agendas. The total net assets of the 117 progressive immigration groups we identified were $194.7 million or almost *thirteen times* greater than the net assets of the 9 conservative immigration groups, which totaled $15.1 million. The total annual revenues of the progressive immigration groups—the funds they receive annually to spend on advocacy for their causes—amount to $306.1 million, while that available to conservative groups is $13.8 million. In other words, the total funds annually available to the Left for advocacy on immigration are more than *twenty-two times* greater than the conservative environment.[32]

The situation is similar in regard to groups engaged in advocacy on other critical national issues such as the environment. We were able to identify 553 environmental groups on the left compared to only 32 conservative groups that promote market-friendly approaches to environmental problems. The net assets of the progressive environmental groups total $9.53 billion compared to the $38.2 million in net assets of the conservative groups or a ratio of over 249 to 1. The annual grants awarded by the 32 conservative groups to environment-related issues total $1.2 million. The annual grants awarded by the 553 progressive environmental groups total $555.4 million. In other words, progressive environmental groups award grants almost 462 times more than do the conservative environmental groups.[33]

There is yet another dimension to the political universe that functions under the IRS codes. Under IRS code 527, organizations may gather tax-exempt funds to directly influence elections if they do not attempt to sway voters to particular candidates. Among the most influential of these 527s is the aforementioned Democracy Alliance, the collective of eighty millionaires led by George Soros. Although it was founded in April 2005, as a result of the Stein PowerPoint, its origins really lie in the formation of a unique political coalition organized by Soros to shape the 2004 presidential election. In the run-up to that election, Soros put together a group of billionaires and Democratic political operatives and created a network of 527s, so powerful the *Washington Post* described it as a "Shadow Party." Its agenda was to seize control of the Democratic election campaign from a party apparatus it felt was in inept hands.[34]

The newly enacted campaign finance reform laws deprived both parties of soft money contributions, draining the Democratic Party of financial resources. It was Soros who had put together and financed the coalition that successfully lobbied to enact campaign finance reform.[35] This was a calculated effort to create the opening for the 527 network Soros then put together as the Shadow Party to collect the contributions the Democratic Party no longer was legally eligible to receive, and thus to shape the message of the presidential campaign. It also provided the Shadow Party with a hammer over Democratic legislators who could no longer depend on the same level of financing from the official party for their individual campaigns. Soros, more than any other individual, is thus responsible for the Democratic Party's recent shift to the left.

The network that Soros put together consisted of progressive billionaires, government unions (SEIU, AFCSME), grassroots radical organizations like ACORN, and political operatives like former presidential adviser Harold Ickes and former White House chief of staff John Podesta, head of the then newly created Center for American Progress, a policy think tank. The political juggernaut that was formed concentrated a power the likes of which had never before been seen in national election campaigns.

Providing venture capital to fund the Shadow Party's campaign were five left-wing billionaires—Soros, Progressive insurance head Peter Lewis, Hollywood mogul Stephen Bing, and California savings-and-loan CEOs Herbert and Marion Sandler. According to the election records, the collective investment of all 527s active in the 2004 campaign, Democrat and Republican, was $440 million. But of the $440 million total, a staggering 70 percent went to Democratic-leaning groups.

One Shadow Party 527, the Media Fund, spent $57 million on broadcast and television advertising in battleground states attacking President Bush and supporting his Democratic opponent John Kerry. Another Soros-linked 527 group, America Coming Together, spent $78 million on get-out-the-vote efforts. By the time the campaign was over, between them the Media Fund and America Coming Together outspent their nearest two Republican counterparts by a factor of three to one. Between 2004 and 2008, 527s generally spent almost $1.5 billion, most of it in support of Democratic candidates.

Despite the record infusion of money by the Shadow Party, the Democrats lost the 2004 election. Out of the disappointment of defeat, the Democracy Alliance was born. The idea behind the group was straightforward: by investing even more money in entities such as MoveOn.org, Americans Coming Together, and Media Matters, progressives could create an alternate structure within the Democratic Party to move it even farther to the left, and recapture Congress and the White House. To that end, the Democracy Alliance set about to continue the Left's massive spending, its members donating some $100 million to left-wing groups and activists even before the 2008 primary season kicked off in earnest.

The organization spearheading the Shadow Party's effort to reshape the Democratic Party is Podesta's Center for American Progress. Created with $3 million in seed money from Soros, the center was originally billed as a progressive "think tank." Its role in American politics, however, has been far more expansive. The center has become a 38-million-dollar-a-year permanent campaign headquarters for the Democratic Party left, helping to launch partisan attack projects like Media Matters, Think Progress, and Campus Progress and systematically insinuating itself as the emerging brain center of the Democratic Party itself.

Another critical Shadow Party component is made up of the two most powerful government unions, the Service Employees International Union (SEIU) and the American Federation of State, County and Municipal Employees (AFSCME). Although union power across the board has declined precipitously since World War II, government unions have been a notable exception. In 2009, union members working in government jobs outnumbered those working in the private sector for the first time. Government unions are a dominant force at the local level, where with the help of the Democratic politicians their campaign funds serve to elect, they have secured generous benefit and pension packages, subsidized by the taxpaying public, which have driven states like New York, New Jersey, and California to the brink of bankruptcy.

These government unions provide another financial arsenal for the Left. During the 2008 presidential election cycle, labor unions funneled some $400 million in campaign contributions to Democratic candidates, most prominently Barack Obama. The SEIU alone spent $85 million during the 2008 election to support Democratic candidates, including $60.7 million earmarked for Obama. (Said SEIU president Andy Stern, "We spent a fortune to elect Barack Obama— $60.7 million to be exact—and we're proud of it."[36, 37]) Bolstered by Big Labor's contributions, Obama raised the union flag, staking out a union-friendly platform that emphasized his support for everything from raising the minimum wage, to the so-called Employee Free Choice Act to eliminate secret ballots in union organizing elections, to the Davis-Bacon Act, which requires federal construction contractors to pay inflated union wages on projects, which dramatically raises the cost of building public hospitals and schools.

A less heralded but no less important pillar of the left-wing money machine is the university system. While the Left has long focused on the money behind conservative think tanks, it is less inclined to notice that the country's biggest think tank—the university—is almost exclusively the province of the political Left. Entire academic fields of the university—women's studies, ethnic studies, black studies, peace studies, postcolonial studies, and American studies—have been transformed into indoctrination and recruitment centers for progressive agendas and organizations.[38] The curricula in these departments, as a matter of course, instill in students a left-wing perspective on the evils of capitalism and Western civilization, teaching that America is governed by race, gender, and class hierarchies at home, while acting as an imperial predator abroad. Numerous studies, both liberal and conservative in origin, show that university faculties are between 80 and 90 percent composed of academics who vote Democratic and align themselves on the left side of the political spectrum.[39]

There is no conservative Harvard or conservative Shadow Party, nor any systematic conservative effort to fund local organizations as perpetual protesters behind a society-transforming agenda. Nor are conservative political organizations heavily funded by federal programs. While it is beyond the scope of this book to examine the full range of federal funding of the progressive and conservative actors in these battles, the relative balance reflected in two areas examined in this study are quite instructive. Our research shows that 247 progressive environmental 501(c)3s (i.e., activist organizations) received $568.9 million in federal grants on an annualized basis in the years 2008–2010.[40] In the same period, only 7 conservative environmental groups received federal grants and these grants totaled only $728,190.[41] A similar pattern exists in the area of immigration reform. While 111 progressive immigration 501(c)3s received $325.3 million in government funding in the same years, the lone conservative immigration group to receive a federal grant was the recipient of $18,090 in government funds.[42]

In researching the private foundations that make up the core of the New Leviathan, our team looked at the individual annual reports and records of more than ten thousand foundations. All the data uncovered can be found at DiscovertheNeworks.org, a comprehensive encyclopedia of the Left, produced under the auspices of the David Horowitz Freedom Center, a 501(c)3 foundation based in Southern California. Profiles of the major progressive foundations, including all those mentioned in this book and its appendices, can be found on the Discover the Networks website.

THE pages that follow describe five critical areas of public policy— by no means the only areas—where the network of left-wing funders and activists has moved radical agendas and ideas from the political margins to the political mainstream and made them the official policies of the Democratic Party. They begin with an account of how, by funding and orchestrating the political career of Barack Obama, this network was able to create its own presidential candidate to implement its agendas.

2.

THE MAKING OF
A PRESIDENT

Presidential campaigns are showcases for candidates, providing an opportunity to introduce their identities and ideas to the nation's voting public. But Barack Obama's successful run in 2008 was most notable for his persistent efforts to declare what he was not. Primarily what he was not, according to Obama and his surrogates, was a man with deep ties and debts to the political left. The point was most determinedly drummed home on "Fight the Smears," a website set up by the Obama camp to rebut distortions of the candidate's record dating back to his time as a community organizer in Chicago.[1] Alleged connections to left-wing groups and individuals were "exaggerated" and "tenuous," if not "outright false." Those who focused on such links should be dismissed as shallow "partisans" and "ideologues." The message was clear: where Obama's radical background was concerned there was nothing really to see.

Belying the campaign's defensive hardball, however, was the inconvenient truth that Barack Obama was entirely a product of the left-wing political culture and its institutional base. From the very outset, his political career was nurtured, shaped, and funded through the organizational infrastructure that progressives had built, and which recruited and then schooled him as a "community organizer" and finally transformed him into a major political figure. It was the Left that trained Obama, gave him employment, provided him with political opportunities, and then launched his career in the Illinois Senate. It was the Left, too, that forged the relationships and laid the groundwork for the grassroots support that Obama would harness to such successful effect on Election Day 2008. And it was the left-wing money machine that provided the funding for it all.

As a graduate student at Columbia University and at the time a self-identified Marxist, Barack Obama attended the Socialist Scholars Conferences held in New York between 1983 and 1985. Obama would later cast these conferences, which featured some of the most ideologically extreme voices on the left, as one of many intellectual distractions that he took in during his time in New York. He would also distance himself from the revolutionary politics celebrated at the conferences, insisting that he was always suspicious of the "dogma and excesses of the left and right." Despite those denials, the evidence assembled by Stanley Kurtz through assiduous research in left-wing archives, makes inescapable the conclusion that these conferences had a much more formative impact on Obama's later attitudes than he is today willing to acknowledge.[2] More important, the conferences served as Obama's first introduction to the concept of community organizing, and to the Left's leading personalities and political parties. It also introduced him to the Left's newly devised strategies for implementing radical change in a democratic society by introducing "non-reformist reforms"—in other words, without appearing to be radical. The Socialist Scholars Conferences were Barack Obama's entrée into a world of organizers and organizations that would become the training ground and then the foundation for his political career.

Although most of Obama's time as a community organizer was spent in Chicago, his first engagement in this world of radical politics was in New York. In the spring of 1985, Obama worked as an organizer for the New York branch of the Public Interest Research Group (U.S. PIRG). Officially styling itself as a "nonpartisan" organization, U.S. PIRG was in fact the brainchild of Ralph Nader, and its causes were the familiar concerns of the political left.[3] New York PIRG was also Obama's gateway to the essentially political work of community organizing, a job description that Obama already understood. According to his PIRG supervisor, Eileen Hershenov, Obama even in those early days had a solid grasp of the radical strategies that underlay community organizing—specifically, how the Left used the "community" umbrella to advance its radical agendas.[4] Thus he was comfortable discussing everything from the tactics of Saul Alinsky,[5] the theoretical guru of the new strategies, to the organizing strategies that had been tried and failed by socialist groups like Students for a Democratic Society during the 1960s.[6] As Hershenov would recall, in her discussions with Obama they "were thinking about how you engage the world: what works coming out of the Sixties, what structures and models worked and what didn't."[7]

The structures and models of the Left that worked, according to those gathered at the Socialist Scholars Conferences and in the organizational universe where Obama now found himself, were strategies of moderation in pursuit of radical goals, of "boring from within"— working within the "system" in order to undermine it. These were tactics devised by European Marxists such as André Gorz, who was a theoretician who came up with the idea of "non-reformist reforms." Such reforms were designed to be game-changing, to alter the nature of the market system, taking the anticapitalist struggle to new levels. As Gorz himself put it, these reforms, which he also called "anti-capitalist reforms," can be "sudden, just as they can be gradual," but they all share one common aim: they must be "strong enough to establish, maintain, and expand those tendencies within the [capitalist] system which serve to weaken capitalism and to shake its joints." Whatever form the reforms took, in other words, the ultimate goal was to bring capitalism to its knees and to transform the system from within.[8]

American Marxists Richard Cloward and Frances Fox Piven had become famous among the Socialist Scholars Conference leftists, for example, by advancing a strategy of "breaking the bank" by overloading its welfare rolls.[9] In a seminal 1966 article in the *Nation* titled "The Weight of the Poor: A Strategy to End Poverty," Cloward and Piven advocated a series of massive "welfare drives" in large cities that would swell the welfare rolls, cause widespread disruption in welfare agencies, and sow financial chaos in local and state governments. This deliberately engineered "political crisis" would create a political environment more favorable toward socialist policies.[10] This strategy formed the mission of Cloward and Piven's National Welfare Rights Organization, whose leaders later created ACORN, an organization in which Obama would play a major role, and which in its turn would play a major role in his rise to the presidency. Both organizations could trace their ideological origins to another proponent of the strategy of undermining capitalism internally, American leftist Saul Alinsky.

A self-identified "professional radical," Alinsky had written an indispensable guide for community organizers based on how to conduct a war against the free-market system by working inside it.[11] His 1971 book, *Rules for Radicals*, would become a bible for left-wing activists (and is a manual to this day recommended on the official website of the National Education Association as a guide for the nation's unionized teachers). Obama was formally trained in the Alinsky principles at Alinsky-created institutions and went on to join a network of organizations dedicated to Alinsky-style radicalism, which became his political base in Chicago.

It was in Chicago that the Left's organizational and political infrastructure would enable Obama's political career to take off. Between 1985 and 1988, he served as the director of the Developing Communities Project (DCP), a coalition of left-wing churches that was working to organize the black community on Chicago's South Side.

Obama's job with the DCP served as introduction into both the world of community organizing and the controversial tactics Alinsky had devised. Bankrolled by leading left-wing foundations, the DCP was firmly rooted in Alinsky's radical vision of community organizing. Thus, a key sponsor of the DCP was the Catholic Campaign for Human Development (CCHD), one of the country's largest sponsors of this kind of radical activism.[12]

First founded in 1969 as the Campaign for Human Development, the CCHD traced its roots to Alinsky's alliance with radicals in the Catholic Church. Accordingly, the CCHD adopted both Alinsky's anticapitalist agenda and his aggressive organizing tactics. Poverty, the CCHD claimed in true Alinskyite fashion, was rooted in capitalist America's "social and economic structures and institutions."[13] (As part of its effort to spread the radical gospel in Chicago's South Side, the CCHD was also a longtime funder of ACORN, ending its sponsorship only in 2009 when open support for the group became politically controversial after a series of scandals.) The DCP was actually an affiliate of another CCHD-sponsored initiative, a network of community organizing groups and organizer training centers called the Gamaliel Foundation.

Gamaliel was founded in 1980 by Gregory Galuzzo, a former Jesuit priest and Alinsky disciple. Modeled on Alinsky's methods, Gamaliel supports a variety of left-wing causes—from opposing restrictions on immigration to opposing national security legislation like the USA PATRIOT Act—all under the guise of fostering a "more democratic society."[14] Gamaliel has also received grants from the most powerful philanthropies on the left, including the Ford Foundation, the Carnegie Corporation and George Soros's Open Society Institute.[15] Yet another left-wing foundation involved with the DCP during Obama's time there was the Woods Fund, which provided the money that activist and organizer Gerald Kellman, another Alinsky follower, used to hire Obama for the job.

The Developing Communities Project brought Obama into the orbit of Chicago's left-wing political establishment and its constellation of radical groups. Among those groups was the United Neighborhood Organization (UNO), the Latino counterpart to ACORN. Together, Obama's DCP and the UNO made up the two major components of the Gamaliel Foundation. Known for its aggressive pressure and protest tactics, including public harassment of politicians who stood in the way of the group's political agenda, the UNO favored publicity stunts like packing town halls with hundreds of disgruntled activists to berate and hound politicians until its demands were met. In 1985, for instance, UNO activists shadowed Illinois governor James Thompson in school buses until he released $24 million in state funding for inner-city schools.[16] The UNO also collaborated on a number of confrontational political actions and rallies with Obama and his DCP activists. It was Obama's involvement with these radical groups that first brought public attention to the then-unknown community organizer.

Obama's political star continued to rise as a result of his involvement with another institution, the Midwest Academy, which was a major training center for radical activists with a political pedigree to match.[17] The Midwest Academy was run by veterans of 1960s radicalism and the Socialist Scholars Conferences, and it trained organizers in the Alinsky strategies. It was funded by a roster of big-budget left-wing foundations, such as the John D. and Catherine T. MacArthur Foundation and the Open Society Institute, and in 2008, it had net assets of just over $654,000, the latest year for which figures are publicly available.

The Midwest Academy was founded in 1973 by leftists Heather Booth and her husband, Paul, a former national secretary of Students for a Democratic Society. Booth was a onetime president of Chicago's Citizen Action Program (CAP), formed in 1969 by trainees from Saul Alinsky's Industrial Areas Foundation, and went on to become an executive of the government union AFSCME.[18]

As the chief sponsor of community organizing in Chicago, the Midwest Academy played a critical role in advancing Obama's career. Not only was he mentored, funded, and promoted by activists affiliated with the academy, but in 1992 Heather Booth used her considerable influence to have Obama appointed director of Project Vote, an ACORN-run registration drive targeting black voters. It was his first major political role.[19]

Though billed as "nonpartisan," Project Vote was a wholly-owned subsidiary of the Left, as a look at its twenty-two-member steering committee in Chicago reveals.[20] Among its members was Madeline Talbott, the head of ACORN's Chicago branch; her husband, Keith Kelleher, an ACORN leader and the head organizer of SEIU Local 880; Kim Bobo, a staffer at the Midwest Academy; Obama's incendiary anti-American pastor at the Trinity United Church of Christ, Reverend Jeremiah Wright; and Wright's radical comrade in the cloth, Father Michael Pfleger. Today, Project Vote's claims to nonpartisanship remain as deceptive as ever. The Marxist theoretician Frances Fox Piven, one of the architects of the "breaking-the-system" strategy adopted by the community organizing Left, currently serves on its board of directors.[21] Another board member, Renee Brereton, is a veteran of the Catholic Campaign for Human Development, which funded Obama's DCP, and the lead organizer at the Gamaliel Foundation.[22]

Above all, Project Vote was an auxiliary of ACORN. In the heat of the 2008 presidential campaign, when scandals made the organization politically toxic, the Obama campaign scrambled to deny any connection between Obama's organizing work on Project Vote and ACORN's political activities. Project Vote founder Sanford Newman wrote an exculpatory letter to the *Wall Street Journal* in which he insisted that Obama's work at Project Vote had no connection to ACORN, which was a "separate" organization. Newman acknowledged that ACORN and Project Vote had collaborated on some initiatives, but he claimed that this did not happen "until after Mr. Obama's tenure [with Project Vote] had ended."

That distinction may have helped deflect some of the criticism from the campaign, but as researcher Matthew Vadum has documented, it was false. As early as 1992, ACORN and Project Vote had worked together on voter registration drives, refuting the claim that there was no collaboration between the two groups until after Obama had moved on. In addition, national ACORN leaders like the husband and wife team of Keith Kelleher and Madeline Talbott made up Project Vote's leadership. As ACORN's leader in Chicago, Talbott personally headed Chicago ACORN's campaign to intimidate banks into making high-risk loans to low-credit customers—a policy whose disastrous consequences would not be fully evident until the 2008 financial crisis.[23] This was a prime example of the Cloward-Piven strategy of breaking the capitalist system from within—the very strategy that ACORN's predecessor, the National Welfare Rights Organization, was formed to advance.

There are other examples of overlap between ACORN's and Project Vote's leadership ranks. For instance, Maxine Nelson, ACORN's national secretary, is a past president and director of Project Vote. That the organization was largely an extension of ACORN was already plain during Obama's years at Project Vote. As author Stanley Kurtz has noted, "despite his denials in 2008, Obama's 1992 Project Vote alliance was deeply entangled in ACORN's broader organizing work."[24] That entanglement was so deep that by 2003, ACORN abandoned the illusion of the groups' respective independence and assumed managerial control of Project Vote. Now officially an ACORN subsidiary, Project Vote proceeded to use ACORN's vast network of local chapters to launch a massive registration and mobilization drive of low-income and minority voters prior to the 2004 presidential election.[25]

Obama's time at Project Vote is also notable for the light it sheds on the nexus between ACORN and the SEIU—an alliance that would prove pivotal for Obama as he sought the presidency in 2008. That alliance is both intimate—according to one former Labor Department employee, the SEIU and ACORN were so close that they once considered sharing member dues—and long-standing. Before it declared bankruptcy in 2010, ACORN counted on its official membership list SEIU Locals 100 in Arkansas, Louisiana, and Texas, and SEIU Locals 880 in Illinois and Indiana. Since then the Locals 880 have merged with another SEIU local, but tellingly the merged SEIU organization's Chicago mailing address is the same as that of the national headquarters of ACORN Housing. As an examination of Project Vote's leadership committee during Obama's time there shows, ACORN and the SEIU often shared the same personnel and leadership.

It is no coincidence that ACORN founder and former National Welfare Rights Organization leader Wade Rathke is also a lead organizer of SEIU Local 100 in New Orleans and heads it to this day. Rathke is also a member of the SEIU's national executive board.[26] Andrew Stern, the former head of the SEIU, also sits on ACORN's Independent Advisory Council. With its many contacts inside ACORN, the union often relies on the organization to do its dirty work. According to ACORN whistleblower Anita MonCrief, the SEIU paid an ACORN chapter in Washington, D.C., to harass an international equity firm called the Carlyle Group because the firm did not hire union workers.[27]

Both the SEIU and ACORN went on to play key roles in helping Obama capture the presidency. The SEIU spent nearly $60 million and provided some hundred thousand supporters to aid Obama's presidential campaign and even funded ACORN's voter registration drives. In 2008, the SEIU made nearly $200,000 in contributions to ACORN for such projects. Meanwhile, Citizens Services Inc., an

ACORN subsidiary, conducted "get-out-the-vote" projects for the Obama campaign, receiving more than $800,000 from the campaign for such services—expenditures the campaign then misleadingly described in its Federal Election Commission disclosure report as going toward less partisan work like polling and staging events.[28] Once Obama was elected, ACORN and the SEIU once again came together to form Health Care for America Now, a coalition of left-wing groups lobbying in support of the Obama administration's push for socialized health care.

Obama's position as director of Project Vote was only one of the roles he would occupy in the network of organizations created by Alinsky radicals. In 1992, the year he joined Project Vote, he was also appointed to the advisory board of Public Allies. Taxpayer funded through AmeriCorps and the Corporation for National and Community Service, Public Allies was designed to connect young activists with left-wing organizations, nonprofits, and government agencies. The Chicago branch of Public Allies was effectively an adjunct of the Midwest Academy, and Obama's colleague on the advisory board was Heather Booth.[29] The connection to the academy was also a family affair. In 1993, thanks to Obama's recommendation and his growing reputation as a community radical, his wife, Michelle, would become the executive director of the Chicago branch of Public Allies.

In recognition of the importance of the Midwest Academy in the development of his career, Obama used his influence on several left-wing foundations to which he had matriculated to secure funds for the organization. The academy was also instrumental in Obama's political ascent in helping him to surround himself with a network of left-wing allies and advisers who would go on to influence his career right up to and including his presidency.

Foremost among these figures, early on, was Democratic state senator Alice Palmer, a veteran of Chicago politics, who also had ties to the Midwest Academy.[30] Palmer represented Illinois's Thirteenth District, including large parts of Chicago's South Side, and was a prominent fixture in the world of leftist Chicago politics. In 1986, she attended the Twenty-Seventh Congress of the Communist Party of the Soviet Union and later touted the Soviet dictatorship as a model for the United States to emulate.[31] When she announced in 1995 that she would be leaving her post as state senator to run for a congressional seat, she chose Barack Obama to be her replacement. For the still unknown politician, Palmer's endorsement was priceless, conferring instant credibility on a candidate with whom many in her district were not yet familiar. Without Palmer's passing of the torch, it is all but inconceivable that Obama could have achieved his first elected office as Illinois state senator in 1996.

Another political ally in Obama's first electoral campaign was the "New Party," a Marxist organization, whose endorsement he sought and secured. The New Party was composed of members of the Democratic Socialists of America (DSA)—one of the key organizers of the Socialist Scholars Conferences—along with members of the Committees of Correspondence for Democracy and Socialism, a Communist Party splinter group. The New Party offered Obama a convenient way to solidify support among radical activists who might have remained skeptical. ACORN was also a major force behind the New Party and helped launch it in 1992 as a bridge between radicals and the Democratic Party mainstream.[32]

During his 2008 presidential run, Obama's campaign dismissed allegations of his ties to the New Party as right-wing smear.[33] Yet the evidence for Obama's relationship with the party came from a primary source. According to *New Ground*, the newsletter of the Chicago chapter of the Democratic Socialists of America, Obama got the New Party's endorsement in exchange for a promise that he would have a "visible and active relationship with the NP."[34] By 2008, it was clearly not in Obama's best interests to admit that relationship. But there can be little doubt that his alliance with the New Party played a role in gaining his first legislative seat.

Among the activists associated with the Midwest Academy that were instrumental in Obama's first run for electoral office were the radical power couple, former SDS leaders Bill Ayers and his wife, Bernardine Dohrn. The Ayers' living room provided the launching pad for Obama's political career when Alice Palmer introduced Obama as her designated successor at the couple's home in Chicago's tony Hyde Park neighborhood.[35]

During the 2008 presidential campaign, attention was drawn to the fact that Ayers was unrepentant about his past participation in the Weather Underground, a cult that claimed responsibility for more than a dozen bombings between 1970 and 1974. In a notorious interview in the *New York Times*, which appeared on September 11, 2001, Ayers said, "I don't regret setting bombs . . . I feel we didn't do enough."[36] When the predictable backlash occurred, both Obama and Ayers made concerted efforts to obscure the closeness of their friendship. Obama insisted that Ayers was just a "guy who lives in my neighborhood," while Ayers claimed that he hardly knew the presidential aspirant.[37]

This was disingenuous, to put it mildly. The public record is quite clear on their political friendship and working alliances, and whatever differences they had (if any) did not prevent Ayers from helping Obama rise up the rungs of Chicago politics, nor Obama from actively furthering Ayers's political projects. The reception and fund-raiser that Ayers and Dohrn held for Obama in their living room in 1995 was just a small aspect of their collaboration. Far more important was the instrumental role Ayers played in bringing Obama onto the board of the multimillion-dollar Chicago Annenberg Challenge, a left-wing foundation that distributed educational grants and was pursuing Alinsky politics in the Chicago K–12 schools.

The Annenberg Challenge was in no small part Ayers's creation. In 1993, conservative billionaire Walter Annenberg, a onetime publisher of *TV Guide*, announced an ambitious plan to spend $500 million to reform inner-city schools in America. Ayers saw a political opportunity in the challenge. As a professor of early childhood

education and the leader of a movement to teach "social justice" to
K–12 students, Ayers was a hero to educational progressives. Thanks
to the political clout of the Left in the Chicago school system, Ayers
personally cowrote the "Annenberg Challenge" grant proposal for
Chicago's public schools. The application was successful, and Chicago
received $49.2 million from the Annenberg Foundation, with the
understanding that it would raise double that amount through private funding in the years ahead. Ayers was able to provide matching
funds with the aid of a network of left-wing foundations, among them
the billion-dollar John D. and Catherine T. MacArthur Foundation,
the billion-dollar Joyce Foundation, and the Woods Fund of Chicago.
Out of this seed money—and Ayers's efforts to secure it—the Chicago
Annenberg Challenge was born.[38]

As the creator of the Annenberg Challenge, Ayers played a key
role in assembling the board that hired Barack Obama to serve as its
inaugural chairman, a post Obama held for six crucial years before
stepping down in 2001.[39] During these years the Annenberg Challenge distributed 210 grants, ostensibly with the goal of improving
education in Chicago's public schools. Yet the "education" grants
that the Challenge handed out often had more to do with political
activism—and especially a politically infused multiculturalism—than
with educational reform.

For instance, the Challenge sank $650,000 into an initiative called
the New Schools Multicultural Network. As part of the project, students in a predominantly Hispanic neighborhood on Chicago's Southwest Side received help in, of all things, Spanish language proficiency.
For Hispanic students to receive instruction in a language many of
them already spoke, rather than in the English language that might
help them succeed academically, was a typical example of multicultural political correctness.

Another Challenge-sponsored project, the South Side African Vil-
lage Collaborative, received $27,500 to place six "village elders" in
ten South Side schools, including Michelle Obama's alma mater,

Bryn Mawr Elementary. As journalist Stanley Kurtz has observed, such programs were typical of the Afrocentric "rites of passage movement" promoted by activists at the time. Kurtz points out that schools involved with such programs "featured 'African-Centered' curricula built around 'rites of passage' ceremonies inspired by the puberty rites found in many primitive African societies."[40]

With their often explicit subtext that African tribalism was superior to Western democratic cultures, and that American society was racist and oppressive, these curricula were the educational equivalent of the sermons delivered by Obama's pastor, the Reverend Jeremiah Wright, whose rancid orations routinely demonized America as a country that God should damn. It is no mere coincidence that some of the leading Afrocentrist ideologues in Chicago were invited to address both Annenberg Challenge–funded teacher training sessions and Wright's congregation at Trinity United Church.[41]

As well as overseeing the funding of such radical programs, Obama used his position to repay Ayers's political favor in appointing him to chair the Annenberg Challenge board. During Obama's chairmanship, the fund gave $264,000 to an Ayers-run initiative called the Small Schools Workshop. The director of the workshop was Michael Klonsky, a founder of the Marxist-Leninist Communist Party and Ayers's former comrade in Students for a Democratic Society, of which he was at one time national chairman. Klonsky would go on to write a "social justice"–themed blog for the Obama campaign's official website, which was quickly expunged once Klonsky's past radical affiliations surfaced.[42] Because the seed money for the workshop initially came from the left-wing Joyce Foundation, to whose board Obama had also been appointed, Obama approved the funding for Ayers's program twice.[43] Altogether, the Small Schools Workshop received almost $2 million from the Joyce Foundation and the Woods Fund when Obama sat on their boards.[44]

In light of its politicized funding ventures, it is no surprise that the Annenberg Challenge proved a failure in the one area—education—

it was specifically tasked to improve. Stanley Kurtz reports that, "[the Annenberg Challenge's] in-house evaluators comprehensively studied the effects of its grants on the test scores of Chicago public-school students. They found no evidence of educational improvement."[45] Those results were confirmed by a University of Illinois at Chicago study, which found that the Challenge's money did nothing to improve student achievement at grantee schools.

On the contrary, the study found that in promoting politicized curricula, the Annenberg Challenge Fund may have actually damaged students' educational outcomes. As measured by classroom behavior and social competence, students in Challenge-funded programs proved "weaker" than their peers at comparable schools in the Chicago public school system. Tragically, after an intensive immersion in multicultural curricula, students were actually less well adjusted to the school environment—no surprise given the indoctrination in anti-Western, not to say anti-American attitudes.[46] Obama registered his own vote of no confidence in the educational reform campaign he sponsored, when he sent his daughters to the exclusive and private Laboratory School run by the University of Chicago.

Nonetheless, Obama's time as chair of the Annenberg Challenge provided a major boost to his political career. The Ayers-Obama collaboration also extended to the Woods Fund, a left-wing foundation on whose board they both served between 1999 and 2002.[47] The Woods Fund had its origins in the Woods Charitable Fund, a foundation created in the 1950s by Lincoln, Nebraska, telephone company executive Frank Woods to support the arts and civil rights causes. By the early 1990s, however, its funding had veered dramatically to the left under the stewardship of Ken Rolling, a former Midwest Academy staffer who was also director of the Annenberg Challenge during its six-year existence.

Under Rolling's leadership, the Woods Charitable Fund became a cash cow for radical groups like ACORN, whose "homesteading" campaign of illegal housing seizures was financed by Woods Charitable Fund dollars.[48] The Woods Fund also underwrote Chicago's network of radical community organizing groups, including the Midwest Academy and the Gamaliel Foundation. It was this shift toward more ideologically driven giving that ultimately forced a schism within the Woods Charitable Fund. The original Woods Charitable Fund remained in Nebraska, where it continued to underwrite traditional charities for the arts, while the Chicago entity would become known as the Woods Fund of Chicago, providing patronage for radical community organizing groups. In the financial split that followed, the Woods Fund of Chicago retained 70 percent of the Woods family's original endowment.[49] In 2005, the now wholly radical Woods Fund had assets of nearly $69 million.[50]

In line with its goal of shaping public policy through community activism, the Woods Fund supported Obama's early work as a "community organizer," and in 1998 Obama became the chair of the Woods Fund board. It was during his time on the board that ACORN and the Midwest Academy became the largest recipients of Woods Fund grants. The Woods Fund would also make several grants to Jeremiah Wright's Trinity United.[51]

Obama would prove adept at using the Woods Fund to his own political advantage, wielding his influence to win allies in unlikely places. One example was Obama's friendship with Rashid Khalidi, a former press agent and adviser to Yasir Arafat's PLO. Khalidi was close to Obama while the two were professors at the University of Chicago in the 1990s. In 2001 and 2002, when Obama was serving on its board, the Woods Fund gave $110,000 in grants to the Arab American Action Network (AAAN), the organization headed by Khalidi's wife, Mona. Khalidi then came to Obama's rescue at a crucial moment when he was trying to gin up electoral support among Chicago's Palestinian community, which was skeptical of Obama's views on Israel. The endorsement of an anti-Israel activist like Khalidi would prove politically useful. As a prominent figure, who had repeatedly referred to Israel as a racist state and excused Palestinian terrorism as an understandable reaction to Israeli oppression, Khalidi's credentials among Palestinian activists was not in doubt.

Khalidi used his standing to help Obama in 2003, when the future president attended an Arab American Activist Network–sponsored farewell dinner with Ayers, Dohrn, and Khalidi.[52] Khalidi told the mostly Palestinian crowd that "You will not have a better senator under any circumstances." It was just one example of many when Obama's base of support in the political left, backed by its formidable financial resources, would serve him well at a pivotal moment in his political career.

Obama's colleagues on the Woods Fund board were also instrumental players in Chicago's political network. For instance, Obama's tenure on the board coincided with that of Chicago activist and civic official Howard Stanback. Stanback later served on the board of directors of the Shorebank Neighborhood Institute, the nonprofit affiliate of ShoreBank, a community development bank created to serve the minority communities on the South and West Sides of Chicago. Although the bank declared insolvency in August 2010, a victim of the financial recession, it courted controversy by providing a loan to Jeremiah Wright's Trinity United Church of Christ. The loan was used to finance Wright's ten-thousand-square-foot, $1.6-million retirement home in suburban Chicago. It also provided a $10-million line of credit to Trinity United.[53]

ShoreBank was linked both to the progressive funding network and, indirectly, to Obama's political progression in Chicago. One of the bank's directors, before it went out of business, was Adele Simmons, the former president of the John D. and Catherine T. MacArthur Foundation. Along with William Ayers, Simmons helped handpick the board of the Chicago Annenberg Challenge on which Obama served.

In addition to their professional work on foundations like the Woods Fund, William Ayers and Obama had numerous social interactions that were directly related to their joint agendas. In 1997, Ayers and Obama spoke together on a panel about juvenile justice.

The panel was organized by Michelle Obama, then an associate dean of student services at the University of Chicago. Ayers and Obama found much to agree on in this area, which was a focus of the ex-terrorist's new activism. Obama wrote a glowing review of Ayers's 1998 book, *A Kind and Just Parent: The Children of Juvenile Court*, for the *Chicago Tribune*. In the book, Ayers portrays juvenile crimi-nals, including those who commit serious crimes like murder, as vic-tims of a callous and dysfunctional juvenile court system that imposes adult penalties for children's crimes. In Ayers's account, these juvenile criminals are harshly treated by a system that is itself rooted in "the inequities, the historical legacies of oppression and privilege" that in his view constitute American society.[54] In a section of the book about his Hyde Park community, Ayers mentions Obama by name as one of his neighbors, along with Muhammad Ali and Louis Farrakhan.[55] Obama praised the book as a "searing and timely account of the juve-nile court system."[56]

Personal associations with Chicago leftists in the orbit around the Midwest Academy were an important part of Obama's career trajec-tory. Just as vital were the roles played by influential left-wing charities like the Joyce Foundation. Established in 1948 by the late Beatrice Joyce Kean, whose family made a fortune in lumber, the Joyce Foun-dation initially focused its philanthropy on apolitical causes like hos-pitals and health organizations.[57] Following Kean's death in 1972, however, the foundation increasingly invested its assets—nearly $800 million as of 2009—in left-wing agendas such as campaigns against global warming, environmentalism, gun control, and Alinsky-style community organizing.

It was in the latter capacity that the foundation had funded the Developing Communities Project for which Obama worked, provid-ing him with full-time employment. The foundation also gave Obama his first foothold in the world of left-wing philanthropy, naming him to the Joyce board in 1994.[58] The foundation later became a major con-tributor to Ayers's Annenberg Challenge. Deborah Leff, the president

of the Joyce Foundation, was among the principal figures who, along
with Ayers, provided crucial support for Obama's election bid to the
Annenberg Challenge board.

At the time, Obama was an associate at a small law firm, and
the least distinguished member on the Annenberg Challenge board,
which included presidents of Ameritech and the University of Illinois.
It is a tribute to the organized influence of the Left's political network in Chicago that despite his lack of accomplishment at the time,
Obama was nonetheless welcomed onto the board, his first significant
position in Chicago's political establishment.[59] In exchange, Obama
used his position on Joyce's board to steer funds toward the radical
network, including to groups like ACORN.

As important as his rise to eminence on the boards of the Annenberg Challenge and the Woods Fund among the constellation of organizations around the Midwest Academy was his role in the grassroots
ACORN. ACORN had been founded in Little Rock, Arkansas, in
1970. Its founder, Wade Rathke, was a protégé of the leader of the
National Welfare Rights Organization that Marxists Cloward and
Piven had helped to create. ACORN not only adopted the Cloward-
Piven strategy of "breaking the bank" by flooding the welfare rolls
but adapted it as a strategy to overwhelm America's poorly monitored
electoral system.

Within a few decades, ACORN had become the largest and most
powerful radical group in the country, boasting "two radio stations,
a housing corporation, a law office, and affiliate relationships with a
host of trade-union locals."[60] Until recently, ACORN also claimed
175,000 dues-paying member families and more than 850 chapters in
70 US cities. ACORN's explosive success was significantly underwritten by the US government, which has lavished at least $79 million in
federal funds on ACORN and its affiliates since 1994. As recently as
2009, 10 percent of ACORN's $25 million annual budget came from
Washington.[61] ACORN's other distinction, in the early 1990s, was to
serve as the bridge between the world of community organizing from

which Barack Obama came and the world of mainstream politics that he was about to enter.

Obama first came into contact with ACORN in 1993. Having just returned to Chicago after graduating from Harvard Law School, he was recruited to run a voter registration drive for the ACORN affiliate Project Vote.[62] As director of Project Vote in Illinois, Obama worked directly with ACORN leaders like Madeline Talbott. When he became a presidential candidate, Obama would deny Project Vote's ties to ACORN, which was then under investigation for voter fraud and other criminal activities, and the connection would be strenuously denied by the 2008 campaign. In 1992, however, Obama and ACORN were still very much allies, and Talbott called him "a kindred spirit."[63] Later, Talbott would use her connections to promote Obama among writers and journalists covering Chicago politics as he sought to win the Democratic nomination for Illinois senator.

Obama's connection to ACORN became even more significant in 1995, when he was made the organization's attorney. In that capacity, Obama sued to force Republican governor Jim Edgar to implement the so-called Motor Voter Act in Illinois. The Motor Voter Act allowed citizens to register to vote when they were applying for motor vehicle licenses or social services. It was a product of pressures by radicals in the voter registration movement, originally organized by Richard Cloward and Frances Fox Piven during the Reagan administration, and was an attempt to apply their strategy of breaking the system to the electoral process.

At the time of its passage, Obama and other backers of the Motor Voter Act insisted that it was necessary to prevent the potential disenfranchisement of voters who were minorities and poor. As a result of the Motor Voter Act, *Wall Street Journal* editor John Fund observed, election monitors "were under orders not to ask anyone for identification or proof of citizenship. States also had to permit mail-in voter registrations, which allowed anyone to register without any personal contact with a registrar or election official. Finally, states were limited in pruning 'dead wood'—people who had died, moved or been convicted of crimes—from their rolls." The result, Fund notes, was an "explosion of phantom voters," and the kind of election fraud for which ACORN was later indicted.[64]

In the brief that Obama filed on ACORN's behalf in the Motor Voter Act case, Obama wrote that "A significant number of ACORN members are registered to vote, but have not voted in the last two preceding calendar years because of a lack of candidates addressing their needs or for other reasons."[65] The "other reasons" for irregularities in the voting patterns of ACORN members did not become more widely known until the 2008 presidential campaign, when heightened scrutiny of the organization revealed a systemic pattern of voter registration fraud and compelled at least fourteen states to launch investigations into ACORN's practices.[66] Its well-merited reputation for corruption had garnered ACORN so much bad publicity by the summer of 2010 that the organization was moved to change its tarnished name to Community Organizations International.

In the 1990s, ACORN's days of infamy were still in the future, however, and Obama enjoyed a political success as its "public-interest" lawyer in the Motor Voter case. That success bound him even closer to ACORN. He became a trainer of ACORN staff and received political support from the organization in turn. In 1996, on a questionnaire listing groups that provided key support for his campaign for the Illinois State Senate, Obama listed ACORN first in order of importance.[67] As a board member of the Woods Fund, Obama made sure that grants were given to ACORN. Once elected to the US Senate in 2004, Obama became a leading opponent of voter identification laws to ensure that those who vote are actually eligible to do so. The overturning of voter identification laws remains a signature ACORN cause. As late as 2007, Obama was paying public tribute to the group's role in his career in a speech to ACORN's leaders. "I've been fighting alongside of ACORN on issues you care about my entire career. Even before I was an elected official, when I ran Project Vote in Illinois,

ACORN was smack dab in the middle of it, and we appreciate your work." ACORN's political arm would endorse Obama for president shortly thereafter. Despite the candid admission by Obama, his campaign's "Fight the Smears" website continued to insist that "ACORN was not part of Project Vote,"[68] and a pliant press for the most part gave him a sympathetic pass.

Memorializing its special relationship with Obama, ACORN today runs a training program called Camp Obama. In the camp, aspiring community organizers are trained in the tactics that Obama learned before them. Another program, Obama Organizing Fellows, is designed to train would-be activists in how to "organize in a community, working in conjunction with grassroots leaders and campaign staff."[69] In addition to getting an introduction to community organizing techniques, trainees learn how to incorporate them into successful political campaigns. Obama himself made savvy use of such acolytes during the 2008 election. His campaign employed hundreds of seasoned organizers hailing from a wide range of left-wing groups—from unions to community activists to environmental campaigners—who used ACORN-style tactics to build a successful grassroots campaign that turned out younger voters and African Americans to support Obama in record numbers.[70]

If Obama's alliances with groups like ACORN remain poorly understood, the credit must go to Obama campaign efforts like "Fight the Smears" and a media that shared his progressive agendas and was willing to look the other way or gloss over compromising details about Obama's commitments to the radicals who created him. Meanwhile, conservative critics who did the hard work of researching the facts about Obama's Chicago career were simply ignored.

The evidence is irrefutable and overwhelming that Obama's path to the presidency was paved every step of the way by a network of radical organizations and political figures, and the network of multimillion-dollar foundations behind them whose plan was to work within the system and present a moderate face, in order to advance an agenda of radical change. This was the strategy outlined at the Socialist Scholars Conferences that the youthful Obama had attended in New York, where he had received his formal introduction into the company of radical organizers and absorbed the socialist vision that underlay the rhetoric about grassroots activism, participatory democracy, and "community organizing."

This was also the political outlook of the Developing Communities Project, where Obama first made a name for himself as a community organizer and where his work was paid for by leading funders of the political left. It was the agenda of ACORN, whose Project Vote registration drive marked Obama's debut in the world of political activism. It was also the guiding agenda of the Midwest Academy, whose extensive association of well-connected leaders and organizers provided the mentors, funders, and supporters of the political novice, promoting him from the obscurity of his early organizing days to the prominent boards of large left-wing foundations whose own surfaces as creations of American capitalism were equally deceptive. It was the agenda of the countless left-wing allies and advisers who promoted Obama's career in Chicago and helped to launch his career as a state legislator and then as a national figure, the same allies who would provide the funding and troops for the ground war of his presidential campaign until at last America—the country they had so long attacked—would be led by one of their own. As candidate Obama himself put it, during his victorious presidential run: "We are the ones we have been waiting for."

3.

THE PROGRESSIVE
MONEY MACHINE

The Woods Fund, which was instrumental in making the career of Barack Obama possible, had been run by the Woods family until the member most active in the foundation, Frank H. Woods Jr., died in 1980.[1] With the family's influence diminished, control of the previously traditional charity fell into the hands of leftist staffers, including veterans of the Midwest Academy, who hijacked its agenda and pushed the foundation aggressively to the left. Soon the Woods Fund was ideologically indistinguishable from the radical groups it was now funding, including Tides, ACORN, and an assemblage of Alinsky-inspired community organizations.[2]

The Woods Fund trajectory—an apolitical, even conservative, foundation swerving dramatically to the left—was to repeat itself throughout the philanthropic culture. The Pew Charitable Trusts were created by the philanthropy of oil tycoon and Christian conservative J. Howard Pew in 1957 to educate Americans on the "values of the free market" and the "paralyzing effects of government controls on the lives and activities of the people." But in the 1980s, the Trusts fell under the sway of progressives like neurosurgeon Dr. Thomas Langfitt, who used his position as president to channel the foundation's wealth toward left-wing political causes. Pew's political transformation continued under Langfitt's selected successor, Rebecca Rimel, who had never been shy in expressing her hopes of shifting Pew's grants to the left. In 1991, for instance, she had told the *Foundation News* that she wanted to "infuse the spirit of the Sixties" into Pew's work. Rimel got her chance to do just that in 1994, when she took over as Pew's president and CEO. In her first annual report, Rimel announced that the foundation would now be pursuing a "new template" in making grants.[3] What that meant soon became clear as Rimel purged most of the foundation's conservative staff members, ended the support for conservative causes, and turned Pew Trusts into a reliable ally of the progressive left.[4]

Pew Trusts is now the largest funder of the left-wing Tides Center, which acts as a middleman directing funds from multiple sources to hundreds of radical groups while concealing the sources of the funds.[5] Between 1990 and 2002, Pew Trusts donated nearly $109 million to Tides.[6] Pew Trusts also funds anticapitalist groups like the Institute for Policy Studies, a pro-Castro think tank that opposed America's efforts to roll back communism during the Cold War and since 9/11 has been a staunch opponent of America's war on terror.[7] Its in-house "scholars" have included anti-American radicals Noam Chomsky, Gore Vidal, and Richard Falk. Pew Trusts also funds such radical groups as Earth Justice and the anarchist and violent Ruckus Society.[8] In addition to funding radical organizations opposed to free market societies, Pew Trusts uses its resources to advance its own left-wing agendas. In recent years, the foundation has been spending its funds to support campaigns promoting the threat of global warming and calling for expansive government controls to curb the threat.[9]

Other foundations started by staunch pro-capitalist conservatives experienced similar turns. The John D. and Catherine T. MacArthur Foundation was established in 1970 by the billionaire insurance and real estate mogul John MacArthur, who granted the foundation's trustees a wide berth to manage its funds. As he told one director, "I figured out how to make the money. You fellows will have to figure out how to spend it."[10] But while MacArthur was a conservative, those who ended up controlling his foundation were anything but.

Shortly after its establishment, the foundation became consumed by a bitter power struggle between the conservative members of the board, who included officers in Bankers Life and Casualty, John MacArthur's insurance company and the source of the foundation's fortune, and MacArthur's progressive-minded son, J. Roderick "Rod" MacArthur. The company's representatives on the board were conservatives and wanted the foundation to support the principles of limited government and liberty. President and board chairman Robert Ewing, an associate of John MacArthur at Bankers Life, explained, "We're mostly a bunch of Midwestern businessmen devoted to free enterprise and opposed to more government controls. That's the way we operate our business and that's the way we'll run our foundation."[11] Another board member stressed that they were "determined to avoid the internationalist, liberal-oriented pattern of philanthropy established by such big Eastern foundations as Ford, Rockefeller and Carnegie."[12]

But the conservatives' vision for the foundation ran up against the opposition of Rod MacArthur. Not only should foundations not shrink from government, he insisted, but they should lead it as its "social conscience" and amplify its efforts where possible. When President Reagan called on the private sector to take on social responsibilities instead of the government, MacArthur struck a defiant pose. "I personally think that both we and other foundations should refuse to pick up where the government is pulling back," MacArthur declared.[13] Complaining that the government was "doing little enough as it was," he argued that "private foundations should not encourage the government to go backwards. We should be out there at the forefront, ahead of where the government thinks it's safe to be."[14]

Political differences between MacArthur and his fellow board members soon ignited a fiery legal battle, with MacArthur demanding that most of the other trustees be removed. Rod MacArthur ultimately won the war for the reins of the foundation, as the board gradually came under the control of liberals and progressives. Today it is occupied by such left-wing appointees as Jamie Gorelick, former deputy attorney general in the Clinton administration, and boasts a grant-giving agenda to match. By 1997, the foundation's giving was so skewed to the left that the Capital Research Center commented its grants "have come to exemplify progressive philanthropy."[15]

One of the signature MacArthur programs—the so-called genius awards—illustrates the point. Promoted as honoring creativity, in practice they are almost invariably awarded to creativity on the left. At least four members of the editorial board of the tiny socialist magazine *Dissent*, for example, have won the MacArthur genius award.[16] As a result, one critic has poignantly observed, the one distinction uniting the recipients of the "genius" grant is that the "selection of each would have embarrassed John MacArthur."[17] The foundation also supports a number of anticapitalist organizations, prominent among them Global Exchange, a Marxist group and primary sponsor of the anti-World Trade Organization riots in Seattle. MacArthur has also given special awards to the anti-American leader of Global Exchange, Medea Benjamin, who is its executive director and who once described landing in communist Cuba where she took up residence for five years as entering the "kingdom of heaven." Benjamin received the MacArthur Foundation's Writer's Fellowship, even though she is a political activist and her only book is a political manual printed by Global Exchange.

The famous fortune of capitalist titan John D. Rockefeller Sr. also fell into the hands of heirs who used it to fund an assortment of left-wing causes. The Rockefeller Brothers Fund was instituted in 1940 for Rockefeller's five grandsons. The fund first gained influence in 1956, when it created the Special Studies Project to analyze and issue recommendations on American public policy. The common theme of its reports was that government should have more involvement in foreign and domestic policy. One report called for increasing government support of the arts and was one of the main documents used in the creation of the National Endowment for the Arts in 1965.[18]

In 1967, the Rockefeller Brothers fortune created the Rockefeller Family Fund, which soon became a vehicle for the charity work of the Rockefeller "cousins"—representing the next generation, heavily influenced by the political trends of the 1960s.

In time, as their fathers and uncles passed on, several cousins took their places in the Rockefeller Brothers Fund, pushing the latter even further to the left.[19] The Rockefeller Brothers Fund's current chairman is Steven Rockefeller, son of former governor Nelson Rockefeller. Steven Rockefeller is an emeritus professor of religion at Middlebury College and a lifelong socialist and environmentalist.[20] Along with former Soviet premier Mikhail Gorbachev, Rockefeller drafted the "Earth Charter," an anticapitalist manifesto that condemns capitalism for the world's social, economic, and environmental ills. The document laments that, "the dominant patterns of production and consumption are causing environmental devastation, the depletion of resources, and a massive extinction of species."[21]

Today Steven's radicalism informs much of the Rockefeller Brothers Fund's philanthropy, which has underwritten such radical groups as ACORN, the World Social Forum, and the Institute for Policy Studies. As of 2009, the fund had $729 million in assets and awarded annual grants totaling $31 million. Of these, a significant share fund the environmental movement, with grants worth hundreds of thousands going to groups promoting the threat of global warming. For instance, the Fund has given $400,000 to the National Environmental Trust for a "global warming public education campaign," another $400,000 for anti-global-warming activism to the British branch of the World Wildlife Fund, and $50,000 to the Institute for Policy Studies for a project advocating global-warming regulations in Maryland.[22] The idea that capitalism is the enemy of the environment also seems to have been embraced by the Rockefeller Family Fund, which among other environmental causes has sponsored a movement to require large corporations to list their "environmental liabilities" as part of their corporate balance sheets.[23] Capitalism may have created the endowments of the two Rockefeller funds, but today these foundations seem to define themselves in opposition to the free-market system that allowed their grandfather to assemble his immense wealth.

Not only inheritance but also marriages have led to a reversal of direction for many prominent dispensers of philanthropic wealth. Conservative Republican Ray Kroc used proceeds from his McDonald's hamburger empire to create a foundation in his name. But his widow, Joan B. Kroc, has used those funds to sponsor left-wing agendas that would have repelled her politically conservative husband. Ray Kroc was a strong supporter of the US military, who once announced that McDonald's franchises would fly the American flag twenty-four hours a day in a display of support for American forces in Vietnam. By contrast, the Joan B. Kroc Foundation, which is the successor to Kroc's original trust, has become a leading sponsor of "peace studies," an academic field distinguished more by its antimilitary and anticapitalist politics than by its scholarship.[24] During the 1980s, the foundation became a leading sponsor of antiwar and nuclear disarmament groups, handing out hundreds of thousands of dollars in grants to leftist nonprofits like the Center for Defense Information, the Beyond War Foundation, and the Union of Concerned Scientists.[25] Joan Kroc later established an Institute for International Peace Studies in her name at the University of Notre Dame, which sparked controversy by offering a faculty position to Tariq Ramadan, grandson of the founder of the Muslim Brotherhood, who was banned at the time from entering the United States because of his involvement with terrorist organizations.[26] In its political transformation, the Kroc Foundation followed the path set by Joan Kroc herself, who became a devoted patron of the Democratic Party and in 2004 donated $236 million from her estate to the left-leaning National Public Radio.

The fate of the Kroc fortune was paralleled in the fate of the Howard Heinz Endowments. The foundation was created by H. John Heinz III, a Republican senator from Pennsylvania and an heir to the ketchup fortune. When Heinz was killed in a plane crash in 1991, the endowment's $1.3 billion in assets came under the control of Heinz's widow, Teresa. In 1995, she married Senator John Kerry, a left-wing Democrat from Massachusetts, and began to steer the endowment's philanthropy, which donates $140 million annually, toward activists on that side of political spectrum and to furthering her new husband's political ambitions in the Democratic Party.

In keeping with her long-standing involvement with environmental causes, many of the endowment's grants are now directed toward progressive environmental groups, some with extreme agendas. For instance, the foundation has supported the Berkeley, California-based Ruckus Society, an anarchist group that trains environmental activists in civil disobedience and has engaged in violent protests. The Ruckus Society traces its origins to the eco-terrorist group Earth First!, which became notorious for sabotage tactics like tree spiking, which risked serious harm to timber workers. Heinz Endowments has also funded environmentalist organizations like the Earth Island Institute, founded by David Brower after his politics proved too radical for the Sierra Club.

Heinz Kerry has also used foundation funds to celebrate environmental radicals, creating the Heinz Awards, and a $250,000 cash prize, to honor figures like Paul Ehrlich, an environmentalist doomsayer whose prophecies of ecological disaster in books like the 1968 *Population Bomb,* which predicted mass starvation in the next decades, turned him into an environmental icon despite the failure of the prediction to materialize.[27] Heinz funds have also been used to sponsor activism in public schools. The foundation gave $140,000 to an organization that trains Pittsburgh schoolchildren to engage in "policy advocacy" on environmental issues.[28]

Heinz Endowments has funneled millions to support political activism through the Tides Center, to which it has given at least $8.1 million.[29] The foundation also underwrites far-left groups like PAX Christi USA, which views America's war on al-Qaeda as "unjust." PAX Christi received a $100,000 grant from Heinz.[30] Another group funded by Heinz, Advocates for Community Empowerment, calls the U.S. Constitution "a slave and empire form of governance."[31]

Despite the clear injunction of the IRS code that bars tax-exempt foundations from funding partisan causes, Heinz Kerry has also used foundation funds to advance her husband John Kerry's political career and to sponsor opposition to his political rivals. In 2004, Teresa Heinz Kerry used the cover of allegedly apolitical groups to provide $250,000 in foundation money to help fund the Democratic National Convention that nominated her husband. In addition to funding her husband's political convention, Heinz also funded far-left activists who disrupted the Republican political convention that year.[32]

This funding came through a Pittsburgh-based organization called the Thomas Merton Center. In 2002, the Heinz Endowment gave $100,000 to the Three Rivers Community Foundation "to support the work of grassroots organizations actively engaged in promoting social, racial and economic justice." According to the Three Rivers website, the Thomas Merton Center was one of the "groups that have received the greatest cumulative total of Three Rivers funding over the years."[33]

The Thomas Merton Center is an umbrella organization of thirty-five left-wing groups. In February 2004, the Thomas Merton Center announced that it planned to send protesters to the Republican National Convention in New York City the following September. The center's organizers wrote, "In Pittsburgh, Global Justice Now, a project of the Thomas Merton Center . . . will be organizing multiple buses for the RNC events while the Pittsburgh Organizing Group (POG) is considering what type of direct action tactics are feasible during the RNC."[34] It went on to explain that "Every group mobilizing wants to oppose the convention and thousands of people will be in NYC to physically disrupt to the maximum extent possible the functioning of the RNC, . . ." In the event, activists affiliated with the center—and at least partially funded by Heinz Endowments—attempted to block Republican delegates' buses from getting to the convention center, interrupted several speeches on national television, and harassed the delegates and some of the convention speakers.[35]

No shift to the left, however, was as significant as that which had taken place inside the Ford Foundation even prior to these other developments. The foundation was formed in 1936 by Edsel Ford, the only son of industrialist and auto magnate Henry Ford. The primary purpose of the foundation was to dodge the IRS's steep estate tax. In 1935, the federal government raised the tax on estates over $50 million to 70 percent, but the law retained a provision for a tax exemption for bequests to charitable, religious, and educational organizations. The Fords responded by creating a foundation in January of 1936. The arrangement placed 95 percent of company stock under the charge of the foundation. Although Edsel Ford initially envisioned small-scale philanthropic goals, the massive endowment of company equity made the Ford Foundation the largest and most influential charitable organization in the world, until it was surpassed by the endowment of the Bill and Melinda Gates Foundation in 2006.

Its sheer size makes Ford as financially powerful as an arm of a reasonably sized government—with one important difference: as a private foundation, it lacks the constraints of government, and in particular its accountability. Foundations like Ford and the recipients of their largesse are the only political players in America who don't have to answer to a constituency. They shape our society, culture, and politics but are self-perpetuating and answer to no one but themselves. By contrast, state and federal governments are constrained by a multitude of laws and oversight committees when they dispense money, and ultimately are responsible to the electorate. If government programs fail or go awry, the electorate can demand changes and get them. There is no electorate for foundation executives and there are no shareholders to exercise control over the foundations themselves.

In contrast to profit-making corporations, which are the only private institutions of comparable weight and influence, tax-exempt foundations are ideological and their investments reflect the partisan agendas of one side of the political spectrum. Unlike profit-making corporations, tax-exempt foundations don't have to compete or provide services that are desired by large publics in order to survive. As long as they don't violate IRS rules that bar direct contributions to candidates and parties, tax-exempt foundations can operate without constraints.

Profit-making corporations are subject to market forces and pay a price if they alienate any section of the population. Within wide limits (as, for example, funding terrorists) tax-exempt foundations have no such constraints. Unlike corporations, foundations are ideological, and typically do not support actors on both sides of controversial issues. In contrast, profit-making corporations typically make political contributions to both major parties, typically avoid controversies, and take stands only on issues that directly affect their narrowly defined economic interests and with rare exceptions avoid identification with any ideology. Foundations are thus unique ideological autocracies at the heart of American society. Absent checks on their power and influence, they can and do disenfranchise larger and larger segments of the population.

Edsel Ford died from cancer in 1943 at the age of forty-nine;

Henry died in 1947. In the years following the founder's death, the foundation also became unmoored from the conservative views of the Ford donors. In 1951, the foundation began receiving millions of dollars in dividends from the massive endowment of stock left it by Henry and Edsel. Almost overnight the foundation was transformed into the country's largest and most influential philanthropy. At the time, young Henry Ford II was preoccupied with reviving the company that had foundered under years of mismanagement, and he could not devote attention to running the foundation. To oversee its newly lavish budget, Ford turned to Paul Hoffman, former president of the Studebaker Corporation and a liberal Republican.[36]

Hoffman was made the foundation's president in 1951 and immediately launched its political realignment with a symbolic change of location, moving the foundation from the Ford Company's base in Dearborn, Michigan, to a location near his home in Pasadena, California, as well as to New York City. These geographic changes heralded a shift in the nature and direction of the foundation's charitable giving that would take a dramatic turn in 1966, when McGeorge Bundy became the Ford Foundation's president and engineered its political transformation into a radical force in American life.

A liberal Republican and onetime Cold War warrior who had served as a national security adviser to Presidents John F. Kennedy and Lyndon Johnson, Bundy hailed from the coterie of foreign policy advisers and intellectuals—ironically dubbed "the best and the brightest" by journalist David Halberstam—who had initially advocated American intervention in Vietnam but who came to regret their support for the war and migrated to the left politically.[37] Bundy brought that political outlook with him to the helm of the Ford Foundation. Under his direction, Ford became a leading sponsor of progressive causes—expanding welfare, nuclear disarmament, environmental advocacy, and the creation of "civil rights" interest groups that emphasized ethnic identity and ethnic power—"multiculturalism"—over integration and assimilation into the American culture. Ford gave as much as $300 million a year, every year, throughout the 1960s to support such causes.[38]

Intentions notwithstanding, Ford's sponsorship of radical causes frequently proved destructive to those it was intended to help. In 1967, on the advice of academic radicals in New York, Bundy aligned Ford with members of the black power movement to establish a community-run set of schools in the predominantly black Ocean Hill–Brownsville section of Brooklyn.[39] Between 1967 and 1968, Ford gave over $900,000 to fund New York City schools as part of its "community control experiments."[40] In theory, the Ford-funded project was supposed to empower minority communities and improve inner-city education by giving minority parents full control over their school districts. In practice, it proved divisive and counterproductive.

When the mostly black school board fired the mostly white (and largely Jewish) teachers in the district, it precipitated a bitter and drawn-out fight with the teachers' union, which came to its members' defense. Many of the newly appointed teachers under the program were not remotely qualified for the job. Often the Ford-backed schools were staffed with black power militants who were antiwhite and anti-Semitic, further fueling the tensions.[41] One notorious poem by a teacher appointed through the Ocean Hill–Brownsville program read: "Hey Jewboy, with the yarmulke on your head / You paleface Jewboy, I wish you were dead."[42] Some of the new teachers were white graduate students with no teaching experience, who were drawn to the project for political reasons. As a result, education at participating schools deteriorated. When the project was terminated after three years, minority students at Ocean Hill–Brownsville schools actually performed worse on reading tests than before the project began.

Undiscouraged, the social engineers at Ford bankrolled the black power movement a second time when they steered grants to the Cleveland chapter of the Congress of Racial Equality (CORE) to support its voter registration drive among blacks. Ford funds paid for black youths to attend classes at CORE's headquarters. These classes, which were ostensibly about black history and heritage, stoked racial division by teaching what one disgusted black councilman described as "race hatred."[43]

Most notoriously, Ford grants to CORE helped tip the balance in Cleveland's mayoral race to elect Democrat Carl Stokes, a politician linked with the radical black power movement, as the city's first black mayor in 1967. In what many saw as a partisan effort, Ford gave CORE a grant of $175,000 with $30,000 going toward voter registration efforts aimed exclusively at black voters. Buoyed by the registration drive, Stokes was able to prevail in a tightly contested race.[44] These registration drives were the seeds that led to the creation of organizations involved in similar efforts nationally such as ACORN.[45]

Ford's "march to the Left" would ultimately provoke a bitter falling-out between the foundation's staff and trustees and most particularly Edsel Ford's son Henry Ford II, the last member of the Ford family to serve on the foundation's board. In 1976, a disillusioned Ford terminated his thirty-four-year-tenure with a protest against the leftward course his family's foundation had pursued. In a stinging letter of resignation, Ford excoriated the trustees for using Ford funds to support left-wing causes while abandoning the commitment to free enterprise that had made possible the profits from which the foundation was created and the funds that it dispensed in its grants: "The foundation exists and thrives on the fruits of our economic system. The dividends of competitive enterprise make it all possible. A significant portion of the abundance created by U.S. business enables the foundation and like institutions to carry on their work. In effect, the foundation is a creature of capitalism—a statement that, I'm sure, would be shocking to many people in the field of philanthropy. It is hard to discern recognition of this fact in anything the foundation does. It is even more difficult to find an understanding of this in many of the institutions, particularly the universities, that are the recipients of the foundation's grant programs."[46] Ford wryly observed, "that the system that makes the foundation possible very probably is worth preserving."[47]

Ford's warning fell on deaf ears.[48] Under McGeorge Bundy's leadership, the foundation made what it considered "civil rights" causes a priority. In fact, what it supported were left-wing agendas within the civil rights movement. Because the foundation's staff members were more and more politically partisan, even within the narrow definition laid down by the IRS guidelines governing its tax exemption, they resorted to a combination of audacity and finesse in pursuing their agendas. In particular, they had to convince moderate board members that the foundation should be using its funds to bankroll groups and agendas the IRS might regard as inappropriate beneficiaries for a charitable organization.

That task fell to Sanford Jaffe, the director of Ford's Government and Law Program from 1968 to 1983. Prior to his appointment, Jaffe had served as the executive director of the "Select Commission on Civil Disorder," established in 1968 by New Jersey's governor, Democrat Richard Hughes. The commission published a study examining the underlying causes of the violent and destructive riots that had erupted in the predominantly black inner-city of Newark in the summer of 1967. Like the President's Advisory Commission on Civil Disorders initiated by President Lyndon Johnson, the New Jersey commission concluded that white racism and systemic inequities were the primary causes of the criminal events in Newark. As Jaffe later put it, the riots were sparked by "the inattention to the needs and aspirations of the black community, and the absence of opportunities available across the board."[49]

Blaming urban riots on poverty and racism rather than the breakdown of families and community moral structures reflected a rapidly forming consensus on the left. The commission's report's prescriptions were of a similar cast, proposing vast increases in government welfare programs as a "solution" to the "root causes" of the violence, in particular lack of income. That both the riots and the poverty were the likely result of disintegrating family and community structures in the inner city was a conclusion of the report filed by Democrat Pat Moynihan and commissioned by Lyndon Johnson. The Moynihan Report, as it became known, was quickly buried under claims by the Left that it was "racist" in "blaming the victim."[50]

The newly forming liberal consensus was reflected in the Select Commission's recommendation of a government takeover of inner-city schools to improve the woeful state of education for Newark's black youth.[51] In response to the commission's findings, Governor Hughes proposed that New Jersey absorb 100 percent of the welfare costs from counties and municipalities across the state while at the same time pumping massive infusions of aid to cities like Newark.[52]

Republicans in the state legislature would eventually cut the figure down to a still-substantial 50 percent in the final version of the aid package, but the governor's decision to implement the commission's findings began a cycle of fiscal recklessness that put New Jersey in straitened economic circumstances. Nearly thirty years later, skyrocketing out-of-wedlock birth rates, endemic dependency and escalating crime rates led a Democratic president, Bill Clinton, to sign a massive welfare reform bill recognizing that many of the problems of the inner-city "underclass" had been fostered if not created by the government programs designed to remedy them.

The challenge faced by Jaffe and the other progressives at Ford was to promote the agendas of left-wing Democrats while camouflaging their political nature, thus conforming to the legal requirements of a tax-exempt organization. Aware that this was uncharted territory and legally problematic, Jaffe wondered how he might insulate the Ford Foundation from "criticism both from some people on the Ford board and a lot of people from the outside."[53] The strategy he devised was to form a Public Interest Law Advisory Committee of the Foundation. Composed of four ex-presidents of the American Bar Association, the committee would assess grants and lend the stamp of nonpartisan prestige to an increasingly political grant-making strategy. When the foundation's grants then came under attack for their political nature, Jaffe could tell the board, "Look, I got the advice of these four people."[54]

The strategy was so successful it initially helped diffuse opposition even from critics on the board like Henry Ford II. In order to win Ford's approval, Jaffe made William Gossett, the Ford Motor Company's general counsel, one of the members of his advisory committee. As Jaffe would later recall, "That became a key element to say to Henry Ford if he had a problem, 'Well, Bill Gossett, your lawyer, thinks that this is a worthwhile enterprise, he's joining us in looking at it.'"

Protected by layers of carefully orchestrated legitimacy, Jaffe's approach cleared the way for Ford to fund the creation of left-wing public-interest law firms, where previously the board might otherwise have been reluctant to endorse such nakedly partisan grants. As further insurance, Jaffe made sure that every firm would have a "litigation committee" composed of the kind of white-shoe lawyers that served on Ford's board. That way, if the firms Ford backed were to endorse partisan liberal causes, Jaffe could claim that it was all approved at the highest levels. "We'd say, 'Now, wait a minute, they have a distinguished board and besides that they have a litigation committee and they cannot file a lawsuit unless the litigation committee's approved it.' Now look who's on the litigation committee. Arthur Goldberg, you know, was a former Supreme Court justice, this person and that person are all senior partners at law firms."[55] As one critic notes, "The program's officers did all they could to give this potentially explosive program a smooth, establishment veneer."[56]

Internal critics may have been appeased by Jaffe's strategy—temporarily, in the case of Henry Ford II—but there also remained concerns that the foundation's support for organizations with a political agenda could invite unwanted attention from the federal government. The foundation's nonprofit tax status could be jeopardized if it funded groups allied with progressive movements and causes. According to the relevant provision of the IRS tax code, known as 501(c)(3), nonprofits eligible for tax deductibility must be dedicated to education and charity and not to partisan causes, and must not "attempt to influence legislation."[57] As Ford's president McGeorge Bundy wondered, "What if somebody hassles us about the charitable nature of this?"[58] But the foundation found an important loophole in the tax code: public-interest law firms did not fall directly under the requirement prohibiting 501(c)(3) political advocacy and thus their funding by Ford could not technically be construed as politically motivated. It was a discovery that would leave long-lasting effects on American politics and institutions.

In recent years, the Ford Foundation's penchant for funding radical causes has been so extreme that even liberals otherwise supportive of Ford and its philanthropy have spoken out against some of its giving. In 2003, the *Jewish Telegraphic Agency* reported that the Ford Foundation was funding scores of anti-Israel and Palestinian advocacy groups and nongovernmental organizations, many of which engaged in anti-Israel agitation and some of which overtly supported and promoted anti-Israel terrorist groups.[59]

In 2000, for instance, Ford awarded a grant to a group called the Palestinian NGO Network. One year later, the group was at the forefront of a bigoted campaign seeking anti-Israel resolutions at the 2001 UN World Conference Against Racism in Durban, South Africa. Ford also awarded $100,000 to a group called the Al Mezan Center for Human Rights in Gaza. The grants were ostensibly designed to support "community-based advocacy work on economic, social and cultural rights in Gaza." But in fact the Al Mezan Center's advocacy work was carried out in close collaboration with radical organizations like the International Solidarity Movement, a pro-terrorist organization notorious for its efforts to obstruct Israeli security forces in the Palestinian territories. The Al Mezan Center also operated a website condemning Israeli offensives against the Islamic terrorist group Hamas.

Yet another group, which received $365,000 worth of funding from the Ford Foundation, was the Jerusalem Media and Communication Centre. According to the foundation, the grants were for "media services for the foreign press and a weekly electronic magazine," as well as "enhancement of media activities related to the crisis situation." But the center's idea of media activities included maintaining a website that promoted six Palestinian terrorist groups, among them the People's Front for the Liberation of Palestine, Islamic Jihad, and Hamas.

Revelations of the extremist recipients of Ford's grants in the Middle East ignited a backlash in the United States. Even liberal Democrats like New York Rep. Jerold Nadler threatened to convene a congressional investigation if the foundation didn't end its support for such groups. Under intense scrutiny, the Ford Foundation apologized, withdrew funding for one Palestinian grantee, and forced all future grantees to sign an agreement that they would not "promote or engage in violence, terrorism, bigotry, or the destruction of any state."[60]

To repair its strained ties with liberal Jews, the foundation also hired Stuart Eizenstat, a former Clinton official with connections to the Jewish community, to "help promote a new policy forbidding grant recipients from supporting terrorism or bigotry."[61] Despite this aggressive damage control, the most notable aspect of the funding scandal is that, in the absence of a protest, including from many liberal supporters of the foundation, Ford would have continued to fund anti-Israel groups that promoted terrorism.

Ford is the most striking example of how far once-conservative foundations have strayed from their original intent. Progressive foundations are so dominant in the philanthropic field that they are able to shape the direction of other funders, whose governing bodies are still those appointed by their original funders. An example of this is the transformation of the Colorado-based Daniels Fund, a $1 billion philanthropy created in 2000 from the estate of cable television tycoon Bill Daniels. Daniels was a conservative Republican who had sought the Republican nomination for governor of Colorado in 1974. In starting his foundation, he identified the Daniels Fund's areas of giving but did not leave any instructions about how its operations were to be conducted.

That task was taken up by the fund's first president, Phil Hogue, who once worked for Daniels at Daniels & Associates. Hoping to figure out a direction for the foundation, Hogue sought advice from the most prominent and what he believed to be the most successful foundations in the country, all of which by that time also happened to be on the left, despite the fact that they were all created from the fortunes of extremely conservative men: the Ford Foundation, the Rockefeller Foundation, the MacArthur Foundation, and the Pew Charitable Trusts. As a result of their advice, the Daniels Fund's operating policies—everything from the proper role of the board, to grant-giving criteria, to grant processing—became modeled after the policies in place at major left-wing foundations. Heeding the counsel given by Ford and the others, the Daniels Fund also adopted their view that its board, which happened to include a number of outspoken conservatives, should be marginalized in favor of a staff of professionals culled from the field of philanthropy—a field dominated by the Left. The Daniels Fund thus hired a staff of industry professionals and allowed them to determine the mission of the foundation that Bill Daniels's fortune had created. Under the operating procedures that were adopted from other players in the philanthropy business, staff could make grants of up to $50,000 without board approval.

In short order, the sixty to seventy progressive staff members who had been hired to run the Daniels Fund were turning down funding requests from conservative groups and causes even as they approved funding for liberal ones, often without the knowledge of the board. Although Phil Hogue had not been driven by ideology in seeking advice from the left-wing foundations, and although he did not intend to remake the Daniels Fund in their image, the end result of following their advice and imitating their operational policies was just that.

One conservative recalls a panel on philanthropy he attended at Harvard where Hogue was a participant and observed him eagerly soaking up their advice. "The Harvard people were tickled pink that they had such a receptive student in Hogue and that he was going to set up a state-of-the-art foundation based on their strictly 'neutral' and 'nonideological' expert advice. I knew we had lost Daniels when I met a former Rockefeller program officer at a reception who had just been hired at Daniels. Who can quarrel with foundation expertise acquired at one of the nation's best! And I'm sure all the while Hogue thought he was just doing the most professional job he could in carrying out Daniels's will. That's why the Daniels story is more than ordinarily instructive in the annals of Lost Foundations."[62]

Today, the Daniels Fund invests $50 million a year in such traditional charitable causes as care for seniors, substance abuse counseling, and assistance to people with physical disabilities. The foundation does support some causes that are identifiably libertarian or conservative, especially on K–12 education reform, giving money to initiatives like vouchers and charter schools. But those familiar with the Daniels Fund's operations say that this is the legacy of the dwindling number of conservatives on the board and, in the absence of a strong champion, likely will not be sustained in the future. When the foundation recently sponsored an ad campaign on Denver news stations critical of K–12 education in the Denver area, it stirred a backlash from the local education establishment and the teachers' unions. Rather than defend the content of the ad, the foundation decided to pull it and end the campaign. Recounting the Daniels Fund's political transformation, one conservative grumbles, "It's a prime example of the way we lose good money. It isn't that someone sets out to make them liberal. It's that someone sets out to make them professional and respectable, which means consulting with the Ford Foundation and others. The result is the same: a left-wing foundation built with right-wing money."[63]

The network of progressive foundations built with right-wing and left-wing fortunes now exceeds over a hundred institutions, with assets of over $100 billion, the largest concentration of money available for political purposes ever amassed, and more than ten times the size of its conservative counterpart.[64] It has spawned a secondary network of 501(c)3 policy think tanks and advocacy groups that number in the thousands, and that, in areas of critical social and political import, can deploy resources that exceed those of their conservative rivals by as much as a hundred to one.[65] The consequences of this new institutional leviathan for the ideas, policies, and eventually laws that shape the American polity and determine its future are—and already have been—momentous. They are explored in the chapters that follow.

4.

DECONSTRUCTING THE AMERICAN IDENTITY

Before his campaign for the presidency inspired a new caution in his speeches and more centrist tone in his pronouncements, Barack Obama was not diffident about identifying himself as a political leftist. Yet even as his speeches came under national scrutiny and their tone became more moderate, less guarded comments he had made earlier in his career were notable for the lack of attention they received. One of these occurred during Senator Obama's keynote to the convention of the National Council of La Raza in July 2007. Despite the explicit racial overtones of the name ("La Raza" means "the race" in Spanish), no one questioned the presidential hopeful's association with a radical group despite the fact that he was then styling himself as a "postracial" candidate. Nor were there objections when Obama described La Raza as a "bottom-up, grassroots movement that can transform a nation," or when he promised that he would "never walk away from the 12 million undocumented immigrants" in America—which was how the Left referred to illegal aliens—or even when he suggested that the inability of the "undocumented" to communicate in their new country was actually the fault of Americans and the "language barriers we refuse to break down."[1]

The lack of a reaction to Obama's radicalism was hardly a mystery. The reason his statements failed to raise eyebrows whether among the press or among Democratic Party officials was that they had long since become a conventional wisdom for self-described liberals who were prominent among America's cultural elites. This was not the case in the America that existed from the founding until the 1980s, when obedience to the nation's laws and assimilation to its language and culture were accepted conditions of becoming an American. Until then, no one described illegal immigrants with the evasive term "undocumented." The term suggests an immigrant who has lost his papers, not one who never applied for them.

By the same token, immigrants were expected to learn English. It would have been unthinkable to suggest that it was up to Americans to accommodate the linguistic preferences of foreigners immigrating to their country—let alone those who had forced their entry into the country illegally. This was the consensus not only among native-born Americans both liberal and conservative, but also among immigrant communities and their organizations, such as the grassroots Hispanic civil rights groups that were the forerunners of La Raza.

All this began to change as a result of the upheavals of the 1960s, when multibillion-dollar funding organizations, and in particular Ford, came under the direction of increasingly liberal and then overtly left-wing staff. Despite its authorization as a tax-exempt foundation set up to promote the general (nonpartisan) welfare, Ford had created an army of progressive "public-interest" law firms, designed to advance the agendas of the political left. Among these tax-exempt advocacy groups were the Mexican American Legal Defense Fund

(MALDEF), the National Council of La Raza, and the Puerto Rican Legal Defense and Education Fund. With the backing of the Ford Foundation, these groups were empowered to fundamentally transform the public debate about immigration, both legal and illegal, and ultimately shape national policy to reflect agendas that originated on the political fringe and, in the absence of Ford money, would probably have remained there.

MALDEF was the brainchild of Latino activist and lawyer Peter Tijerina, a member of the San Antonio, Texas, chapter of the League of United Latin American Citizens (LULAC), the country's oldest Hispanic organization. Representing a traditional outlook, LULAC was created to defend the civil rights of new citizens and emphasized cultural and political assimilation and pro-American patriotism. Both themes were reflected in LULAC's code, which stated: "Respect your citizenship; honor your country, maintain its traditions in the minds of your children; incorporate yourself in the culture and civilization."[2]

Peter Tijerina, by contrast, was inspired by the example of the radical Latino activists who came to prominence during the cultural ferment of the 1960s. Preaching "brown power" and "Chicano power," they urged Latinos to embrace their ethnic origins, reject assimilation, and confront America's "racist" and "oppressive system" along with their ethnic elders who had betrayed the Latino cause through assimilation. Speaking for the new radical generation, labor leader—and Saul Alinsky acolyte—Cesar Chavez called for a "social revolution" against "pretty, perfumed sellouts."[3] Tijerina himself was galvanized by the example of Latino militant Reies Tijerina (no relation), a New Mexico–based preacher who led a series of violent actions in the 1960s to occupy land he claimed rightfully belonged to Hispanics but had been stolen by "Anglo" ranchers and lawyers. Reies Tijerina would be arrested and serve prison time following an armed 1967 raid on a New Mexico courthouse, in which two police officers were shot, but the incident spawned national headlines and made Tijerina a role model for the Chicano left.

Seeking to emulate his model, Peter Tijerina conceived the idea for a more confrontational alternative to LULAC. In 1967, he approached the Ford Foundation for support in setting up a new Chicano rights organization based on the premise that Mexican Americans were an oppressed minority. It was not an obvious appeal. Despite an often difficult immigrant experience, Hispanics in the United States had never been subjected to the kind of systemic racism suffered by African Americans. There were no Jim Crow laws for Mexican Americans, and the recently passed Civil Rights Acts had ended all forms of legal segregation and outlawed segregation.[4] Black leaders immediately took issue with the new Latino activists' claims that the plight of Mexicans paralleled theirs and required a civil rights organization based on those claims.

Nevertheless, the Ford Foundation leadership welcomed Tijerina's request and endorsed his radical indictment of American pluralism. Ford president McGeorge Bundy announced the foundation's acceptance of the radical perspective in a formal statement equating the situation of former slaves who had suffered more than a half century of legal segregation in the American South and had been systematically discriminated against across the country with Mexican Americans who did not share this history: "In terms of the legal enforcement of rights, American citizens of Mexican descent are now where the Negro community was a quarter-century ago."[5] In 1968, on this faulty premise, the Ford Foundation granted Tijerina's Mexican American Legal Defense Fund (MALDEF) nearly $2.2 million over five years.

In June of the same year, the Ford Foundation also established the Southwest Council of La Raza (later the National Council of La Raza) with a $630,000 grant. The National Council of La Raza was billed as a community organizing effort to help the "barrios to help themselves." Despite the civic-sounding mission, La Raza's agenda, like its leadership, was politically radical—a Latino version of the Alinsky grassroots movements. Maclovio Barraza, the founding chairman of

La Raza's board of directors, had been cited by the federal government's Subversive Activities Control Board as a Communist Party member. Barraza claimed that Mexican Americans in the Southwest were victims of an American system that made them one of "the most disadvantaged segments of our society."

La Raza's first executive director, Herman Gallegos, was a community organizer who had worked with Alinsky to set up a local chapter of the Community Service Organization, the California-based Mexican American political action group that served as a forerunner to MALDEF and La Raza. In the 1960s, Gallegos became a consultant for the Ford Foundation and urged it to provide financial support for groups like La Raza. In later years, he would wield that same influence on the boards of other prominent foundations, including Rockefeller, which had increasingly come under the influence of left-wing heirs and staffers.

With Ford's financial backing, MALDEF and La Raza quickly outgrew their humble beginnings. During the first three decades of MALDEF's existence, Ford provided almost all of its funding, a king's ransom for what had begun as a modest organization totaling $25 million.[6] Ford funding also provided the radical MALDEF with a mainstream imprimatur, helping the organization draw additional millions from foundations like Carnegie and Rockefeller and from corporations like Anheuser-Busch, Coca-Cola, AT&T, and Verizon, among others. As a result, having started as a fringe civil rights group in San Antonio, Texas, with no national impact, MALDEF became a nationally influential advocacy group with regional offices in Atlanta, Los Angeles, San Antonio, Chicago, and Washington, D.C.; a satellite office in Sacramento; and program offices in Phoenix, Albuquerque, and Houston. MALDEF today has net assets of $7.9 million, an annual budget of $6.2 million, and a staff of seventy-five, among whom are twenty-two attorneys, and is without question one of the two most important rights advocates speaking for Mexican Americans.

The other is La Raza, equally a Ford Foundation creation. When it first began in 1968 as the radical Southwest Council of La Raza in Phoenix, the organization had modest ambitions. It was supposed to apply the funds Ford provided to support community organizing efforts and develop local Hispanic leadership.[7] Thanks to $30 million in Ford grants through 2002, and the ancillary grants of foundations and companies that followed Ford's lead, La Raza has become a major political organization on a national scale. Today La Raza boasts that it is the "largest national Hispanic civil rights and advocacy organization in the United States." With net assets of $46.6 million, La Raza claims more than three hundred affiliate organizations in forty-one states and a connected network of "30,000 groups and individuals nationwide."[8] Mindful of that influence, Democratic presidential aspirants, including Barack Obama, now seek La Raza's backing and make a show of supporting its political agendas.

Even more impressive than their size is what MALDEF and La Raza, backed by Ford Foundation funds, have been able to accomplish. In one generation they have radically transformed the immigration debate in America, which now features widely accepted direct attacks on the very idea of national sovereignty and the de facto elimination of any requirement for citizenship rights.

As the leading Hispanic advocacy organizations, MALDEF and La Raza have each been called to testify at congressional hearings more than one hundred times since the 1970s.[9] Much of their policy agenda has been passed into law—whether in the form of federally funded bilingual education; in-state tuition rates for illegal immigrants; the granting of driver's licenses regardless of immigration status; the establishment of "sanctuary cities"; and amnesty for illegal immigrants.

Through their advocacy campaigns, these groups have radically distorted the concept of citizenship rights, transforming them into "human rights" as though the establishment of such rights had nothing to do with the existence of a nation-state that was committed to those rights. These were rights once reserved for actual citizens and legal residents. But today they are widely presumed to apply to those in the country illegally with no commitment to preserving them. As former MALDEF president Vilma Martinez has said, "Our definition of Mexican-American has expanded to encompass not only the citizen, but also the permanent resident alien, and the undocumented alien."[10] No other country in the world, including and especially Mexico, would accept such a definition regarding any immigrant group.

In keeping with their campaign to erase the distinction between citizens and foreigners who are in the United States illegally, MALDEF and La Raza lawyers have waged a relentless assault on local and national attempts to enforce existing American immigration laws. Most brazenly they have promoted "sanctuary city" policies that prevent police from checking the immigration status of criminals, verifying resident status in the workplace, or securing the nation's borders. MALDEF's opposition to border enforcement efforts is so effective it routinely trumps national security concerns. In the 1990s, for instance, MALDEF opposed a US government campaign to stop the flow of illegal drugs across the US-Mexico border because it would mean heightened border security. After the September 11 terrorist attacks, MALDEF's radical legal team led the opposition against Operation Tarmac, an INS crackdown on illegal aliens employed in secure sections of the nation's airports.[11]

Most significantly, MALDEF and La Raza, supported by a network of left-wing organizations and foundations (including the ACLU and the Center for Constitutional Rights), have succeeded in defining the parameters of the immigration debate on their terms by labeling opponents of their radical agendas "anti-immigrant" nativists and racists, while deriding critics of their antisovereignty, antisecurity agendas as "McCarthyites." Typical was a 2008 campaign called "We Can Stop the Hate." Launched by La Raza with the assistance of MALDEF and the George Soros–funded groups Media Matters and the Center for American Progress, the campaign was designed to silence critics who raised alarms about mass illegal immigration into the United States and who opposed amnesty for illegal immigrants and open borders.[12] The campaign made no attempt to answer the substantive concerns of the critics—for instance, the presence of an estimated 12–20 million illegal immigrants in the country; the budget-breaking economic burdens placed on social services and education provided by municipalities and states; the disproportionate crime and gang activity associated with illegal immigrants (illegals account for over 29 *percent* of prisoners in Federal Bureau of Prisons facilities and are the fastest-growing segment of the federal criminal population);[13] or the fact that illegal immigration is perceived by Hispanic radicals as a way to reclaim the southwestern United States for Mexico and that, demographically, politically, and culturally, this *reconquista* movement is already under way in that part of the country.[14]

Instead, the La Raza campaign set out to demonize its opponents, dismissing such concerns as the "rhetoric of hate groups, nativists, and vigilantes."[15] Crude as these tactics may seem, such smear campaigns have been successful in forging an orthodoxy on immigration issues, which coincides with the radical agendas of Ford's offspring, MAL-DEF and La Raza. The result is the wholesale sabotage of the idea of citizenship and national sovereignty—unparalleled in any other nation and a prime agenda of what the Hudson Institute's John Fonte describes as "transnational progressives"—activists who consider themselves "citizens of the world" and denigrate national loyalties and patriotism as "reactionary" and unenlightened.[16]

With the election of Barack Obama, many of these radical agendas now have a powerful advocate in the federal government. In April 2010, the Arizona legislature passed SB 1070, a law making illegal immigration a state crime and giving state police broader powers to detain illegal immigrants when they were stopped for an unrelated infraction. The statute was designed to implement existing federal law, which remained unenforced, and was a belated response to an

illegal immigration crisis—exacerbated by years of lack of enforcement—that has devastated the southern border states, and Arizona in
particular.

As a direct consequence of mass illegal immigration, Arizona has
experienced an explosion in crime, including kidnappings and drug-
related felonies. In 2010, the Department of Justice's National Drug
Threat Assessment reported that there had been 267 kidnappings in
Phoenix in 2007 and 299 in 2008, with the victims usually connected
to immigrant smuggling groups or drug traffickers.[17] Moreover, illegal
immigrants made up a disproportionate share of the state's prison population. Arizona has also grown more dangerous for legal residents. In
March 2010, a rancher in Arizona's Cochise County, a border area
associated with illegal immigrant crossing and drug smuggling, was
gunned down on his property. The suspected murderers were illegal
immigrants.[18] Against this background, SB 1070 was a reasonable step
to restore the rule of law.

Yet the backlash that greeted SB 1070 was anything but reasonable. MALDEF pronounced the law "unacceptable," and progressives
following its lead lambasted SB 1070 as intolerant and "draconian" in
its supposed subversion of rights.[19] Almost without exception elected
officials of the national Democratic Party adhered to the MALDEF
line, with Colorado congressman Jared Polis going so far as to declare
that the law was "reminiscent" of Nazi Germany and likening Arizona
to a "police state."[20] These charges were echoed by the Obama White
House, which went on the warpath against the Arizona law. The president claimed the law would "undermine basic notions of fairness that
we cherish as Americans,"[21] while the Justice Department launched
a lawsuit to prevent SB 1070 from going into effect. In July 2010, a
federal judge bowed to MALDEF's demands and blocked key provisions of the law.

In fact, the text of SB 1070 was copied nearly verbatim from
the existing but unenforced federal law.[22] That it could touch off a
national controversy was a commentary on how far the immigration

debate had shifted. That it would elicit opposition from the Justice Department, the chief law enforcement agency in the land, indicated how powerful the Left's influence had become.

No such debate could have taken place prior to the Ford Foundation's creation of MALDEF and La Raza as generously funded radical organizations. Ford had made these groups the effective voice of the Hispanic community, although there is no evidence that either of them—both almost exclusively dependent on Ford and other non-Hispanic support—could make a credible claim to this role in the absence of Ford's support. As author Linda Chavez notes, "[T]he Ford Foundation virtually created the infrastructure of the contemporary Hispanic policy movement," while Henry Santiestevan, a former head of La Raza, concedes that "without the Ford Foundation's commitment . . . the Chicano movement would have withered away in many areas."[23]

Nonetheless, the optical illusion created by Ford's largesse enabled MALDEF, La Raza, and the reformed LULAC to introduce the agendas of the radical left into the American mainstream and make their views on the issues of national borders and immigration the official position of the Democratic Party. As a result, today the country does not have a national debate between conservatives and liberals over immigration but rather a debate between conservatives and leftists who want to deconstruct American sovereignty and the traditional notion of citizenship rights.

MALDEF and La Raza not only pushed the mainstream American debate on immigration to the left, but in the process of doing so radicalized Hispanic groups once distinguished by their political moderation. A prime example is LULAC, whose traditional approaches to immigration and citizenship had offended radicals like Peter Tijerina and inspired them to start MALDEF. Where once liberal groups like LULAC had touted the virtues of patriotism, legal immigration, and cultural assimilation, by the 1980s that view of citizenship had become the province of so-called reactionaries and the political right.

Echoing the MALDEF/La Raza rhetoric of Chicano separatism, LULAC officials now stridently declared, "We cannot assimilate! We will not assimilate!"[24] In point of fact, LULAC began receiving Ford Foundation funding in 1981. With Ford behind it, LULAC joined MALDEF and La Raza, as the country's three most influential Hispanic organizations.

On the other hand, despite its acceptance by national media and the Democratic Party, the rejection of traditional notions of citizenship by Ford-funded groups like MALDEF is not the mainstream sentiment of the Hispanic community. On the contrary, prominent Mexican American leaders have long assailed these organizations for warping the Hispanic community's traditional views on immigration issues. The late San Antonio congressman Henry Gonzalez, a liberal Democrat, repeatedly condemned groups like MALDEF for their attacks on American pluralism and cultural assimilation, likening them to white segregationists that activists of his generation had fought against. In a speech before the House of Representatives, Gonzalez characterized their agenda as the "belief that racism in reverse is the answer to racism and discrimination" and that "simple, blind, and stupid hatred is an adequate response to simple, blind, and stupid hatred."[25]

Gonzalez vowed to oppose those groups as he had other racists, but his efforts were neutralized by the massive progressive network, which Ford and the left-wing foundations funded. Because of these funds and their influence, moderate voices like Gonzalez's were drowned out by the sectarian radical chorus. Nor was the wider Hispanic community able to influence the agendas of the Ford-sponsored organizations. Despite purporting to represent that community, organizations like MALDEF and La Raza were effectively independent of it and not accountable. Their money came from corporations and wealthy left-wing foundations with no Hispanic base. Even as they postured as the authentic voice of Hispanic Americans, MALDEF and La Raza remained aloof and unresponsive—indeed often hostile to the Hispanic American community's concerns.

The success of Ford's radical intervention into the politics of Mexican Americans was paralleled by its intervention into the politics of another Latino community. In 1972, the Puerto Rican Legal Defense and Education Fund (PRLDEF) was founded with a Ford seed grant. The New York City–based organization was created with the stated aim of providing legal support for Puerto Ricans and the wider Hispanic community.[26] But over the following three decades, PRLDEF came to push the same radical agendas as its sister Ford organizations, MALDEF and La Raza—from bilingual education, to racial quotas in hiring, racial gerrymandering of voting districts, and amnesty for illegal immigrants. One of PRLDEF's campaigns involved representing plaintiffs in lawsuits against the New York City police and sanitation departments. When Hispanics performed worse on hiring exams than their white counterparts and were denied jobs as a result, PRLDEF sued the departments for hiring discrimination and alleged "cultural bias" on their exams.

Like MALDEF and La Raza, PRLDEF's agenda would have a transformative effect on American policy and institutions, most prominently through its efforts to nurture a cadre of left-wing Latino lawyers to influence public policy and opinion. The most significant of these lawyers was future justice Sonia Sotomayor, an alumnus of PRLDEF's board, and the first Puerto Rican American to be elevated to the Supreme Court.

Handpicked by José Cabranes, a Puerto Rican lawyer who was her mentor when she was a student at Yale, Sotomayor served on the PRLDEF board for twelve years, her entire legal career prior to becoming a federal judge in 1992. In that time, Sotomayor served as vice president and chair of PRLDEF's litigation and education committees. As a board member she promoted the foundation's core view that Puerto Ricans—despite their exemption from federal income taxes (even while receiving billions in federal assistance) and their effective dual citizenship (even while being exempted from military service) were an oppressed minority in the United States, requiring the intervention of a group like PRLDEF to safeguard their rights in an official system stacked against them. As Sotomayor herself described its mission, PRLDEF protected the "civil and human rights of disadvantaged Hispanics." Like other radicals, Sotomayor did not specify which "human rights" she believed were not already included in America's constitutional framework, unless it was the right to enjoy the privileges of citizenship without going through a legal immigration process.

During her Supreme Court confirmation hearings in the summer of 2009, Sotomayor professed ignorance of PRLDEF's political positions and distanced herself from statements she had made in the course of her career that betrayed her radical beliefs. One potential stumbling block to her confirmation by the Senate was her involvement in a legal case brought by PRLDEF against the New York City Police Department in the 1980s. Representing black and Hispanic sergeants, PRLDEF filed suit against the department over its allegedly "racist" promotion exam. Test consultants to the department demonstrated that there was nothing racist about requiring police sergeants to show competence in standard English. But PRLDEF prevailed in court, engineering a radical redesign of the exam to allow more minorities to achieve a passing grade, while degrading existing department standards.[27] As a federal judge, Sotomayor followed PRLDEF's precedent of racial favoritism in her ruling in the case of *Ricci v. DeStefano*, the controversial New Haven, Connecticut, racial discrimination case.[28] In the proceedings, Sotomayor refused to overrule a decision against white New Haven firefighters who had passed promotional exams for lieutenant and captain positions, yet were denied the promotions because the city deemed that not enough minorities had been able to pass those same exams.

More broadly, Sotomayor adopted both PRLDEF's racial essentialism and its indictment of the American system as unjust to minorities. On more than one occasion she has said that a "wise Latina" could "more often than not reach a better conclusion than a white male who hasn't lived that life," as though interpretation of the law is a racial matter, in effect rejecting the idea that judges can apply the law fairly regardless of race—an idea that is integral to a system in which equality before the law is a foundational principle.[29]

Under questioning by Republican senators during her confirmation hearings, Sotomayor backed away from these statements and insisted against all evidence that her words had been taken out of context. But the Democratic majority prevailed and Sotomayor was confirmed. Once seated on the nation's highest court Sotomayor made clear that her views remained those of the PRLDEF radicals. In a speech at the University of Chicago Law School, she criticized her colleague Chief Justice John Roberts for advocating "colorblindness" in American laws. Sotomayor insisted that "our society is too complex to use that kind of analysis."[30] Sotomayor also claimed that America suffers from "structural problems" that prevent full racial equality from being realized.[31] She failed to explain how full racial equality is possible in a multiracial society in the absence of color-blind laws.

That the political left has been able to exert so much influence on American public policy and institutions, transforming the nature of the immigration debate and placing one of its spokespeople on the Supreme Court, is a testament to the power of Ford and its foundation networks.

These networks that are composed of tax-exempt 501(c)3 organizations are not small. If one defines progressive immigration groups as those that support radical departures from traditional immigration policies and notions of sovereignty, that refer to illegal aliens as "undocumented immigrants," that support granting illegals rights traditionally reserved to citizens, and that oppose enforcing existing immigration laws or otherwise restricting immigration—there are 117 such progressive 501(c)3s with net assets of $194.7 million.[32] By contrast, as of 2009 there were only 9 conservative groups focusing on immigration, whose net assets came to $15.1 million. The National Council of La Raza, just one of the progressive groups, had assets of $46.6 million as of 2009. By contrast, the largest conservative immigration group, the Federation for American Immigration Reform (FAIR), had just $9 million in net assets.[33]

To sum up: In the political battle over America's borders, its immigration policies, and its sovereignty, the political left can rely on *thirteen times* the private financial resources available to its conservative opponents. But thanks to the pressures of the political left, government has also entered this battle, and on the side of the antiborder radicals. The federal government in fact provides $325.3 million in funding to 501(c)3s that advance the progressive agenda and only $18,090 to one 501(c)3 supporting the conservative agenda.[34]

FORD'S interventions into issues directly affecting the Latino community are but one facet of its unique role in the national debate on sovereignty, ethnicity, and race—in effect on the meaning of America's social contract. The idea at the center of this debate is "multiculturalism," a concept that the Ford Foundation played a decisive role in establishing throughout America's educational system at all levels. Multiculturalism—the claim that cultures are equal or that their differences do not matter—poses a direct challenge to the idea that there is a distinctively American culture, which makes its pluralistic democracy possible.

The multicultural claim is a calculated challenge to American exceptionalism as a nation whose identity is built on the integration of diverse ethnicities and their assimilation to a common social contract. That integration hinges on the assumption that while we are hyphenated Americans, we are Americans first. In other words, integration can only take place within a common culture and under America's color-blind standard of equality before the law. In the 1960s, these concepts were subjected to sustained assault by radical activists under the multicultural banner. This movement was funded, legitimized, and abetted by Ford bureaucrats and advanced by the battery of organizations Ford created. These organizations—both academic and activist—attacked the idea of objective standards insisting that all standards were group based and group biased, and that one man's standard was another's oppression.

The multicultural idea worked its way into American politics through the university. A succession of Ford grants in the late 1960s and 1970s helped establish the fields of black studies and women's studies as political parties within the university, and then spread to other interdisciplinary fields committed to radical agendas. These new pseudodisciplines celebrated ethnic, racial, and gender separatism and fostered group allegiances over a core American identity. Their common theme was the race-gender-class oppression of designated "minority" groups by American capitalism. Within a few decades their sectarian teachings became the educational standard throughout American schools.

The very first black studies program was created in 1967 at San Francisco State College as a concession to a radical student strike that shut down the school and set the pattern for other politicized curricula that followed. The program dispensed with traditional academic subjects like science and math in favor of so-called black science and black math that emphasized racial consciousness and racial agendas.[35] A second black studies program was created at Cornell University in 1969 when the school bowed to shotgun-wielding black student radicals who occupied the Administration Building and demanded a Black Studies Department and the right to appoint their own professors. The demands were mostly granted.[36] Following this template, women's studies programs were created around the principle that gender differences were not biologically based but "socially constructed" as part of a system of race, gender, and class hierarchies that oppressed racial minorities, women, transgendered individuals, and workers. At their core, each division of the new multicultural curricula constituted an assault on the idea of a common national identity and on America as a society based on principles of equality and individual rights.

After establishing itself in American universities, the multicultural concept forced its way into America's political and legal culture. MALDEF won the first major legal battle for multiculturalism in the early 1970s when it filed a voting rights lawsuit on behalf of Puerto Ricans living in New York. MALDEF's suit argued that English literacy tests discriminated against Puerto Ricans as a class of people. The courts agreed, allowing MALDEF to establish the radical legal precedent that holding elections in English—the official language of the United States—was an act of oppression that disenfranchised Hispanic voters.[37] By 1975, groups like MALDEF could successfully campaign to amend the 1965 Voting Rights Act to force jurisdictions with significant numbers of Hispanics to provide voting materials in Spanish. Instead of Hispanics integrating into American culture, as had been the goal of traditional approaches, they were to be encouraged to remain separate and granted special treatment on the basis of their ethnicity. That Ford underwrote this multiculturalist assault was particularly ironic, since Henry Ford had been a strong advocate of assimilation, even setting up a school for his immigrant employees to learn English.[38]

In 1992, the distinguished liberal historian Arthur Schlesinger Jr. wrote a jeremiad describing the multiculturalists' assault on the American founding, which he titled *The Disuniting of America*. Schlesinger noted that groups like MALDEF had profoundly undermined America's historical unifying creed of *e pluribus unum* (Latin for "out of many, one"), in favor of a multicultural ideology where ethnicity and race are irreducible categories: "Instead of a transformative nation with an identity all its own, America in this new light is seen as preservative of diverse alien identities. Instead of a nation composed of individuals making their own unhampered choices, America increasingly sees itself as composed of groups more or less ineradicable in their ethnic character. The multiethnic dogma abandons historic purposes, replacing assimilation by fragmentation, integration by separatism. It belittles *unum* and glorifies *pluribus*."[39]

This reversal of American fortunes—really a throwback to the status societies that the American Revolution had rejected—was another testament to the power of the political left and its funders at Ford.

5.

REDEFINING NATIONAL SECURITY

Immigration was not the only issue where coordination among left-wing funders helped to mainstream agendas designed to undermine the American system. At the height of the Cold War, a similar orchestration of goals by left-wing funders and nonprofits fueled a radical effort to weaken America's security and degrade the nation's military defenses.

Spearheading the attempt to redefine national security objectives was a group of large funding institutions organized by the Ploughshares Fund for that specific purpose.[1] Ploughshares was created in 1981 by a wealthy San Francisco activist named Sally Lilienthal to support a "nuclear freeze movement" and thus to oppose NATO's decision to place medium-range missiles in Europe. The decision to install the missiles was actually NATO's response to an aggressive military buildup by the Soviet Union, whose illegal occupation of Eastern Europe had been the casus belli of the Cold War. Sally Lilienthal's agenda mirrored the objectives of the Soviets, which was to freeze America's nuclear forces in Western Europe and thereby protect the military advantage the Kremlin had gained by placing SS-20 missiles in Eastern Europe.[2] These missiles amplified the massive superiority of forces the Soviet bloc already had on the ground, tipping the balance of power and posing a serious threat to the security of the West.

If successful, the mission of the Ploughshares Fund would have tipped the balance of power permanently against the United States. This mission was in keeping with the Left's basic approach to the Cold War, which was to pressure disarmament measures on the United States but not its Soviet adversary. To advance this agenda, the Ploughshares Fund pooled donations from wealthy individuals, families, and foundations, such as Rockefeller and Stern, to underwrite—and almost single-handedly create—a left-wing movement opposed to American defense policies, which was led by spokesmen as prominent as presidential contender Senator Edward Kennedy. The "nuclear freeze" movement came together under the banner of promoting "peace." Its modus operandi was to arouse and then exploit the public's fear of nuclear annihilation.

Despite professing to oppose all nuclear weapons everywhere, however, the movement focused its opposition and protests squarely on the United States and the Reagan administration. It directed particular ire at Democratic Party legislators who were anti-Communists and supported a strong defense posture against the Soviet enemy. This focus reflected the movement's core belief that the United States rather than the Soviet Union was primarily to blame for the threat of nuclear war.

The disarmament movement sought to roll back and ultimately eliminate America's capacity for nuclear self-defense but not to check the aggressive designs of the Soviet bloc.[3] Virtually no attention was paid to the continuing Soviet occupation of Eastern Europe, or its recent military aggression in Afghanistan.[4] Insofar as nuclear freeze campaigners acknowledged Soviet political repression and belligerence, it was only to draw a false equivalence between the United States and its Soviet rival. In the classic tradition of "fellow-travelers," nuclear freeze campaigners consistently claimed that the USSR was more willing to make peace and disarm than the United States.

The American nuclear freeze movement had strategically important international allies. Mobilized by Europe's large Communist and Socialist parties, and a broad "united front" of the Left, two million people poured into the streets of European capitals like Amsterdam, Berlin, and Rome to protest the proposed emplacement of American missiles. There were no demonstrations opposing the Soviet-installed weapons that had tipped the balance of military power in the first place. Progressives regarded the Soviet weapons as a defensive response to the "threat" from the West.

At a crucial juncture of the Cold War, Ploughshares and its allies were nearly able to turn the tide of the conflict between Western democracy and Soviet totalitarianism in the latter's favor. They were ultimately thwarted because of the resolve of President Reagan and Britain's prime minister Margaret Thatcher, supported by a public whose political common sense was well to the right of Ploughshares and the freeze advocates.

Nevertheless, the movement did succeed in weakening American security and encouraging Soviet obstinacy. By stoking fears of a nuclear holocaust and concerns about the alleged saber rattling of the Reagan administration—relentless themes of the Soviet propaganda offensive—the freeze movement created a crisis of public confidence in America's nuclear arsenal. By 1984, according to a survey conducted by the Public Agenda Foundation, an anxious electorate had been persuaded that "nuclear war is unwinnable, unsurvivable."[5] The same report found that "the public is now having second thoughts about the dangers . . . of an assertive posture."

As long as the Cold War lasted, Ploughshares devoted the lion's

share of its budget toward "peace" initiatives like nuclear disarmament treaties and partisan efforts to foster "voter awareness" about
the nuclear arms race."[6] The Cold War came to an end when the
Soviet occupying forces were withdrawn from Eastern Europe, liber-
ating its captive peoples. Russia was exposed as the brutal occupier of
the region and its expansion into Eastern Europe as the real source of
the Cold War conflict. These developments, however, failed to engen-
der any second thoughts among the political leftists at Ploughshares
or cause them to revise their anti-American agendas.

Twenty years later, Ploughshares was still investing most of its
funds on political projects designed to portray the United States as
the source of international tensions and the prime culprit in creating the ground for a nuclear Armageddon.[7] By 2011, its thirtieth
anniversary, Ploughshares had disbursed over $60 million on these
agendas thanks to the support of leading left-wing funders—the Ford
Foundation, the Carnegie Corporation, the John D. and Catherine
T. MacArthur Foundation, the Rockefeller Foundation, and George
Soros's Open Society Institute. By then the Ploughshares board featured such notables as actor Michael Douglas, left-wing author Reza
Aslan, and former Nebraska senator Chuck Hagel—a Republican
opponent of the war in Iraq.[8] High-profile support and name recognition helped the Ploughshares Fund grow to more than $35 million in
collective net assets, making it the largest grant-making foundation
in the United States focused on national security issues.[9] It is notable
here that there is no comparable network of national-security-focused
foundations on the conservative side of the spectrum as that organized
by the Ploughshares Fund, which includes 64 progressive foundations
with collective assets of $31 billion (these are listed in Appendix VII
of this volume). Given its ability to draw on these resources, it is little
wonder that Ploughshares has remained such a potent force in American politics.

Financial support from the funders' network Ploughshares created has enabled it to continue championing its signature cause of

degrading America's nuclear and ballistic missile defenses, without reciprocation from other military powers. When the Obama administration canceled plans for a missile defense shield in Central Europe in September 2009, the decision drew praise from Moscow and reproach from America's recently liberated allies in Eastern Europe who felt betrayed by Washington's action. When the cancellation was announced, Ploughshares boasted that its influence had "informed the decision" by the Obama administration.[10]

Ploughshares continues to fund radical pacifist and nuclear disarmament advocacy groups like the radical Peace Action Network,[11] Physicians for Social Responsibility,[12] and Win Without War.[13] Win Without War was established in 1982 as the Women's Action for Nuclear Disarmament, a constituent element of the nuclear freeze movement. Today, Win Without War is a coalition of groups that support a more "progressive national security strategy" and whose members include an array of left-wing organizations such as Greenpeace, MoveOn.org, and the National Organization for Women.[14] Leaders of these groups also oversee many of the Ploughshares Fund's projects. The fund's Peace and Security Initiative is implemented by left-wing activists like Susan Shaer, the former head of Win Without War.[15]

Because of its failure to learn the crucial lessons of the Cold War—in particular that the cause of the conflict was Soviet aggression and its solution American power—Ploughshares has continued to regard America as the world's chief security problem. There has been one significant change however: the fund has moved from the political margins to the liberal mainstream—so much so that its views on a wide range of national security issues are essentially indistinguishable from those of the Democratic Party.

During the Iraq War, for instance, congressional Democrats joined Ploughshares in branding the war a strategic blunder. One of the harshest critics of that war was Joseph Cirincione, the current president of the Ploughshares. A longtime antinuclear activist and a former director for nuclear policy at the George Soros–funded Center for American Progress, Cirincione emerged as a vocal opponent of the US military campaign in Iraq. In a coauthored 2004 paper, Cirincione dismissed the Bush administration's case for war as "dubious" and suggested that the military campaign to depose Saddam Hussein "does not serve U.S. national security interests."[16] Although the regime of Saddam Hussein had violated the truce it signed in the first Gulf War and seventeen United Nations resolutions designed to enforce that truce, and although the Iraqi dictator had used weapons of mass destruction against his own people and neighboring states, the statement concluded that it was really the United States that had undermined international law by regarding Saddam as a threat, even while acting to enforce the UN edicts.

Cirincione's opposition became even more strident as the war continued, and by 2007 he was claiming that Bush administration officials had "repeatedly misled the press" and manipulated intelligence reports to fit their case for war—charges that, though demonstrably false, were echoed by Democratic politicians.[17] In 2007, on the other hand, when newspapers reported that Syria was building a nuclear reactor with assistance from North Korea, Cirincione angrily rejected the story as baseless propaganda pushed by American and Israeli hardliners.[18] Intelligence officials later produced video evidence of the Syrian–North Korean cooperation.[19]

Cirincione's less-than-clear-sighted analysis of a critical proliferation issue did not prevent him from becoming an adviser on nuclear policy to Barack Obama during his 2008 presidential run. Precisely how much influence Cirincione and Ploughshares were able to exert on the president became evident in February 2011, when Obama signed into law a Ploughshares-promoted cause—the new Strategic Arms Reduction Treaty (START) with Russia.[20] Republicans concerned about the security consequences of drastic cuts to America's nuclear deterrent opposed the treaty. But it was the Ploughshares view that prevailed within the Democratic Party and the Obama administration to become American policy. The following March, Obama further revealed the extent of Ploughshares's influence on his national security plans when he announced a review to find ways that the United States could reduce its nuclear weapons stockpiles beyond the already large cuts he had committed to by signing START into law.

The fact that the left-wingers at Ploughshares have come to wield inordinate influence on America's national security policy is in no small measure due to the unprecedented sums it can command, as well as to its aggressive approach in sponsoring antimilitary groups. According to George Perkovich, a vice president at the Carnegie Endowment for International Peace, "The Ploughshares Fund moves faster than almost anyone else. More traditional foundations usually need a very clear sense of a prospect's institutional history. Ploughshares sees a promising person and puts its money down."[21]

Ploughshares's appetite for radical agendas helped to sustain causes that might otherwise have been little more than political sideshows. In 2006, for instance, Ploughshares made a grant of $100,000 to the *Bulletin of Atomic Scientists* for a campaign involving its so-called Doomsday Clock, a symbolic clock-face ticking toward a nuclear doomsday. The clock's "five minutes to midnight" message, which stayed in place for nearly fifty years, had long since made it a running joke.[22] ("*I have* to hurry up and finish shopping, it's five minutes to midnight on the Doomsday Clock!")

In 1999, Ploughshares became the model for the Peace and Security Funders Group, a vast network of individual philanthropists, private and public foundations, charitable trusts, and other grant-making programs.[23] Like its parent organization, the Peace and Security Funders Group brings together sixty-four philanthropic organizations and individuals, including such major funders as the Ford Foundation, the John D. and Catherine T. MacArthur Foundation, George Soros's Open Society Institute, the Carnegie Corporation of New York, and the Tides Foundation. Together they provide the Peace and Security Funders Group with a war chest of over $31 *billion* in total assets.[24] That is a sum larger than the defense budgets of Greece, Colombia, and Poland combined. Since the Pentagon is barred by law from defending its programs in public relations campaigns to the electorate, this task is left to the handful of conservative 501(c)3s that have some focus on national security matters and whose assets are a tiny fraction of those available to the left-wing side of the debate.[25] Thus ten conservative think tanks that have a focus on national security policy have assets of just $365.8 million. In short, the Left's resources available to devote to national security issues are more than eighty-four times that of conservatives.[26]

Following the Ploughshares model, the Peace and Security Funders Group directs its prodigious budget toward two main goals, both of them designed to end US military supremacy and weaken US security. The first is disarmament, whose agenda is global in theory but American in practice. The Peace and Security Funders Group pursues the goal of American disarmament by sponsoring groups and supporting measures that promote nuclear and conventional disarmament, by backing restrictions on arms trading, and by pushing for cuts to the US defense budget.[27]

While seeking to scale back America's military capabilities and restrain America's role in global affairs, the Peace and Security Funders Group also seeks to expand the reach of international institutions like the United Nations—dominated by the Islamic dictatorships and the former members of the Communist bloc—as a counterweight to America's global influence. Underlying this agenda is a worldview, which (in the words of journalist J. Michael Waller) "deliberately tends to diminish U.S. influence by promoting more numerous and more powerful international organizations and courts, nongovernmental organizations (or NGOs), and treaties that would constrain the United States while doing little, in practical terms, to restrain regimes hostile to America and to freedom."[28]

The Peace and Security Funders Group's globalist agenda would erode American sovereignty by giving these international organizations an effective veto over US national security, while creating what some on the left refer to as the "multilateral leviathan."[29] The Peace and Security Funders Group may avoid overtly anti-American rhetoric but its vision of a militarily disarmed and internationally diminished America is no less clear and no less destructive.

Despite the radicalism of these agendas, they are now widely shared across the spectrum of American politics. John Tierney, the Walter Kohler Professor of International Relations at the Institute of World Politics, points out that "Many Peace and Security Funders Group policy positions receive support from moderate Republicans, neo-isolationists, libertarians and the center-left of the Democratic Party. In fact, the goal of reducing nuclear weapons was promoted by the Bush Administration, which cut the U.S. arsenal from 6,000 to 2,200 nuclear warheads, the lowest total since the Eisenhower Administration."[30] Acting on advice from Ploughshares, the Obama administration has committed the United States to further shrinking its stockpiles to as few as fifteen hundred warheads. Not only would this slash America's nuclear arsenal to its smallest size in fifty years and dramatically impair its defensive capabilities, it would strain ties with allies for whom the American nuclear umbrella serves as the only guarantor of their security against nuclear powers such as Russia.[31]

The bipartisan acceptance of these disarmament agendas in America's political culture is a testament to the power and influence of the Peace and Security Funders Group and the collective resources that its network can focus on any issue it chooses. America's intervention in Libya in March 2011 reveals that the globalist agenda of tying the hands of the American Gulliver in a web of international arrangements has become the official position of the Obama White House. Instead of an early, decisive intervention when demonstrations erupted in the Libyan capital against the Gadhafi regime, the administration waited three weeks before committing US forces to creating "no-fly zones" in Libyan air space, a delay that allowed the Libyan dictator, Muammar Gadhafi, to deliver crushing blows to his opposition. The White House wait was required to secure the approvals of the

Arab League and the United Nations Security Council. The world's only superpower thus effectively granted veto rights over US military action to a corrupt international bureaucracy made up of adversaries and allies alike, and also to an alliance of Arab dictatorships. When the intervention was finally launched, the international coalition the White House had spent so much time assembling promptly fell apart, as the Arab League withdrew its support and European powers such as Germany refused to take part in the mission.[32]

The Obama administration also insisted on placing its military mission under the control of NATO. In short order, this strategic shirking of responsibility sowed chaos in the military chain of command, leaving the coalition partners unsure about their respective roles and the military objectives of the mission itself muddled at best. A now hostile Gadhafi remained in power at a cost of hundreds of millions to US taxpayers in the midst of a financial crisis.[33]

America's strategically confused intervention in Libya also marked the emergence of the so-called responsibility to protect, or R2P doctrine, another agenda favored by the left-wing funders network. This doctrine first emerged in the 1990s, when the United Nations failed to prevent the massacre of 800,000 Tutsis in Rwanda, arousing the ire of the human rights community. Activists found an influential spokesman for their concerns in Harvard academic and Pulitzer Prize–winning author and left-wing academic Samantha Power. In her book, *A Problem from Hell: America and the Age of Genocide*, Power condemned US officials for excluding moral and humanitarian concerns from American foreign policy objectives under what she considered an overly narrow conception of the national interest.

The "realist" doctrine Power was criticizing had been designed to constrain America from virtually unlimited interventions. Viewed from the perspective of the national interest, there was no reason to invade Libya, which posed no threat to the United States, as even Obama's own secretary of defense conceded.[34] In place of this traditional doctrine, Power urged the adoption of a "right of humanitarian intervention" to stop genocide, which in practice would mean what a particular political administration might interpret as genocide. Under the Power doctrine, great powers would assume a sweeping "right" to interfere in the internal affairs of weaker states, violating their sovereignty. This right would also violate the organizing principle of the United Nations Charter, whose Article 2 states that "Nothing contained in the present Charter shall authorize the United Nations to intervene in matters which are essentially within the domestic jurisdiction of any state."[35]

Ignoring the imperial overtones of a "responsibility to protect," along with the tragic lessons of past open-ended interventions, supporters of the Power doctrine pressed their agenda. They gained their first official support in September 2002, when Canada launched an International Commission on Intervention and State Sovereignty to "foster a global political consensus" for interventions based on the R2P principles. Soon after that, the R2P campaign received crucial backing from leftist financier George Soros. Dismissing concerns about state sovereignty, Soros claimed that although "democracy is an internal affair . . . it often requires a helping hand from the outside,"[36] a rationale familiar in imperialisms of the past. Sovereignty, Soros maintained, "is based on the people," meaning that "the international community can penetrate nation-states' borders to protect the rights of citizens"—as it interprets them. To justify such violations of national sovereignty Soros advocated a new and conveniently vague standard, whose implications were all too familiar: "When the government . . . violates the human rights of the people, the international community has a right to protect the people."

The "international community," of course, was in practice no more than the powers who happened to arrogate to themselves the authority to speak in its name. Just how broadly the right to impose solutions on sovereign states could be stretched was demonstrated in May 2008, when R2P enthusiasts called for intervention in Burma in the wake of a cyclone, after judging the Burmese government's response inadequate.[37]

In March 2005, UN secretary-general Kofi Annan endorsed the R2P doctrine, which was then unanimously adopted by the United Nations in September as part of the organization's World Summit Outcome Document. As a party to the summit, the United States was among the countries that committed itself to the R2P principle of being "prepared to take collective action" to stop atrocities consistent with the doctrine. Still, the document failed to realize the ambitions of R2P supporters because its only concrete provision called for the UN General Assembly to continue considering the doctrine. More would be needed to put the R2P doctrine into action, and left-wing funders stepped in to close the gap between theory and practice.

One of the leaders of this movement to secure R2P's practical implementation was the $79 million Stanley Foundation, a key member of the Peace and Security Funders Group. The foundation was established in 1956 by Iowa engineer and entrepreneur C. Maxwell Stanley to address his "deep concerns about global security and international organizations in an increasingly interdependent world."[38] The foundation's extreme left interpretation of "global security" can be gauged by the fact that its quarterly journal, *Courier*, describes the terrorists of the Iranian-sponsored Islamic army group Hezbollah as "freedom fighters."[39]

A self-styled "world citizen," Max Stanley embodied the modern left's disdain for national sovereignty in general and American sovereignty in particular, an attitude that writer John Fonte has called "transnational progressivism." Consequently, the Stanley Foundation came to regard institutions like the UN, dominated by anti-American dictatorships, as the key to maintaining international security and checking the power of the United States.[40]

The Stanley Foundation was prominent among the left-wing funders who embraced the R2P doctrine, which it described as a "politically potent concept."[41] It played a critical role in generating support for the R2P campaign, sponsoring a conference in 2008 called "Actualizing the Responsibility to Protect." The conference brought together UN officials, UN-affiliated progressive think tanks like the International Peace Institute, whose board of directors includes current UN secretary-general Ban Ki-moon, and NGOs "to reflect on ways of putting the idea into action."[42]

One of the recommendations put forth in the Stanley Foundation conference became particularly striking after the US involvement in Libya. This was to emphasize prevention or more likely preemption—since "avoiding mass atrocities in the first place is the best protection for populations." President Obama would follow this advice almost to the letter in March 2011, when he sought to defend the Libyan war as essentially a preventive action to avoid the slaughter of civilians by the dictator in the rebel city of Benghazi.[43] On the other hand, preventive intervention was exactly what Obama had opposed in Iraq, both as a candidate and senator, even though Iraq posed a military threat to the region and to US interests, and its regime was in violation of seventeen UN Security Council resolutions.

Even as invoked by Obama to justify his policies in Libya, the preventive rationale for the Libyan intervention was highly suspect. Despite the Gadhafi regime's brutal repression and its arbitrary attacks on civilians, there had been no systematic government campaign to massacre civilians in any of the cities captured by his forces and there was no compelling evidence that one was imminent in Benghazi.[44] In acting with the urgency demanded by the R2P doctrine, Obama simultaneously dodged a serious discussion of American national interests, made American power hostage to a fragile international coalition, and embroiled the country in a costly campaign with no defined objective.

Obama was not the first president to lend support to the R2P doctrine, though only Obama acted on it. In June of 2005, President Bush declared the situation in Darfur, Sudan, a "genocide."[45] Bush did not specifically cite an American responsibility to protect civilians in Darfur, but his decision was consistent with the R2P agenda of classifying conflicts in a way that could compel intervention on humanitarian grounds. As would later prove the case in Libya, the reality on the ground was more complicated. Massacres had indeed taken place in Sudan, but even liberal observers like journalist David Rieff noted that, however tragic, the Sudanese conflict did not rise to the level of genocide as traditionally understood, but more closely resembled a civil war.[46]

In short, high-minded idealism about preventing genocide by disregarding national sovereignties was fraught with untold risks. By effectively abrogating national sovereignty, the doctrine formulated by Soros and the roster of supporting progressive foundations and NGOs gave license to unscrupulous governments to have their way with smaller countries, justifying their intrusions by appeals to humanitarian concerns.

Thus, shortly after Obama's Libyan intervention, his partners in the Arab League sent a formal request to the United Nations to establish a "no-fly zone" over Gaza allegedly to protect Palestinians but in fact to prevent the Israeli air force from responding to rocket strikes on Israeli towns and schoolyards by Hamas terrorists. It was not much of a stretch to imagine the Arab League dictatorships invading Israel for a fourth time since its birth on the pretext of saving Palestinians from alleged abuse.

This would be perfectly consonant with the attitudes displayed by progressive sponsors of the R2P doctrine. In a notorious 2002 interview, Samantha Power had called for action along precisely these lines—a massive military intervention on behalf of the Palestinians in order to impose a "solution" on Israel, as though Israel and not the terrorist regimes on the West Bank and Gaza, and three aggressive Arab wars to destroy the Jewish state, were not themselves the source of the problem.[47] Under sharp public criticism for this suggestion, Power disavowed her remarks, insisting that she could not recall their exact meaning. In fact her original statement is striking not only in its clarity but also in its perfect consistency with the internal logic of R2P's rationale and the left-wing politics behind it.

The R2P doctrine may be the most high-profile recent example of how the Left, through its funding networks and 501(c)3 advocacy groups, has been able to undermine America's ability to defend its national interest. But it is by no means the only one. Just as groups like Ploughshares worked to sabotage the United States in its showdown with the Soviet Union during the Cold War, the left-wing network has been effective in creating and empowering organizations that seek to impair America's ability to defend itself against the threat of global Islamic terrorism.

The September 11, 2001, terrorist attacks and the ensuing invasions of Afghanistan and Iraq marked America's belated entry into the war that Islamic jihadists had declared against the West. For the Left and its network of wealthy funders, these events also presented an occasion to recast the United States in the familiar role of villain—much as the Ploughshares Fund had succeeded in doing in the face of the Communist threat. Among the organizations leading the campaign to cast America as the cause of the war that was being waged against it were the American Civil Liberties Union (ACLU) and the Center for Constitutional Rights (CCR). The less well-known latter organization is a legal nonprofit whose clients have included Fidel Castro, Hamas, and the "Blind Sheik" whose terrorist cell was responsible for the first World Trade Center bombing.

Founded in 1920, the ACLU has long styled itself as the country's premier civil liberties group. At the time of its founding, many in the ACLU's leadership were, in fact, self-declared Communists and fellow travelers who turned a blind eye to abuses of civil liberties as long as they took place under the banner of the Left. The organization's founder, Roger Baldwin, famously declared, "I am for socialism, disarmament, and ultimately, for abolishing the state itself as an instrument of violence and compulsion." Corliss Lamont, who served on the ACLU's board of directors for twenty-two years, was a notorious defender of Stalin's Soviet Union even during the years of the show trials and purges.[48]

Today, the ACLU remains as supportive as ever of totalitarian radicals and violent revolutionaries, foreign and domestic. In 2009, the ACLU's Michigan chapter invited Bill Ayers and Bernardine Dohrn, unrepentant former leaders of the terrorist Weather Underground, to deliver a keynote address at one of its meetings.[49] Dohrn also sat on the ACLU's advisory board.[50] The ACLU's political radicalism is hard to miss in its choice of lawsuits and political campaigns, which are intended to weaken American security measures and make it easier for America's terrorist enemies to operate. After the 9/11 attacks, the failure of the intelligence community to prevent them from taking place fueled public support for heightened security measures. This was a reasonable response to the mass murder of three thousand people and the worst terrorist attack in American history. The ACLU responded with an obstructionist campaign to prevent the new measures from being enforced.

For instance, five of the nineteen hijackers had overstayed their visas, something that might have been flagged by a more rigorous system of immigration controls. But when the Justice Department issued an order for adult men from countries in the Arab/Muslim Middle East to register with the Immigration and Naturalization Service or face fines or deportation, the ACLU instantly mounted a campaign to help these men resist the order as "discriminatory." The ACLU persisted in its opposition to the Justice Department's order even when the *9/11 Commission Report* later confirmed that the order had curtailed al-Qaeda's ability to operate in America after 9/11. Along the same lines, the ACLU has opposed any surveillance of radical mosques, despite substantial evidence that they have served and continue to serve as recruiting and fund-raising bases for Islamic terrorism.

Even more revealing of the lengths to which the ACLU will go to oppose American security measures was its campaign against a

Clinton administration measure making it a federal crime to provide material support for terrorism. The most famous opponent of the Clinton law was Professor Sami al-Arian, who was vigorously defended by his ACLU friends even after he was exposed as the North American head of Palestinian Islamic Jihad, a terrorist organization responsible for the murder of more than a hundred individuals in the Middle East, including two American citizens.[51]

The provision banning "material support" for terror was an outgrowth of the 1996 Anti-Terrorism and Effective Death Penalty Act, which was signed into law by President Clinton after the 1995 Oklahoma City bombing. The new law outlawed donations to designated foreign terrorist organizations. At the time, Sami al-Arian was the financial head of Palestinian Islamic Jihad. He was videotaped at a 1991 rally shouting "Death to Israel!" and that same year publicly proclaimed, "Let us damn America, let us damn Israel, let us damn them and their allies until death!"[52] Convicted on a charge of aiding terrorists, al-Arian was deported in 2006.

· From the time of his arrest and throughout his trial, the ACLU spearheaded a campaign to portray al-Arian as a political victim, targeted because he was a Palestinian. Working as part of an unofficial defense team, along with the Center for Constitutional Rights, the National Lawyers Guild, the American Muslim Council, and the Council on American Islamic Relations (CAIR), the ACLU mounted a public effort to defend al-Arian as the victim of a government attempt to silence him for what supporters described as his "pro-Palestinian views."[53]

The ACLU had long before transformed itself into a "progressive" advocacy group, relegating civil liberties to a secondary place in its menu of causes. According to one study of the ACLU's agenda, civil liberties composed 94 percent of the organization's cases in 1948; by 1987, that number had dropped to 45 percent.[54]

By reinventing itself as a left-wing organization, the ACLU was able to attract the support of the Left's megafoundations. In 1999, the ACLU received a $7 million grant from the Ford Foundation for its endowment fund, one of the largest gifts by Ford in its entire history.[55] The ACLU is the beneficiary of even larger gifts from George Soros's Open Society Institute, which in 2007 made a $12 million contribution. Cashing in on its high-profile reputation as a civil liberties champion, the ACLU Foundation's net assets had risen to $197.6 million by 2009.[56]

Since the 9/11 attacks the ACLU has used its funds to oppose virtually every effort by the United States to prosecute a war against its terrorist enemies abroad and keep the populace safe at home. In October 2001, a bipartisan majority in Congress passed the antiterrorism PATRIOT Act. Among other crucial security provisions, the legislation tore down the legal barriers that had prevented law enforcement, intelligence, and national security agencies from coordinating their efforts prior to 9/11, and which most certainly created vulnerabilities that made the attacks possible. Thanks to the PATRIOT Act, US authorities have been able to thwart at least twenty-nine terrorist plots since 9/11, including the 2002 "Lackawanna Six" plot in which information sharing between drug and counterterrorism investigators, made possible by the act, allowed authorities to crack down on a terrorist cell in Buffalo, New York.[57]

From the beginning, the ACLU portrayed the PATRIOT Act as draconian, intrusive, and unconstitutional, a "chilling grab of authority and further diminution of constitutional checks and balances on law enforcement," even though it contained many safeguards to protect civil liberties and had secured support in both parties, among liberals and conservatives alike. The lawsuits the ACLU began to file against the PATRIOT Act helped to erode the law's legitimacy in the eyes of the lay public, while an ACLU-led campaign outside the courts helped to persuade local and state governments to pass resolutions condemning the PATRIOT Act as a "threat to fundamental rights and liberties" and refusing to cooperate with Homeland Security officials in enforcing the act's provisions.[58]

A partner in the ACLU's anti-PATRIOT Act campaign was the Massachusetts-based Bill of Rights Defense Committee.[59] The BRDC is funded by the Open Society Institute and associated foundations and draws support from across the spectrum of left-wing activist groups. Its board includes a staff attorney for MALDEF, since its attack on the PATRIOT Act is focused on keeping America's borders porous. David Cole, a pro bono attorney with the Center for Constitutional Rights, and the leading opponent of the ban on material support for terrorism, sits on the BRDC advisory board. As of April 2011, with the help of left-wing groups engaged in local politics such as ACORN, the BRDC had succeeded in persuading a total of 414 local and county governments, including eight state legislatures, to pass resolutions denouncing the PATRIOT Act and pledging not to cooperate with Homeland Security in tracking and monitoring illegal aliens.[60]

Eventually this progressive juggernaut was successful in eroding the bipartisan support for the PATRIOT Act. During the act's original passage, just one Democrat, Wisconsin's left-libertarian Russ Feingold, voted against it. But thanks to the tireless efforts of the anti–PATRIOT Act campaign, by the time key provisions of the bill came up for extension in February 2011, congressional support for the law had eroded. Democrats in the House voted against extending several of the bill's provisions, and Republicans were no longer unified in their support, with twenty-six voting against.[61]

Michelle Richardson, the ACLU's legislative counsel, declared she was "glad to see there is bipartisan opposition to the PATRIOT Act 10 years later." The ACLU was in no small part responsible for the change.[62] As a result of the ACLU's campaign, three critical surveillance provisions were initially dropped from the act: one measure permitting roving wiretaps on phones, one that gave the FBI court-approved access to library records relevant to a terrorism investigation, and one that permitted secret intelligence surveillance of non-US "lone wolf" residents not known to be affiliated with a specific terrorist organization. Although Congress eventually extended these measures, the ACLU had succeeded in calling their legitimacy into question.[63]

While the Left had made significant strides in undermining the congressional consensus behind the PATRIOT Act, it nonetheless failed to convince the general public, which polls showed consistently supportive of the law.[64] Thus, the well-financed campaign not only undermined the credibility of a demonstrably effective antiterrorism law but in doing so disenfranchised a general public that wanted its protections in place.

The ACLU's sustained assault on the PATRIOT Act is part of a broader campaign by the Left to oppose national security measures and make it more difficult to gather vital intelligence, which would enable the government to prevent terrorist attacks. In December 2005, the *New York Times* disclosed classified details of the National Security Agency's domestic surveillance program. One element of the program, instituted in the aftermath of the September 11 attacks, authorized the government to intercept e-mails and phone calls sent by foreign nationals already identified as terrorists to people in the United States.

The ACLU marshaled its legal forces to kill the program, calling it "illegal spying" and filing suit to prevent it from going into effect. In August 2006, the ACLU achieved its goal, when Detroit district court judge Anna Taylor Diggs sided with the ACLU and ruled the program unconstitutional. Critics quickly pointed out that Judge Diggs had a clear conflict of interest that should have prevented her involvement in the case. At the time of the ruling, she was a secretary and trustee of the Community Foundation for Southeastern Michigan in Detroit, an organization that had given at least $125,000 to the Detroit chapter of the ACLU since 1999.[65] Diggs's ruling was overturned by an appeals court in 2007, but the leaks had already drastically weakened the program by alerting the terrorists to its existence, allowing them to take countermeasures. Eventually this reality and the continuing attacks from the "civil liberties" left forced the administration's hand. In January 2007, President Bush decided not to reauthorize the program.[66]

President Bush's failure to reauthorize the surveillance program persuaded many that it had been misguided from the start. Not until years later did its importance become apparent. In 2009, the inspectors general from America's five leading national security and intelligence agencies—the Department of Defense, the Department of Justice, the CIA, the NSA, and the Office of the Director of National Intelligence—conducted a comprehensive review of the NSA's surveillance program and found that it had indeed been highly useful as an early detection tool for national security agencies tracking terrorist suspects and helping them to identify terrorist networks and potential threats to American security.[67] Former CIA director Michael Hayden testified that had the program been in place prior to 9/11, hijackers Khalid Almihdhar and Nawaf Alhazmi almost certainly would have been identified and arrested.[68]

Influential as the ACLU was in undermining the government's counterterrorism efforts, the organization represented just one of an army of progressive groups that joined in lockstep to oppose national security measures. Altogether, some 126 left-wing organizations had joined the campaign against the PATRIOT Act, ranging from 501(c)(3) groups like the Center for American Progress and MALDEF, to radical groups like International Answer and the International Socialist Organization, to NGOs like Amnesty International and Human Rights Watch, to networks like the Peace and Security Funders Group.[69] In turn, these groups were backed by funders like the Ford Foundation, the Open Society Institute, the Tides Foundation, the MacArthur Foundation, the Annie E. Casey Foundation, and others in the progressive funding network.

Opposing antiterrorist legislation is not the only way the ACLU and the network have been able to damage America's ability to defend the country against terrorism. The so-called rights coalition has long viewed America as an aggressive predator in global affairs. Staying true to Roger Baldwin's anti-American ideals, the ACLU has positioned itself on the side of the alleged victims of American oppression, both nation-states like Communist Cuba and individual terrorist suspects and detainees.

It was for this purpose that the ACLU created the John Adams Project in November 2008. Composed of a team of ACLU lawyers, the project was created to oppose the Bush administration's efforts to bring charges against high-profile terrorist detainees involved in the 9/11 attacks through the military commissions system at Guantanamo Bay, Cuba. The project's name was an attempt to put a patriotic spin on what many would regard as an unpatriotic effort. Early in his career as a lawyer, John Adams had represented British soldiers charged with killing American colonists during a 1770 riot in Boston—somewhat different from al-Qaeda terrorists picked up on the field of battle in a war they had declared on the United States. The purpose of the $8.5-million project was to shut down the military commissions system and close the detention facility in Guantanamo. As ACLU executive director Anthony Romero put it, the organization's goal was to "blow up" the system his government had put in place to defend American citizens.[70]

To that end, the ACLU accused the government of illegally holding the terrorist detainees and challenged the legality of the proposed military commissions. Opposing the ACLU challenge, the Bush administration maintained that terrorists should be designated unlawful enemy combatants and treated accordingly as wartime enemies. Consequently it held that they should be tried in the military justice system, not granted the rights of US citizens in federal court. This assertion was entirely in keeping with legal precedent. As Jack Goldsmith, a former assistant attorney general in the Bush administration's Office of Legal Counsel and a sometime critic of the administration, pointed out in his 2007 book *The Terror Presidency*, the administration was acting in accordance "with a long-held U.S. position that terrorists and other enemy fighters who did not wear uniforms or carry

their arms openly would be denied POW status" under the Third
Geneva Convention. This was also the position that administrations of
both parties had taken since at least the 1980s, long before al-Qaeda
or the Taliban existed.

The ACLU was so successful in promoting the view that the
military commissions system at Guantanamo was illegitimate that it
became part of the policy agenda of the incoming Obama administration. As one of his first acts as president, Obama announced that he
would close the Guantanamo Bay facility by the end of his first year
in office. In the fall of 2009 Obama further announced that the September 11 mastermind, Khalid Sheikh Mohammed, and four other
accused plotters would be tried in a criminal court in New York. The
president was so committed to this course that he was willing to over-
look the fact that pretrial proceedings in the military commissions
system were already under way and Khalid Sheikh Mohammed was
prepared to plead guilty.[71]

It was not surprising that the ACLU's campaign had made inroads
inside the administration. Attorney General Eric Holder was an activist in the left-wing network that led the opposition to Guantanamo.
In 2008, he was a keynote speaker at the national convention of the
American Constitution Society, a Washington, D.C.–based "think
tank" that is the left-wing version of the conservative Federalist Society and is funded by the Ford Foundation and the Open Society
Institute, among others.[72] In his remarks, Holder denounced Guantanamo as "an international embarrassment" and claimed that the Bush
administration's national security policies were "needlessly abusive
and unlawful."[73]

Holder was particularly scathing in condemning the administration's refusal to grant prisoner-of-war protections under the Geneva
Conventions to terrorist detainees held at Guantanamo. As a top Justice Department official in 2002, however, Holder himself had taken
that same position, on the sound grounds that American authorities
should reserve the right to interrogate terrorist prisoners to learn

about their cells and future plans. Holder's reversal on this crucial matter of national security was another measure of the influence of the left-wing networks' campaign against US counterterrorism policies generally and the Guantanamo Bay facility in particular.[74]

Once again a broad-based public backlash against the approach the progressive network had promoted forced a change of plans, as the Obama administration abandoned its attempt to try Khalid Sheikh Mohammed in New York and also agreed to keep the military commission system in place. Nonetheless, the ACLU campaign had succeeded in casting doubt on the legitimacy of American detainee policies, and it took a nationwide public reaction to dissuade the Obama administration from implementing the ACLU's policy.

While the John Adams Project failed in its ultimate goal of shutting down Guantanamo Bay and the military commissions trials, it did succeed in damaging the US intelligence community. In 2008, lawyers affiliated with the project tracked down and photographed CIA officers living in the Washington, D.C., area, including some with covert status. They then smuggled the photographs into Guantanamo and surreptitiously gave them to detainees as part of a deliberate campaign to identify CIA officers who had been involved in "enhanced interrogations" of terrorist suspects or had served in so-called CIA black sites overseas. Photos of the CIA officers were reportedly found in the cell of al-Qaeda terrorist Mustafa al-Hawsawi, the paymaster of the 9/11 attacks who was captured together with Khalid Sheikh Mohammed in 2003 and interrogated by the CIA before being transferred to Guantanamo Bay.[75] Not only did the John Adams Project lawyers put the lives of covert operatives and their families at risk, but they may have also broken a number of laws in the process, including the Intelligence Identities Protection Act.[76]

The ACLU's partner in these attempts to sabotage national security policies was the Center for Constitutional Rights. The center was founded in 1966 by left-wing lawyer William Kunstler, a former director of the ACLU, whose more notorious clients included the Black

Panthers, the Chicago Seven conspirators, and convicted murderer Leonard Peltier. The center has defended Castro's Cuba and Hamas, and one of its prized lawyers, Lynne Stewart, was convicted of collaborating with the mastermind of the original World Trade Center bombing to further his terrorist activities.[77]

The center's longtime president is Michael Ratner, a political radical who cofounded the Lawyers Committee Against U.S. Intervention in Central America in the 1980s and in support of the Communist insurgencies there. Ratner was a key figure in organizing the Committee in Solidarity with the People of El Salvador, an organization created by Cuban intelligence to support the Communist guerrillas.[78]

Although the Center's $7.9 million in assets are substantially smaller than the ACLU's, it too has been able to call on the support of the Left's top funders, including the Ford Foundation (which has given the Center for Constitutional Rights $825,000 since 2002), the Tides Foundation, George Soros's Open Society Institute, and Atlantic Philanthropies, a fund run by Soros protégé and former Open Society Institute vice president Gara LaMarche.

Despite its name, the Center for Constitutional Rights is even less about defending the Constitution than the ACLU is about defending civil liberties. The center's primary agenda has been to defend political forces at war with the United States and most recently to limit the ability of the United States to defend itself against Islamic jihadists. As author Marc Thiessen notes, the center's efforts "have tied America's hands in a web of lawsuits that have restricted the ability of the U.S. military and intelligence communities to effectively prosecute the war on terror."[79]

One way the center has advanced its agenda is through its Global Justice Initiative. The counterpart to the ACLU's John Adams Project, the initiative has solicited millions of dollars as well as hundreds of pro bono lawyers from top-tier law firms to support the center's campaign to represent detainees at Guantanamo Bay. The Global Justice Initiative also has a direct link to the White House through Attorney

General Eric Holder, whose former firm, Covington and Burling, has been prominent among those participating in the defense of sixteen of the detainees. Since the beginning of the war on terror the center has coordinated over five hundred pro bono lawyers, many from elite white shoe law firms, to file suit on behalf of captured terrorists.

In 2004, the center won a major legal victory when the Supreme Court ruled in the case of *Rasul v. Bush* that foreign fighters captured in Afghanistan could challenge their detention in US courts, triggering a surge in habeas corpus cases. The center also directly represents terrorist detainees, among them Jose Padilla, the so-called dirty bomber dispatched by Khalid Sheikh Mohammed to blow up apartment buildings in American cities; Mohamed al-Qhatani, the would-be "twentieth hijacker" who did not take part in the 9/11 attacks only because he was turned away by immigration agents at an Orlando airport; and Majid Khan, an al-Qaeda operative who was trained by Khalid Sheikh Mohammed to carry out suicide terror attacks in America.[80] An estimated 25 percent of the detainees whose release has been secured through the lawyers' efforts have returned to the battlefield to wage war against the United States and its allies.[81]

But it is not just captured terrorists whose cause CCR has taken up. Terrorists still actively engaged in fighting the United States have also found an ally in the organization and its lawyers. In 2010, CCR joined forces with the ACLU to file a lawsuit seeking to end a US government program authorizing the killing of accused terrorists like the radical Muslim cleric Anwar al-Awlaki, a US citizen and al-Qaeda operative, whose militant sermons were attended by three of the 9/11 hijackers and inspired Fort Hood shooter Nidal Malik Hasan, with whom Awlaki communicated regularly, and whose deadly 2009 shooting rampage he praised.[82] "Christmas Day bomber" Umar Farouk Abdulmutallab also identified Awlaki as one of his al-Qaeda trainers and spiritual advisers. Awlaki called on Muslims to assassinate non-Muslims, including a young female cartoonist in Seattle and the novelist Salman Rushdie, and he was a leading recruiter of terrorists seeking to carry out attacks against America. Despite his résumé as a sworn and lethal enemy of the United States, the Center for Constitutional Rights and ACLU tried to prevent the US government from killing this archterrorist and others like him. Awlaki was finally killed by a US drone in September 2011.

The "Guantanamo bar," as it has come to be known, is bankrolled by the Left's megafunders. Money from Soros's Open Society Institute has gone to aid not only groups like the Center for Constitutional Rights but also to individuals like CCR attorney Lynne Stewart, who was sentenced to ten years in prison in July 2010 for helping to pass messages from her client, the "Blind Sheikh" Omar Abdel Rahman, to his terrorist followers in Egypt instructing them to commit acts of violence.[83] That Stewart had been aiding a convicted terrorist—Rahman was sentenced to life in prison in 1996 for his involvement in the 1993 World Trade Center bombing and in several failed bombing plots in New York—did not prevent Soros's Open Society Institute from contributing $20,000 to her defense.[84] Open Society Institute officials hailed Stewart as a "human rights defender."[85]

An even more significant measure of the radical left's ability to move its national security agenda from the margins to the center stage of American politics through the support of funders like Ford and Soros is the fact that President Obama's platform on entering the White House (and before encountering a public backlash) included a progressive wish list on these matters. The administration promised that terrorists captured abroad would receive civilian trials and would be accorded rights once reserved for American citizens. It promised to shut down Guantanamo Bay and to end military commissions to try terrorist detainees. It vowed to dramatically slash America's nuclear arsenal. It rejected a range of Bush-era counterterrorism policies that had kept the country safe since 9/11, and it disclosed the classified operations of America's intelligence agencies, destroying several of them in the process. Finally, it fulfilled its promise to subordinate US policy and military forces to the authority of international institutions under the doctrine of "responsibility to protect." On all these fronts, President Obama attempted to implement the Left's goals, which were designed to weaken America's defenses and ability to protect its citizens, although popular opposition meant that he was not always successful.

6.

SOCIALISM BY STEALTH

Barack Obama entered office amid the worst economic recession since the Great Depression. Financial markets were tumbling, unemployment was rising, and a $1.2 trillion deficit loomed. In this dismal economic climate, leading Republicans and Democrats alike urged the new president to make the economy his chief domestic policy concern. Democrat Steny Hoyer, then the House majority leader, observed that "Whether you're a Democrat, Republican or an Independent, all the polls reflect that the economy is the major issue."[1]

Polls did indeed bear this out. A January 2009 Pew poll found that 85 percent of the American people wanted Obama to make the economy his top political priority, with registered Democrats even supporting a focus on the economy ahead of other issues in slightly higher numbers than Republicans. By contrast, health care ranked eighth on their list of priorities.[2] By almost any measure, the economy should have been first and foremost on the incoming administration's agenda.

Yet it was not. In February 2009, just a month after the Pew poll was released, Obama gave his first address to Congress and declared that his focus would be on . . . health care. Even as the country was urging the president to focus on the nation's ailing economy, Obama declared that "we can no longer afford to put healthcare reform on hold."[3]

This was not the first time that Obama had made news on this subject. While running for the US Senate in 2003, he had revealed his support for single-payer universal health care where government is the sole insurer—a socialist plan that would come back to haunt him as the health-care debate unfolded. Nonetheless, the president's decision to make health care a top policy priority—in a time of pressing economic problems and in defiance of the will of the public and members of his own party—signaled a dramatic victory for those elements of the political left who saw socialized medicine as a foot in the door on the way to a socialist state. In short, what neutral observers might have regarded as a case of spectacularly misplaced priorities by a president faced with an economic crisis was in fact a top priority of the Left and a testament to its unrivaled ability to form powerful issue-focused coalitions and build advocacy campaigns that would succeed in "fundamentally transforming the United States of America," as the president himself had promised on the eve of his election.[4]

Historically, government-run "universal" health care has been a hard sell in the United States. Nor has a "right" to health care ever been recognized in America.[5] It is unmentioned in any of the country's founding documents, whether the Declaration of Independence or the Constitution. That is no coincidence. When the founders wrote of citizens' "unalienable rights" to "life, liberty, and the pursuit of happiness," they were referring to natural rights, which exist independent of government,[6] and the rights they enumerated in the Bill of Rights were conceived as limits to government—prohibitions on what government might seek to do. The claim that health care is a right is a historically socialist claim and is a radical departure from America's founding principles.

Even in countries that claim a universal "right" to health care, the actual right is harder to implement than the theory would imply. Government bureaucrats make decisions about the kind of health-care recipients of the "right" are eligible to receive and when they can receive it. All countries with socialized medicine ration health care by forcing their citizens to wait to receive treatments when demand relative to supply is great. Canada has a population smaller than California's, yet 830,000 Canadians are currently waiting to be admitted to a hospital or to get treatment.[7] In England, which is also a country with a "universal" health insurance system, the waiting list is 1.8 million.[8] America's health-care system may be far from perfect, but consignment to a waiting list under a socialized system can be (and often proves) fatal. Consequently, universal health-care systems frequently have worse outcomes for the public they serve. One study of British lung cancer treatments found that "21 percent of curable patients become incurable on the waiting list."[9]

Nonetheless, the actual experience of countries that have made health care a "right" has not deterred the advocates of socialized medicine from pressing Americans to follow their troubling example. Support for universal health insurance has a long history in the post-Roosevelt Democratic Party, including many presidential administrations. But it was the power of the coordinated financial networks of the Left and the secondary advocacy groups they created that finally made socialized medicine more than just a progressive pipe dream.

Prior to the election of Barack Obama, legislation to enact universal health care in America had always stalled politically. In 1945, President Harry Truman proposed a sweeping "economic bill of rights" that included a right to universal health-care coverage, but he found his program thwarted by a Republican Congress and an adversarial

American medical community led by the American Medical Association.[10] In the 1970s, the cause of universal health care was taken up by the late senator Ted Kennedy, who claimed that health care was "a fundamental right and not just a privilege" and proposed legislation, the so-called Health Security Act, that would have made health care a universal government benefit.[11] But despite a rhetorical commitment to support Kennedy's bill from President Jimmy Carter, the bill foundered amid congressional opposition and an economic recession that forced the administration to recast its policy priorities.

Democrats again turned their attention to universal health care in the 1990s, when their efforts bore modest fruit at the state level. In 1991, Democrat Harris Wofford successfully campaigned for Senate in Pennsylvania on the slogan, "If criminals have a right to a lawyer, then working Americans have a right to healthcare." But the campaign for socialized medicine failed at the federal level, most prominently during the Clinton administration's doomed 1993 effort to pass a universal bill. Drafted in secret by a task force led by First Lady Hillary Clinton, the resulting proposal, dubbed "Hillarycare," was a 1,367-page legislative behemoth that if passed would have forced all Americans to purchase health insurance and would have socialized one-seventh of the American economy by forcing private businesses to provide health care for their workers through government-run plans. Hillarycare proved so unpopular that it was pronounced dead-on-arrival when it came before a Democrat-controlled Congress in 1994 and was a key factor fueling the Republican Party's sweep in that year's congressional elections.

While failing time and again to establish universal health care in a single legislative coup, Democrats also employed a gradualist approach that has steadily expanded government's role in health care and brought their vision ever closer to reality, while creating a massive unfunded liabilities problem (benefits promised that are not covered by tax receipts). Frustrated in his attempt to pass universal coverage, Truman settled for signing the Hospital Survey and Construction

Act, which earmarked $4.6 billion of taxpayer money to building non-profit hospitals, which provided care for the poor in exchange for their government subsidies.[12] In 1965, President Lyndon Johnson again expanded government involvement in health care when he signed legislation creating the Medicare and Medicaid programs to provide comprehensive health-care coverage for the elderly as well as the poor and the disabled.

Within a few years, these new government programs had caused health-care-related spending nationwide to surge—a trend that continues to the present day, when the two programs, totaling almost 20 percent of all spending, make up the single fastest-growing expenditure for state and federal governments.[13] As a result, despite the fact that government accounted for almost half of all health-care spending by 2004,[14] it was still not enough to cover the exploding cost of programs like Medicare and Medicaid. The Medicare trustees reported that their program had an unfunded liability of nearly $38 trillion.[15]

To put this figure in perspective, it is more than double the size of the entire US economy.[16] The cost of Medicaid is rising even more rapidly. With a budget of $439 billion in 2010, the program is expected to become the country's most expensive health-care entitlement.[17] Together and individually, these government programs present a growing crisis for America's long-term fiscal health.

The runaway costs of government health-care programs failed to faze progressives in their crusade for a government health-care system. It merely cautioned them to use a piecemeal approach. In 1997, President Clinton passed the Children's Health Insurance Program, which provided health insurance to the children of the poor or near poor. Praised by supporters as providing a "critical safety net," the program marked another step toward creating a socialized medical system because its funding formula left open the option of expanding eligibility for government coverage far beyond the program's intended recipients. In February 2009, President Obama extended funding and eligibility for this program to cover an additional four million children, many of whom did not meet the original income qualifications.[18]

These efforts to institute a health-care reform that would irreversibly change the American health-care system had long been supported by the network of foundations committed to the progressive cause. In 1989, the Ford Foundation published a report called *The Common Good: Social Welfare and the American Future.* In it, the Ford executives concluded that "The national goal should be *universal health coverage* for all Americans." The Rockefeller Foundation had also made no secret of the fact that it was working to "support the transformation of health systems toward universal health coverage."[19] The Tides Foundation described universal health care as one of the organization's "fundamental principles."[20] George Soros's Open Society Institute funded several groups advocating a socialist, single-payer health-care system controlled by the federal government.[21]

The foundation-sponsored campaign gained significant traction in the 1990s, when state governments and then the federal government came under its influence. Prominent among the campaign's funders was the Robert Wood Johnson Foundation. Established in 1972, the Princeton, New Jersey–based philanthropy is a Tides Foundation donor, and a funder of the Children's Defense Fund, on whose board Hillary Clinton once sat, and the New Jersey Institute for Social Justice.[22] It is America's largest philanthropy focused exclusively on health care, and, as a stockholder in the pharmaceutical industry giant Johnson & Johnson, one of the most financially powerful with $8.8 billion in assets.[23]

Politically, the RWJ Foundation has long been a supporter of universal health-care coverage and in the 1990s, under the direction of President Steve Schroeder, it spent millions backing state and national efforts to pass legislation expanding government-provided health care. At the state level, the foundation funded a health-care task force in 1992 that pushed through a universal coverage plan in

Minnesota. The foundation then tried to expand the program on a national scale by leading a campaign in support of the Clinton administration's health-care bill. Although the effort ultimately failed, the RWJ Foundation played a significant role in crafting and promoting the legislation.

Steven Schroeder was a member of the Clinton administration's transition team and recommended candidates for Hillary Clinton's task force on health care, which ultimately drafted the legislation. In addition, the RWJ Foundation spent $690,000 for public community forums in which Hillary Clinton promoted her health-care plan—a move that critics lambasted as blatant partisanship on the part of a tax-exempt and therefore supposedly nonpartisan foundation.[24] Desperate to see the legislation pass, the foundation even gave an unprecedented $2.5 million grant to NBC in May 1994, plus another $1 million for promotion so that the network could produce a two-hour health-care special informing the public of the benefits of Clinton health care.

When its investment in the cause of the Clinton plan failed to secure its passage, the RWJ Foundation stepped up its funding efforts. In 1995, RWJ alone accounted for almost 45 percent of all giving in the area of health policy in America.[25] In particular, the foundation sought to achieve universal health-care coverage incrementally by expanding government-provided coverage for uninsured children. To that end, the foundation funded initiatives like "Covering Kids," which was established in 1997 to reduce the number of uninsured children. Originally a $13 million initiative planned for fifteen states, it soon grew into a $47 million national effort with programs in all fifty states. Later in 1997, taking Covering Kids as a model, the Clinton administration enacted the Children's Health Insurance Program (CHIP) at the federal level. The foundation also laid much of the early organizational groundwork for the passage of a radical health-care overhaul under the Obama administration by sponsoring coalitions that brought together left-wing advocacy groups like Families USA, government unions like the Service Employees International Union (SEIU), and representatives of the business industry like the US Chamber of Commerce.[26]

While RJW was instrumental in building the political foundation for legislation like CHIP, its efforts were amplified by the Annie E. Casey Foundation, another funder that played a key role in shifting health-care policy to the left in the 1990s.[27] Established in 1948 by Jim Casey, one of the founders of United Parcel Service shipping company, the $2.5 billion foundation channeled its grants toward programs and organizations ostensibly intended to help the poor but in fact were designed to further progressive goals. Among the recipients of Casey funds are the Tides Foundation and the Tides Center, ACORN, the ACLU, the National Council of La Raza, the Colorado Progressive Coalition, the Center for Community Change (an organization of Alinsky radicals), the American Institute for Social Justice, Independent Media Inc. (a far left media network), and the Children's Defense Fund. Among the Casey beneficiaries, ACORN sought to expand government-run health insurance at the state level and emerged as a leading supporter of the CHIP program, which in time became a Trojan horse for expanding government health-care coverage.

Socialized health-care coverage was also an agenda of the $5.7 billion David and Lucile Packard Foundation.[28] Created in 1964 by David Packard, a cofounder of Hewlett-Packard, the Packard Foundation had—like many other large foundations—come under the influence of the political left. The Packard Foundation was a donor to the Tides Center, the ACLU, MALDEF, Changemakers, the Children's Defense Fund, the National Council of La Raza, the EarthJustice Legal Defense Fund, the National Abortion and Reproductive Rights Action League (NARAL), the Feminist Majority, and the Alliance for Justice.

Along with the RWJ Foundation, Packard was also one of the principal funders of expanding health insurance coverage for children.

The Clinton administration's passage of the Children's Health Insurance Program spurred the Packard Foundation to increase its support for political campaigns for universal health care. Like the RWJ Foundation, it went on to sponsor political coalitions backing universal health care comprising labor unions and left-wing groups like Families USA.[29]

The financial muscle of these foundations working in and through the 501(c)3 policy groups they supported kept the many-times-rejected universal health-care idea alive and ensured that it was part of the national discussion. But because the idea remained radical in the eyes of the American public, this support was not yet sufficient to push socialized health care across the finish line. Chastened by the much-publicized failure of Hillarycare, mainstream Democratic presidential hopefuls in the late 1990s distanced themselves from universal health-care proposals. During the 2000 presidential election, National Public Radio reported that "while universal healthcare coverage was the buzz word in healthcare reform some years ago, there's been little mention of it this election season, except from Green Party candidate Ralph Nader."[30] When asked if he would support a government-run universal health-care system, Democratic nominee Al Gore categorically rejected the idea. "I am not in favor of government doing it all," he said in 2000.[31] A socialized system remained so unpopular with the public that the 2004 Democratic nominee John Kerry also declined to make universal health-care part of his presidential platform.[32]

Nonetheless, universal health care remained a priority for the Left because it was the quintessential "non-reformist reform"—a reform that would be a game changer, making every American part of a government system that affected their individual lives as a matter of life and death.[33] Within four years after Kerry's defeat, the ground beneath the Democratic Party had shifted and the day of socialized health care had arrived. In the 2008 election, every one of the leading Democratic presidential candidates unveiled their own universal health-care plans.[34]

This was not due to increased enthusiasm for such a radical proposal on the part of American voters or the public at large. The change was very clearly the result of the newly acquired strength of the progressive Leviathan in the form of the Shadow Party that George Soros had put together during the previous presidential election cycle—the network of left-wing foundations, policy organizations, and government unions that had now elected a president who came directly out of their ranks.[35] With the chief executive supporting a socialist plan and offering lucrative deals to corporate players, the pharmaceuticals and other industry giants fell into line. This powerful political juggernaut cleared the way for the passage of the most radical bill in American history.

Spearheading this effort was an organization called Families USA.[36] Although self-described as a "nonprofit, nonpartisan organization," Families USA is a left-wing lobbying group for universal health care.[37] Founded in 1982 with a $40 million endowment from high-tech businessman Philippe Villers, Families USA first came to exert an influence on health-care policy in the 1990s, when it advised Bill Clinton on the issue during his 1992 presidential campaign. Following the defeat of Hillarycare in 1994, the group's cofounder and executive director, Ron Pollack, an attorney and former 1960s radical, joined a presidential health-care advisory commission that recommended a so-called patients' bill of rights. The bill applied to Americans in government-run health plans and added an official imprimatur to the Left's ideological assertion that health care was a "right" to be guaranteed by the state. Families USA also played a key role in the Clinton administration's 1997 passage of the Children's Health Insurance Program, which had further expanded government health-care coverage.

As of 2009, Families USA was armed with $48 million in net assets, the source of which it has kept secret, and would play a critical role in the Obama administration's push for health-care legislation, not least by forging an unlikely alliance that was ultimately successful in prevailing on the administration to follow its lead. In January 2007, Pollack and Families USA had created the Health Coverage Coalition for the Uninsured (HCCU), a disparate coalition of sixteen national organizations to support, if not universal health care, then something as close to it as politically feasible—"to cover as many people as possible, as quickly as possible."[38]

The coalition's historic proposal called for universal health care and proposed an increase in government insurance *coverage* to achieve that goal.[39] The theme of its campaign would be "protecting the uninsured." Among the coalition's member groups were major lobbying organizations like the American Association of Retired Persons (AARP).[40] Closely aligned with the Democratic Party, the AARP has long used its $1.6 billion in assets to invest in progressive causes, including health-care "reform."

In what the HCCU itself described as a case of "strange bedfellows," the coalition included pharmaceutical industry giants like Pfizer Inc. and Johnson & Johnson. In reality, there was nothing strange about these profit-making companies' support for a new health-care bill championed by the Left. As part of any eventual legislation, the giant pharmaceuticals hoped to benefit from expanding the health-care market while making participation *mandatory*, and from special provisions to ban drug reimportation into the United States.[41] Government monopolies can prove very profitable for those included in the monopoly. The pharmaceutical industry has long lobbied to keep such bans in place because the industry stands to lose billions in revenue if Americans are allowed to reimport drugs from Canada, where price controls keep their costs artificially low.

Despite having opposed the ban on drug reimportation as a senator, President Obama promised to retain it in his health-care bill. In return, corporations like Pfizer spent $150 million lobbying for the bill and became willing members of a left-wing health-care coalition.[42] Merging money and political clout, the HCCU played an early role in portraying health care as an urgent domestic policy goal to cover Americans who had "fallen between the cracks"—a position the Obama administration would soon adopt.

Not only did Families USA rally corporate America to the cause of socialized health care, but it served as a vital link between the Left's lobbying groups and the government unions that would go on to play a pivotal role in the health-care debate. For instance, Mary Kay Henry, a member of Families USA's executive board, is also the president of the powerful 2.2-million-member Service Employees International Union (SEIU), the country's largest union of health-care workers, and a charter member of the Shadow Party.[43] Along with other unions representing government employees, the SEIU proved instrumental both in pressuring the Obama administration to pass a radical health-care overhaul and in profiting from the resulting legislation.

Unions were not always a natural constituency for universal health care. When progressive politicians like Theodore Roosevelt proposed a system of compulsory national health insurance at the outset of the twentieth century, legendary labor leader Samuel Gompers, the head of the American Federation of Labor, opposed it on the grounds that it was "paternalistic and repugnant." Gompers believed that union members could get better health care without government involvement and insisted that "workers had to rely on their own economic power rather than the state."[44]

Over time, however, unions came to embrace the cause of government-run health care. That ideological shift became especially pronounced with the rise of government unions, whose increasing power led to a dramatic leftward shift in union leadership in the 1990s. In 1996, progressives seized the reins of power from the old industrial unions and expelled the more moderate old guard from leadership.

The old-guard leadership was exemplified by Lane Kirkland, longtime head of the AFL-CIO. Although a staunch liberal, Kirkland

was also a committed Cold War warrior whose anti-Communist politics had long vexed the progressives in the AFL-CIO, as had his traditional labor views. Kirkland's presidency became a dividing line
between liberals and leftists within the AFL-CIO's leadership. One
crucial difference between Kirkland and the government union leftists was Kirkland's opposition to universal health care.[45] It was during
Kirkland's tenure that the AFL-CIO's health-care committee rejected
a proposal that the union movement support a single-payer plan.[46]

In the AFL-CIO elections of 1996, Kirkland's chosen successor, Thomas Donahue, was defeated by a left-wing coalition led by
John Sweeney, a member of the Democratic Socialists of America
and president of the SEIU. The leadership change signaled a seis-
mic shift within the AFL-CIO, as left-wing government and teachers' unions eclipsed the more moderate craft and industrial unions
and, with them, traditional union philosophy and politics.[47] Sweeney
wasted little time in reorganizing the AFL-CIO's priorities to reflect
the dominance of the government unions.

Chief among those priorities was universal health care. Government unions had made generous health benefits for their members
at taxpayers' expense a key element of the packages they negotiated
with government officials. That they viewed this bounty as a "right"
became evident in the financial crisis of 2008, when states going bank-
rupt tried to renegotiate their contracts and deal with the crippling
economic burdens they entailed. In states like New Jersey, to take one
example, 88 percent of public-school teachers paid nothing toward
their health insurance premiums.[48] Government union members also
enjoyed more access to health care than their private-sector counterparts. Across the nation, 86 percent of state- and local-government
workers had access to employer-provided health insurance, while only
45 percent of private-sector workers did.[49]

Overall union membership was in a precipitous decline. From a
high of 35 percent in the 1950s, union membership had slumped to
just 12 percent by 2006 and 11 percent at present.[50] But the expan-

sionist role for government that Obama and congressional progressives envisioned promised to offer unions a lifeline. If the health industry were even partially nationalized, health-care workers would effectively become government employees. They too would then enjoy more job protections and benefits than their counterparts in the private sector while being immune from market competition. As a result, chances of recruiting new union members would increase—a pattern familiar in countries with socialized health-care systems.[51] In Canada, for instance, 61 percent of all health-care workers belong to unions, compared to just 11 percent in the United States.[52] Increasing government involvement in health care would help unions replenish their dwindling membership while maintaining the generous benefit packages that have pushed states and cities across the country to fiscal ruin. Thus, universal health care was seen as a way to achieve by government fiat what unions had failed to achieve on their own: more unionized workers—and, from a progressive point of view, more political constituents for further government expansion.

Passing legislation to expand the government's role in health care was the task that Sweeney set for himself and the AFL-CIO. Sweeney had been the first chairman of the AFL-CIO health-care committee and it was under his leadership that the AFL-CIO became identified with the cause. It was no coincidence that when, as an aspiring senator, Obama announced his support for a single-payer plan in 2003, he did so at an AFL-CIO forum. In keeping with Sweeney's conviction that "the answer is universal healthcare,"[53] the AFL-CIO worked to put the issue into the forefront in the run-up to the 2008 presidential election. In 2007, the AFL-CIO's executive council announced that it was "time to mobilize America behind a concrete plan to enact universal healthcare."[54] The following year, the AFL-CIO did just that. The union spent over $3 million in lobbying the federal government on behalf of causes like universal health care.[55]

Sweeney's enthusiasm for universal health care was shared by his radical protégé at the SEIU, Andrew Stern. Disaffected with what he saw as the insufficiently political direction of the AFL-CIO, however, Stern took his union out of the organization in 2005, while continuing to push hard for national health care. In the same month that Families USA announced its Health Coverage Coalition for the Uninsured in 2007, SEIU launched the "Divided We Fail" coalition— a multimillion-dollar public relations effort to promote health-care legislation.

Divided We Fail's first marketing gimmick was to promote itself as a "grassroots" movement. Nothing could have been further from the truth. With $268 million in revenues in 2009,[56] the SEIU is not only one of the country's largest unions but is also an enormously influential political lobbying organization in its own right. In 2009, Andrew Stern justifiably boasted that the union's $60 million investment in Barack Obama's election had paid off.[57] That fortune bought Stern and the SEIU direct access to the president. During Obama's first six months in office, Stern was the most frequent visitor to the White House and was surpassed by the end of the year only by Anna Burger, known as the "Queen of Labor." Burger was the SEIU's secretary treasurer. Obama's political affairs director, meanwhile, was Patrick Gaspard, a former top lobbyist for the SEIU.[58]

Besides the SEIU, the HCCU included business groups like the Business Roundtable, which represents the CEOs of Fortune 500 companies with a combined $4.5 trillion in annual revenues.[59] Partnering with the paragons of corporate America was perfectly consistent with the counsel given by Stern's and Obama's socialist mentor, Saul Alinsky, to work within the system and push it to the edge— in this instance, by using the leading beneficiaries of capitalism to advance a government takeover of health care, tying all citizens to the state. As Alinsky had said, "whatever works to get power to the people, use it." Of course "the people" who would get the power would be the government unions, government bureaucrats, and left-wing politicians who promoted the new order. Divided We Fail proved adept at doing just that. Before long, the coalition could boast that 360 members of Congress, including Republicans and Democrats, had signed its pledge or endorsed its campaign for universal health care.[60]

Just as Alinsky's pragmatic radicalism guided Divided We Fail, his shrewd grasp of market competition inspired another SEIU-headed coalition to support the universal health-care effort. In *Rules for Radicals*, Alinsky had instructed radicals to use what he called "corporate jujitsu" to achieve their political goals.[61] By bearing in mind "the self-interest of corporations," Alinsky wrote, radicals could appeal to the corporate bottom line to achieve their own ambitions.

The fruits of Alinsky's wisdom could be seen in groups like Better Health Care Together. Founded in February 2007, this organization allied left-wing activist groups like the Center for American Progress, a left-wing think tank headed by former Clinton chief of staff John Podesta, with the Ford-funded League of United Latin American Citizens (LULAC). Also included were unions like SEIU and the Communication Workers of America and corporations like AT&T and retail giant Walmart. The alliance between the famously nonunionized Walmart and the SEIU may seem unlikely, but as Alinsky himself might have predicted, it was not. Walmart was just one of many corporations that lobbied for universal health-care legislation out of self-interest: it would impose new regulations to provide health-care coverage and thereby eliminate competition from smaller retailers, like Target, who would find such coverage too costly to provide.[62] Alinsky's corporate "jujitsu" in action—Better Health Care Together—was now joined by still another.

The new coalition called itself Health Care for America Now. It was created shortly after Obama secured the Democratic nomination in July 2008 and immediately pledged to spend $40 million to make health-care reform a reality. Billed to the public as a "grassroots" campaign, Health Care for America Now was a consortium of powerful left-wing interest groups and labor unions, and key elements of the billionaire-backed Shadow Party. Health Care for America Now's twenty-one-member steering committee included such groups as ACORN, the Center for American Progress, MoveOn.org, the National Council of La Raza, the SEIU, the American Federation of State, County and Municipal Employees (AFSCME), and the United Food and Commercial Workers union.

One of the most influential members of the Health Care for America Now coalition was the Center for Community Change (CCC), a group with deep roots in the world of Alinsky-influenced progressive organizing that nurtured Barack Obama's early political career.[63] A favorite of the Left's leading funders, the CCC received grants from the Woods Fund of Chicago and the Ford Foundation, as well as from health-care-focused funds like the Annie E. Casey Foundation and the David and Lucile Packard Foundation.

Through its Health Rights Organizing Project, the CCC seeks to promote government-run health care and to "expose the harmful role of the private market in our healthcare system."[64] During the health-care debate, the Health Rights Organizing Project served as an important ideological conduit between the Left's health-care campaign and radical community organizers who would play a crucial but little-noticed role in that campaign. For instance, the CCC's executive director is Deepak Bhargava, an outspoken advocate of socialized medicine and a former labor and ACORN organizer.[65]

In the 1990s, Bhargava helped patent the center's strategy of opposing welfare reform not by attacking conservative reformers but by targeting Democrats who might be willing to compromise on that issue.[66] That tactic would be revived during the 2009–2010 health-care debate when progressive activists packed town halls to demand that Democratic moderates support universal health-care legislation, and groups like Health Care for America Now purchased ads designed to pressure Democratic congressmen in swing districts.[67]

Bhargava would go on to direct the National Campaign for Jobs and Income Support, a coalition of two hundred progressive groups formed to advance the Cloward-Piven strategy of flooding welfare rolls by calling for new benefits for welfare recipients.[68] Alinsky's hidden hand was also in evidence on the center's board, whose members include Heather Booth, 1960s radical and former director of the Midwest Academy, which was Barack Obama's political base and sponsor for more than a decade before he became an elected official. In Booth's own words, "Alinsky is to community organizing as Freud is to psychoanalysis."[69]

Booth was a founding member of Democratic Socialists of America and a key figure in the mayoral and Senate campaigns of Harold Washington and Democrat Carol Moseley Braun. In the 1990s, Booth became a health-care outreach coordinator for the Democratic National Committee, in which capacity she played a role in the Clinton administration's failed effort to enact health-care reform. Now the director of the AFL-CIO's health-care reform campaign (her husband, Paul, is an AFCMSE executive), Booth symbolizes the radical leadership behind the health-care agendas of the country's largest union federation and the Democratic Party.[70]

As the phalanx of left-wing funders supporting its goals indicates, Health Care for America Now was not the "grassroots" group that it claimed to be. Headquartered on Washington's K Street, home to the capital's high-powered lobbyists, Health Care for America Now was fueled by millions of dollars from its member groups and their financiers. Not only did each member of the Health Care for America Now steering committee have to put up an initial contribution of $500,000, but the group also drew from the coffers of leading left-wing funders.

Atlantic Philanthropies, for example, a foundation with $3.3 billion in assets in 2007, provided a $10 million grant to HCAN. Atlantic was headed by Gara LaMarche, a Soros protégé. Soros himself pledged $5 million for the campaign.[71] Health Care for America Now also received support from the Tides Center.[72]

All this largesse fueled a $40 million lobbying campaign in support of universal health care and, ultimately, for the health-care legislation rammed through a Democratic-controlled Congress by the Obama administration. That campaign included national exposure through a $1.5 million ad buy in national print, online, and broadcast media, all part of an eventual $25 million media blitz.[73] Health Care for America Now's massive budget also allowed it to fund hundreds of organizers who mobbed town hall debates about health care across the country, lending an artificial grassroots gloss to a campaign that was in fact orchestrated from above as a project of multimillionaires. Even after the passage of the Obama administration's health-care bill, Health Care for America Now continued to campaign on behalf of the legislation alongside groups like Families USA, which had abandoned even the pretense of political neutrality to join forces in a new advertising campaign with the administration.[74]

Conservative opponents of universal health care also took part in the health-care debate, but their inability to influence the final legislation illustrates the Left's institutional advantage in orchestrating social change—its financial dominance and its far more developed political coordination. In February 2009, one opponent, Rick Scott, the founder of the Columbia Hospital Association, a for-profit hospital chain, created an organization called Conservatives for Patients' Rights. Scott's group made reasonable arguments about the perils of government provision of health care, warning of its consequences for taxpayers and patients and proposing free-market alternatives. Compared to the many left-wing coalitions that had sprung up to support universal health-care legislation, Conservatives for Patients' Rights often seemed like a lone voice for the other side.

Even that one dissenting voice was one too many for the Left, however. Rick Scott had donated $5 million of his own money to the group—the same amount that George Soros had given to Health Care for America Now and a tiny fraction of the tens of millions that left-wing funders had invested in their campaign for health-care legislation. Scott's individual contribution made up one-fourth of the group's planned $20 million advertising budget, a figure that paled in comparison to the $82 million that progressives pledged to spend in support of universal health care, not to mention the $150 million that the pharmaceutical industry spent to support the legislation.[75] (That the industry was actually supporting the Left did not deter the Machiavellians at HCAN from claiming that "big pharma" was their foe in the health-care fight.[76])

Seizing on Scott's $5 million donation, the Left launched a successful smear campaign to marginalize his organization's modest attempt to provide a counterview. Appearing on CNN, Scott was ambushed by left-wing anchor Rick Sanchez, who proceeded to berate him as "the poster child for everything that's wrong with the greed that has hurt out current healthcare system."[77] Sanchez then dismissed Scott as a "multimillionaire investor" out for himself, even though no one questioned the motivations of the billionaires and trillion-dollar corporations who were bankrolling the Left. In a typical attack, *New York Times* columnist Paul Krugman denounced Scott as a "cynical political operator" and sneered that Conservatives for Patients' Rights was a "well-heeled interest group" that was distorting the health-care debate. Krugman failed to notice or acknowledge the fact that leftist groups like Families USA and Health Care for America Now invested more than ten times Scott's contribution to Conservatives for Patients' Rights.[78]

White House press secretary Robert Gibbs also got in on the act, suggesting that Scott's history as the CEO of a privately run health-care company was evidence of his suspect motives, even though health-care company CEOs were a prominent part of the left-wing coalition supporting the Obama plan.[79] Lacking the resources to repel this political siege, Scott's organization soon found itself on life support. Before long, Conservatives for Patients' Rights ceased to exist altogether.

By contrast, Health Care for America Now not only thrived but was able to claim that the coalition and its agenda "are supported by President Obama, Vice President Biden, and more than 190 Members of Congress,"[80] as the Obama administration, backed by congressional Democrats, moved full speed ahead with the socialized health-care plan, which became known as "Obamacare."

Notwithstanding the efforts of one of most powerful lobbies ever mounted in support of a piece of legislation, the radical nature of Obamacare created a fierce national backlash among the voting public. Poll after poll showed that an overwhelming majority of Americans—still committed to American individualism—opposed the health-care plan.[81] That opposition soon fueled a populist revolt that saw Democrats in liberal blue states lose their seats to Republicans who ran on their opposition. Most notably, in Massachusetts, little-known Republican state senator Scott Brown scored an upset victory after campaigning to be the senator whose vote could block its passage.

Not the least irony was the fact that in his campaign against the health-care bill, Brown captured the vacant Senate seat long held by the country's leading proponent of universal health care, Ted Kennedy. Meanwhile, in gubernatorial races in New Jersey and Virginia, voters turned out Democratic incumbents in favor of Republican candidates who opposed Obama's bill. Popular anger at the new law and its dramatic expansion of government also energized a national grass-roots movement, the Tea Party, in opposition.

Although the huge Democratic congressional majorities that had been won in the previous midterm elections ensured passage of Obama's bill, supporters of a single-payer socialized system did not get everything they wanted. Nevertheless, the legislation, which passed in March 2010, marked an unprecedented victory for the political left. It was the largest expansion of American government in four decades, and it radically transformed the American health-care system to more closely resemble the state-run systems of countries like Canada, putting the country on a clear path toward socialized health care.[82] American leftists lauded Obama for fulfilling a long-sought dream. After the president signed the health-care bill into law, Patrick Kennedy handed him a facsimile of the failed Health Security Act that Senator Kennedy had championed, writing at the bottom that Obama had "completed" his father's work.[83] On his father's grave, Kennedy wrote, "Dad, the unfinished business is done."[84]

The Left's business may have been done, but the problems created by Obamacare were just beginning. At over 2,400 pages, the legislation dwarfed Hillary Clinton's 1,367-page proposal, but it contained many of the excesses that had ensured the defeat of her bill. Although falling short of the politically calculated promise of universal coverage—23 million Americans would still be uninsured by 2019—the bill restructured one-sixth of the American economy. As a consequence of Obamacare, the government would be responsible for 52 percent of the country's health spending by 2019,[85] with estimated costs of a budget-breaking $1.05 trillion over ten years, according to the Centers of Medicare and Medicaid Services, assuming the projected figures were realistic, which all previous experience with government health-care systems suggested they were not. The legislation also dramatically enlarged government's reach by forcing Americans to purchase health insurance. Critics of the bill, including Virginia's attorney general Ken Cuccinelli, pointed out that if the federal government could compel Americans to purchase a commercial product, in this case health insurance, there was virtually no limit to its power. And that was exactly the point.

7.

CONTROLLED ENVIRONMENTS

In February 2009, Lisa Jackson, the director of the Environmental Protection Agency in the Obama administration, announced that the agency had identified a dangerous new threat to the American people and the environment: air.[1] Specifically, the agency concluded that carbon dioxide, a key component in air, would now be classified as a harmful "pollutant," one that the EPA would regulate under the Clean Air Act.

Critics quickly pointed out that this new regulatory authority amounted to an unprecedented power grab by the state. After all, Congress had never intended the Clean Air Act to cover carbon dioxide, and the conclusion that it was harmful was itself scientifically suspect. As a naturally occurring gas, CO_2 is essential to life processes like photosynthesis. Nor is it a major threat to the environment. Carbon dioxide makes up only a small percentage of the greenhouse gases in the atmosphere, around 38 molecules of CO_2 for every 100,000 molecules of air. To that concentration, man-made carbon dioxide emissions had added only one molecule every five years.[2] Because the country's principal energy sources came from carbon-emitting fossil fuels, moreover, the costs of the EPA's new regulation would be passed on to American consumers in the form of higher energy costs and increased unemployment.

But anyone following the environmental movement as it has evolved in the last four decades would not have been surprised by the Obama administration's regulatory overreach. Just a week after Obama's victory in the 2008 election, the environmental group EarthJustice released a memo of environmental priorities it urged the new president to take up immediately. Atop the group's list was the demand that the administration "limit CO_2 emissions under the Clean Air Act."[3] Environmental groups like the Natural Resources Defense Council also made it clear that they expected the administration to regulate carbon dioxide through the Clean Air Act, even if it meant bypassing Congress to do so.[4]

It was no accident that the administration's environmental policy priorities converged so neatly with those of environmentalist groups like EarthJustice and the Natural Resources Defense Council, which were far more radical than the country's older and more traditional environmental organizations. This was the direct consequence of their disproportionate impact on the country's political debate, an influence underwritten by a massive investment from left-wing foundations. The financial muscle of these foundations brought the radicals out of the wilderness and into the mainstream of the nation's environmental politics.

The seeds of the modern environmental movement were sown in the political counterculture of the 1960s, although environmental groups had existed long before then. America's oldest environmental organization, the Sierra Club, was founded in 1892, for example.

But these "first-generation" environmental groups were focused primarily on land and wildlife conservation.[5] It was in 1962, seventy years later, that the agenda of the environmental movement began to broaden beyond its traditional concerns with the publication of Rachel Carson's polemic *Silent Spring*, a radical indictment of the chemical pesticide DDT. Factually inaccurate and marked by alarmist rhetoric—a typical chapter title was "Elixirs of Death"—Carson's book became a bestseller and has remained a bible of the modern environmental movement. It launched the emerging environmentalist belief that industry was the environment's enemy and a danger to Americans' health. Ever more expansive government regulations were thus required to protect the American people from industrial threats to natural ecosystems.

That argument could seem compelling when decades of pollution and official neglect had indeed left the country's environmental patrimony in a debilitated state. "People who lived in or near large urban centers could see firsthand how dirty the air was," observes environmental analyst Rich Trzupek. "The evidence ranged from the unnatural color of the sky to the coating of dust that would appear on automobiles parked in the city overnight."[6] Water quality was no less degraded. In 1972, the Potomac River was too dirty to swim in, Lake Erie was dying, and Ohio's Cuyahoga River was so polluted it had actually once burst into flames and burned.

In a bid to reverse the damage, the Nixon administration passed two landmark environmental laws: the Clean Air Act of 1970 and the Clean Water Act of 1972. The first set emissions standards for industry and car manufacturers. The second set new water quality standards. To enforce these standards, the Nixon administration created the Environmental Protection Agency, which established numeric benchmarks for pollutants in the air and water.

The new regulations had an immediate restorative effect. Air pollution declined dramatically in the years after their passage. The amount of pollutant dust and lead in the air decreased almost a hundredfold, and the concentration of other air pollutants, such as carbon monoxide and ozone, fell sharply.[7] At the same time, the number of water bodies safe for swimming and fishing doubled. Even Lake Erie, once known as the "Dead Sea," became safe to fish again. As the environment rebounded, American industry also became more conscientious. Although the number of cars on US roads has doubled since 1970, smog has declined by one-third. "Aggregate emissions," the sum of all air-pollution categories, have fallen 48 percent since that time.[8] Toxic emissions from industry declined 51 percent from 1988 to 2002, even though petrochemical manufacturers, the chief source of those emissions, increased production during that period.[9]

In the late 1960s, however, this dramatic turnaround was still in the future, and American industry could plausibly be framed as the culprit. The moment was ripe for the emergence of a new, more confrontational environmental movement, and left-wing foundations, in particular Ford, moved in to fill the void. Just as it transformed the immigration debate through the creation of public-interest law firms like MALDEF, the Ford Foundation almost single-handedly created and sustained the radical "second generation" environmental movement that would leave a lasting mark on the country's environmental legislation and regulation long after the environment itself had made its recovery.

The first of these groups was the Environmental Defense Fund.[10] Begun in 1967 with a Ford grant, the fund was a loose group of concerned scientists and birdwatchers opposed to the spraying of DDT because of its alleged toxic effect on humans and birds—a cause directly inspired by *Silent Spring*, Carson's anti-DDT polemic. Led by attorney Victor Yannacone, whose rallying cry "Sue the bastards!"[11] captured the aggressive style of the new environmentalists, the Environmental Defense Fund allied with more traditional groups like the Sierra Club and the National Audubon Society to petition the US government to ban DDT.

Much like the claims in Carson's book, the petition had little

scientific merit. In 1971, a seven-month hearing by the recently created Environmental Protection Agency determined that there was
no conclusive evidence that DDT was harmful either to humans or
birds. The hearing's presiding judge, Edmund Sweeney, concluded in
his summary of the hearings that DDT "is not a carcinogenic, muta-
genic, or tertragenic hazard to man," and its uses "do not have a del-
eterious effect on freshwater fish, estuarine organisms, wild birds or
other wildlife." On the contrary, "the evidence in this proceeding supports the conclusion that there is a present need for essential uses of
DDT."[12]

Those findings were echoed by the American scientific medical community, including the American Medical Association, the
National Academy of Sciences, and the US Surgeon General, which
all opposed a ban on DDT. But in what would become a pattern in
the years to come, the misleading environmental campaign galvanized public opposition and eventually forced the government to act.
In 1972, to appease the political pressure that environmental groups
had mounted to outlaw the pesticide, the Environmental Protection
Agency banned DDT.

This intervention was not only needless, its consequences were
lethal. The pesticide DDT repelled and killed malaria-carrying mos-
quitoes. Two years before the Nixon administration instituted its
ban, the National Academy of Sciences had reported that in just two
decades, the use of DDT had "prevented 500 million human mortali-
ties due to malaria that would otherwise have been inevitable."[13]

The EPA's ban curtailed domestic production of DDT and diminished its supply to the developing world. As a result, despite scientific advances and the advent of new medicines that have led to a
gradual decline in malarial deaths, malaria remains a prolific killer.
In Africa, malaria causes the deaths of between one and two million
people each year.[14] It is the leading cause of death among African
children under the age of five, and 5 percent of African children—
the equivalent of almost three thousand a day—die of malaria every

year.[15] As a result of the ban inspired by Carson's book and the efforts of environmental groups like the Environmental Defense Fund, in the nearly forty years since the DDT ban went into effect, between thirty million and sixty million people have lost their lives—a needless tragedy since DDT's efficacy in preventing malarial deaths had been established well before the ban.[16]

Millions of deaths had no adverse impact on the fortunes of the Environmental Defense Fund, whose influence rose dramatically over the same time span. From a small group of bird enthusiasts, the fund has grown to four hundred thousand members and commands assets of over $132 million. No longer reliant on the Ford Foundation alone, the organization gets nearly half of its revenues through grants from other left-wing foundations, among them the MacArthur Foundation, the Heinz Endowments, and the Joyce Foundation, whose board Barack Obama once graced.[17]

The Environmental Defense Fund is now one of the country's premier environmental groups, exerting direct influence on federal environmental regulations, and benefiting from a revolving door through which its staff joins Democratic presidential administrations and vice versa. In 2009, for instance, Elgie Holstein, a former senior adviser on energy for the Obama campaign and a member of President Obama's transition team, joined the Environmental Defense Fund as the vice president of its project on rivers and deltas.[18] More recently, in January 2011, the Obama administration hired Nat Keohane, an "environmental economist" at the fund, as a special assistant to President Obama on energy and environmental issues in the White House's National Economic Council.[19]

The Environmental Defense Fund's rise to prominence is paralleled by another Ford-sponsored group, the National Resources Defense Council (NRDC), a 501(c)3 public-interest environmental law firm. In 1970, the year the Nixon administration established the Environmental Protection Agency, a $400,000 seed grant from Ford set up the Defense Council.[20] Like the Environmental Defense Fund, the NRDC initially was a bare-bones operation. Staffed by six recent Yale law school graduates, it was a fringe group whose radical motto proclaimed "responsible militancy" in the service of environmentalist agendas.[21] For the first four years of its existence, the NRDC had no members. Ford grants almost single-handedly kept the organization afloat while helping the council to secure its tax-exempt status.

By 2011, the NRDC's early struggles were a distant memory. No longer a peripheral outfit, it had become the largest environmental group in the country, with a staff of 350 lawyers and environmentalists, 1.3 million members, and locations in New York, Washington, Chicago, Los Angeles, San Francisco, and Beijing. NRDC's list of supporters has also expanded, and its $97 million in annual revenues is made up of contributions from the network of left-wing foundations, ranging from the Heinz Endowments to the Turner and MacArthur Foundations.[22] Utilizing the courts and advising government officials, the NRDC is as powerful in many ways as the government's own environmental agency—a reality reflected in the nickname that the NRDC itself had embraced: the "shadow EPA."[23] The NRDC today can and does stake a claim to being the "nation's most effective environmental action group,"[24] with its in-house army of environmental lawyers influencing laws and regulations that affect everything from air and water pollution, to pesticides, nuclear waste, land use, and energy conservation.[25]

NRDC's influence rests in no small part on its high-profile consumer awareness campaigns, which transformed the organization into a serious political force. Often based on misleading information and deploying alarmist proclamations, these campaigns fueled public health scares that triggered new government regulations. Because the general public lacked the scientific background to properly evaluate the NRDC's claims, and because government agencies—as in the case of the DDT ban—routinely bowed to the public pressure generated by the campaigns, the NRDC has ended up wielding disproportionate influence on environmental policy.

Most notoriously, in 1989, the NRDC contracted a famous left-wing public relations firm, Fenton Communications, which had represented the Black Panthers and other radical groups, to launch a consumer awareness campaign against the chemical Alar, a pesticide then used to produce 15 percent of American-grown apples.[26] In the NRDC's overheated account, Alar threatened to cause millions of American children to develop cancer later in life—a sensational conclusion based on the group's dubious extrapolation of a study in which laboratory mice were fed particularly high levels of Alar.[27] After CBS's *60 Minutes* promoted the NRDC campaign in one of its segments, the "Alar scare" became an overnight national sensation. Yet there was still no evidence to justify the charge that trace amounts of Alar caused cancer.

In fact, the National Center for Policy Analysis calculated that an individual was more than three times more likely to be struck by lightning than to contract cancer from any commercial pesticides.[28] A single cup of coffee was twenty times more carcinogenic than all the pesticide residue consumed by an average person in a day. Despite the notable lack of scientific evidence, the NRDC's campaign achieved its goal of expanding government regulation, as the EPA banned the use of Alar.

The EPA's involvement was particularly ironic because the agency later concluded that a person would have to eat fifty thousand pounds of Alar-treated apples per day over the course of a lifetime to develop cancer, thus giving the lie to the NRDC's exaggerated claims of a cancer risk from the chemical.[29] Today, the EPA considers daminozide, the chemical name for Alar, to be of "very low" toxicity and allows its use for ornamental plants, even as it has kept in place the ban on its use for food crops.[30]

But the damage done by the anti-Alar scare campaign had immediate ripple effects throughout the economy. As the American public panicked, schools removed apples from their cafeterias, grocers were forced to throw out apples from their stores, and apple growers suffered massive losses, including bankruptcy. On the other hand, according to the internal memos of Fenton Communications head David Fenton disclosed in the *Wall Street Journal*, the Alar campaign was a bonanza for the NDRC. "We designed [the Alar campaign]," Fenton explained, "so that revenue would flow back to the Natural Resources Defense Council from the public, and we sold this book about pesticides through a 900 number and the *Donahue* show. And to date there has been $700,000 in net revenue from it."[31]

The Alar ban was the NRDC's first major "scare" success, but it was not the last. In 1998, the NRDC again teamed up with Fenton Communications to promote an initiative called "Give Swordfish a Break!" The campaign was presented as a grassroots effort to raise awareness about the overfishing of the supposedly endangered North Atlantic swordfish and to expand federal fishing regulations to cover swordfish. Not unlike the threat of a rarely used chemical in the case of Alar, the swordfish campaign was a hard sell. As one NRDC activist later acknowledged, "If you think it is hard to convince people that global warming is real, try persuading them that the oceans are running out of fish."[32] But the NRDC did not reveal the real reason that this was a difficult case to make: it was untrue. As the National Marine Fisheries Service later confirmed, Atlantic swordfish were not endangered.[33]

Once again the campaign proved a success despite the lack of evidence for its claims. To help make its case, the NRDC enlisted the support of 270 restaurants, who bankrolled the campaign through grants and agreed to stop serving swordfish. Swayed by the scare tactics, restaurants, hotel chains, cruise companies, and airlines decided to remove swordfish from their menus, and the Clinton administration signed new regulations governing swordfish nurseries.

Ultimately, "Give Swordfish a Break!" was part of a larger NRDC strategy to cast a wider net of federal regulations over numerous varieties of seafood, whether they were endangered or not. Thus, the NRDC claimed that, in addition to swordfish, seafood species like cod, scallops, sole, sea bass, sturgeon, redfish, red snapper, and monkfish should now be classified as "overfished." This approach of ever-increasing government regulation—whether it was justified or not—has become a hallmark of the environmental movement.

Under pressure from environmentalists, it has also become the policy of the EPA, which has been influenced by and supported groups like the NRDC regardless of which party occupies the White House. Despite the NRDC's relentless attacks on the Bush administration's environmental record, the group received $2.6 million from the EPA during the first three years of the Bush presidency.[34]

The NRDC has come in for special recognition during the Obama administration. In February 2011, President Obama bestowed the Presidential Medal of Freedom, the country's highest civilian honor, on NRDC founder John Adams.[35] Encouraged by this effective endorsement of its mission, the NRDC has continued to whip up costly environmental scare campaigns based on scant scientific evidence. Most recently, the group has set its sights on bisphenol-A, or BPA, a common industrial chemical that for over fifty years has been used to manufacture plastic products, from beverage containers to baby bottles. Regulatory agencies like the Food and Drug Administration, supported by health and science experts, have repeatedly found BPA to be nonhazardous and safe for industry use. Nonetheless, the NRDC's campaigns have pressured states like California to undertake a lengthy and expensive review of BPA, despite that state's soaring debt crisis.[36]

In addition to launching the two biggest new environmental organizations, the Ford Foundation also helped to transform more traditional environmental groups, inducing them to join the new radical guard. In 1971, Ford created the Sierra Club Legal Defense Fund (SCLDF), to help it remake environmental policy through the courts. Initially wholly dependent on Ford grants, the SCLDF now has 150 employees who staff a "policy and legislation team," nine regional offices around the country, and an international program. Having changed its name in 1997 to EarthJustice, the group today is one of America's leading environmental organizations and radical to its core. It was one of the groups that successfully pushed President Obama to bypass Congress in order to regulate carbon dioxide at the beginning of his term.

It didn't take long for the environmental groups Ford created at the beginning of the 1970s to have a dramatic impact on national policy. That decade saw the enactment of twenty-three major environmental laws, including the Clean Air Act, the Clean Water Act, the National Environmental Policy Act, the Endangered Species Act, and the National Forest Management Act.[37] Some of these regulations proved beneficial, which led to the paradox of a regulatory era in that they actually lessened the need for more regulations. Yet these successes did not lead to a slackening of advocacy for more laws and regulations, but rather—as in the case of CO_2 emissions—an expansion of the nature and scope of the interventions demanded.

Philosophically, the radical environmental movement was an offshoot of Marxism. Just as Marxists claimed that capitalism oppressed man, the radical environmentalists insisted it destroyed nature. One of the early intellectual architects of this school of environmentalism was Marxist academic Herbert Marcuse, a student of the Nazi philosopher Martin Heidegger. Marcuse's anticapitalist theories inspired the New Left's later view that the "degradation" of the environment was a systemic product of industrial capitalism.[38] Those ideas in turn would shape the modern environmentalist movement. In 1969, radical students at Berkeley "liberated" a vacant lot, renamed it "People's Park," and proclaimed themselves a "conspiracy of the soil" to rescue the land from its rapacious property owner—the university, which had reserved the space for future student housing.[39] The radicals then declared a strike for the "non-negotiable demands of the earth" and insisted that trees were no different than other exploited minorities, including American blacks.[40]

In 1970, Yale professor Charles Reich lent additional fervor to the anticapitalist strain in the environmental movement when he pub-lished *The Greening of America,* a bestseller charging that capital-ism had bankrupted American culture and subjected the country to "uncontrolled technology and the destruction of the environment." In a more strident version of Reich's thesis, the New Left anarchist Mur-ray Bookchin argued that "the immediate source of ecological crisis is capitalism" and that "capitalism is a cancer in the biosphere."[41] Book-chin, who became an icon of the new environmental movement, also revealed its political character when he observed that "the color of rad-icalism today is not red (communism), but green (environmentalism)."

It should come as no surprise, then, that a deep-rooted hostility to capitalism animates the country's leading environmental groups and activists. Thus the Natural Resources Defense Council has endorsed a document called the Earth Charter, which blames capitalism for many of the world's environmental, social, and economic problems and maintains that "the dominant patterns of production and con-sumption are causing environmental devastation, the depletion of resources, and a massive extinction of species."[42] Similarly, it is no accident that Carol Browner, the former global-warming czar in the Obama administration, once served as a commissioner of the Socialist International, the umbrella group for 170 "social democratic, socialist and labor parties" whose "organizing document" cites capitalism as the cause of "devastating crises," "mass unemployment," "imperialist expansion," and "colonial exploitation" worldwide.[43]

Expanding the state through regulation is one way that the envi-ronmental movement and its backers have sought to undermine the capitalist system they oppose, but it is not the only one. In recent years they have embraced so-called green jobs, a cause that wraps anticap-italist agendas in an economically friendly label. As billed by their environmentalist supporters, green jobs would shift American energy use toward renewable energy sources like wind and solar power while creating millions of new jobs in the process.

But despite the economic and environmental promise attributed to green jobs, they have a mythic basis, namely that government can "create" jobs using regulatory fiat by subsidizing innovations, in this case non-fossil-fuel energy and energy-efficient technologies, for which there is not yet sufficient demand in the free market.[44] Not the least of the reasons that there is no popular demand for non-fossil-fuel energy is that these sources remain far less efficient and far more expensive than fossil fuels. For instance, while coal can generate 155 million megawatt-hours of electricity a month, renewable energy like wind currently generates as little as 1.3 million megawatt-hours and cannot be transmitted over long distances from the power source. Green energy cannot compete with established energy sources, but it can massively expand the role of the state in the free-market economy.

Green jobs are also economically counterproductive, destroying jobs in the private sector. This is because in order to make the green energy industry competitive, government must subsidize it and must tax consumers and businesses to do so.[45] In favoring green industries, government diverts labor, capital, and materials from economically efficient and productive industries. The experience of European countries with green jobs is instructive. Spain's subsidies of renewable energy have led to the destruction of two private-sector jobs for every "green job" the government creates.[46] In Italy, green jobs were so expensive that for every green job created, five to seven were lost in the general economy.[47] Scotland's experience with green jobs was similar.[48]

But despite being inefficient and economically damaging, the green jobs campaign has found a powerful constituency in the United States: an alliance of environmental groups and government labor unions. Such alliances have a long history on the left. In what some on the left refer to as the first "environmental justice movement," in 1939 radical guru Saul Alinsky created the Back of the Yards Neighborhood Council.[49] Based in Chicago's stockyards, near the slaughterhouses famously chronicled by socialist writer Upton Sinclair in *The Jungle*, the organization brought together labor unions, Catholic groups, and local residents to negotiate with the city's meatpacking industry to clean up garbage and pollution in the community.[50]

The modern heir to Alinsky's environmental coalition is the Blue Green Alliance.[51] Launched in 2006 by the United Steelworkers and the Sierra Club, the fourteen-million-member coalition includes leading environmental groups like the Natural Resources Defense Council and the National Wildlife Federation[52] and ten of the country's largest government unions, among them the Service Employees International Union (SEIU), the Communications Workers of America, the American Federation of Teachers, the United Auto Workers, the United Food and Commercial Workers, and the Sheet Metal Workers' International Association.

Merging the agenda of environmentalists and government unions, the Blue Green Alliance's platform advocates everything from climate change legislation to union-friendly legislation like collective-bargaining rights for government and public service workers and the passage of the Employee Free Choice Act to eliminate secret ballots in union voting. Where the alliance finds the most common ground, however, is in its support for "green jobs." While the expansion of the green economy would hurt ordinary workers by reducing the number of private-sector jobs, it would be a windfall for left-wing environmental organizations and government unions.

The massive new government-subsidized green industry would open the door to more government unionization. Consequently, in 2009 the Blue Green Alliance spent $1.5 million lobbying for agendas like green jobs, a figure that surged to almost $2.5 million in 2010.[53] The Blue Green Alliance is only one member of a national network fueling the campaign for green jobs. Another is the Alliance for Climate Protection, the environmental nonprofit founded by former vice president Al Gore, which in 2008 partnered with the Blue Green Alliance in a campaign promoting green jobs.[54] The organization drew on connections in the world of progressive politics. Maggie Fox, the CEO of the Alliance for Climate Protection, is a past president of America

Votes, a progressive coalition of over forty organizations that is a functional member of the left-wing Shadow Party created by Soros.[55]

The advocacy campaign for green jobs resonated with the Obama administration thanks to another group that linked the green jobs agenda of the environmental movement with the Obama White House. In 2007, environmental activist and self-described communist Anthony "Van" Jones founded the Oakland, California–based Green for All.[56] Supported by funders like the Ford Foundation and the Rockefeller Family Fund, and by environmental groups like the Natural Resources Defense Council, the group lobbied to "build an inclusive green economy strong enough to lift people out of poverty" by "creating millions of quality jobs and careers" and Van Jones became a fellow at the Center for American Progress.

According to Jones, the "green economy" would require a wholesale transformation of the American capitalist system: "We want to move from suicidal gray capitalism. . . . So the green economy will start off as a small subset, and we're going to push it, and push it, and push it, until it becomes the engine for transforming the whole society."[57] Saul Alinsky could not have formulated this gradualist approach to radical agendas any better. That this new government economic engine would arrest the essential dynamism of American capitalism—indeed that it was designed to do so—was openly admitted by Van Jones. In his 2009 book, *The Green Collar Economy*, Jones wrote that mankind must reconsider "the very notion of economic growth."[58] Instead, Jones envisioned a brave new environmentalist world, where the economy would be "designed to maximize well-being—not necessarily wealth." Production for so-called need instead of profit is of course a cherished idea of the Marxist left and a hoary misconception of the role that profit and "production for wealth" play in the economic order of things. If there is no need for a product, there obviously will be no profit. Profit is both a measure of cost efficiency and an incentive to invest. Marxist schemes to "maximize well-being" by eliminating profit through government planning have been responsible for bankrupting whole continents, while capitalist systems built on free-market principles have raised living standards to their highest point in human history.

Despite the discredited radicalism of Van Jones's views, Green for All's lobbying efforts had a decisive impact on environmental policy as soon as the Democratic Party achieved control of the US Senate and House in the elections of 2006. The following year, Green for All helped to pass the Green Jobs Act, which authorized $125 million annually to train workers for employment in a variety of so-called green industries.[59] The group's next major coup came in March 2009, when President Obama brought Jones into the White House and made him his "green jobs czar."

Because of his extreme views, which he was careful to cloak, Van Jones's tenure at the White House proved controversial and short-lived. In September 2009, he was forced to resign his position amid revelations that he had signed a conspiratorial "truther" petition suggesting that the Bush administration had colluded in organizing the 9/11 terror attacks on the World Trade Center. But he had left his mark on the country's economy. In February 2009, when the Obama administration and congressional Democrats muscled through a $787-billion stimulus bill, it allocated $70 billion in taxpayer funds to create the green economy and green jobs whose virtues Van Jones had preached.

Green jobs are an ideological industry founded on what has become the idée fixe of the modern environmental movement and its megarich financers: the allegedly dire threat of "man-made global warming." Global warming is a relatively recent addition to the environmental movement's agenda. But fears of climatic calamity and the necessity of dramatic and comprehensive government action to avert it have been a mainstay of environmentalist politics for decades, even when the specific nature of the calamity has changed. In the 1970s, for instance, the environmental movement was swept up in grim predictions of global cooling. Preceding the apocalyptic rhetoric that marks the modern global-warming debate, a decrease in global temperatures between 1945 and 1970 fueled doom-filled forecasts of global cooling.

Warning that "man's continued pollution is likely to lead to a reduction rather than an increase in global temperature," environmentalists began blaming extreme weather patterns on global cooling and cautioned the public to "brace yourself for another Ice Age."[60] A 1975 *Newsweek* article reported that meteorologists were "almost unanimous in the view" that global cooling was a reality. Disastrous environmental consequences, like a dramatic drop in food production and famines, were certain to follow.[61]

When global cooling failed to materialize in the ensuing decades, environmentalists revised their end-of-times scenarios to focus on a new apocalyptic threat. The same weather patterns and natural disasters that were once adduced as evidence of a dangerous cooling were now presented as evidence of a dangerous global warming.[62] The new agenda first began to gather steam in 1990, when the United Nations' Intergovernmental Panel on Climate Change (IPCC) published its inaugural report on the subject. According to the IPCC report, carbon dioxide emissions from human activities were significantly increasing the atmospheric concentrations of greenhouse gases, resulting in the warming of the earth's surface.

In stark contrast to the IPCC's conclusions, the peer-reviewed science on the subject of anthropogenic (man-made) global warming was far more equivocal. Skeptical scientists pointed out that global warming had occurred between 1918 and 1940, well before the most intensive phase of global industrialization and human carbon emissions.[63] Moreover, the climate period between 1940 and 1965, when human emissions were increasing at their greatest rate, actually saw a global cooling that had led environmental alarmists to prophesy the imminence of a new ice age.[64] Still other dissenters from global-warming orthodoxy pointed out that, for all the alarm about rising temperatures, evidence suggested that the world was actually warmer in the period between A.D. 800 and 1300, long before the industrial era began.[65]

Despite the fact that many of the participating IPCC scientists were not actually climate experts, the IPCC's report was embraced by environmental activists as definitive proof of man-made global warming. The report led directly to the 1992 UN Conference on Environment and Development in Rio de Janeiro, better known as the Earth Summit, the largest conference ever on climate change. Attended by twenty thousand environmental activists, ten thousand members of the media, and heads of state ranging from George H. W. Bush to Fidel Castro, the Earth Summit committed its 154 participating countries to a "non-binding aim" to reduce greenhouse gases with the goal of "preventing dangerous anthropogenic interference with Earth's climate system."

This summit quickly became a showcase for the anticapitalist agenda of the modern environmental movement. In dissenting remarks, President Bush warned the radicals that "the American way of life is not up for negotiation." Yet that was precisely the kind of change the summit's organizers had in mind, most notably its chair, the self-described socialist Maurice Strong. A Canadian businessman and environmental activist, Strong was a fierce opponent of capitalism who had denounced private property as a "social injustice." He opened the summit by denigrating the idea of international sovereignty and advocating "global environmental cooperation" to provide "environmental security" against the alleged depredations of capitalism.[66] Strong then proceeded to lecture the audience that the American way of life had to be changed to satisfy environmentalist demands, warning: "Current lifestyles and consumption of the affluent middle class—involving high meat intake, use of fossil fuels, appliances, air conditioning, and suburban housing—are not sustainable." Carrying his message at the Earth Summit a step further, Strong later that year joined with former Soviet premier Mikhail Gorbachev in launching the Earth Charter initiative, whose anticapitalist manifesto was enthusiastically endorsed by environmental groups like the Natural Resources Defense Council.[67]

The Earth Summit marked a political triumph for the environ-mental radicals and the global-warming agenda, which was given a further boost by the ascent of one the world's leading warming alarm-ists to the second-highest office in the United States. Al Gore had shown an interest in the subject even as a senator. In 1988, he had asked NASA scientist Dr. James Hansen to testify about the warming threat. His appearance at the summit was carefully choreographed by Democrat Timothy Worth, chairman of the Senate's 1988 hearing on climate change. Worth had called the US Weather Bureau to make sure that Hansen would testify on the hottest day of the summer. A sweating Dr. Hansen sensationally asserted before a roomful of tele-vision cameras that the "earth is warmer in 1988 than at any time in the history of measurements" and that he had "a high degree of confi-dence" that humans were responsible.[68]

Like much of what would later pass for a scientific consensus on global warming, Hansen's testimony was problematic. It down-played the difficulty of predicting climate patterns, ignored natural causes as possible explanations for climate changes, and abandoned scientific nuance in order to dramatize the potentially catastrophic consequences if all his assumptions were correct and man-made greenhouse gas emissions were not reduced. Hansen's testimony captured national headlines, inflamed fears about climate change, and ultimately inspired Gore to create a second career of spreading extreme claims about the coming environmental apocalypse.

In 1992, Gore claimed that global warming represented the "highest risk problem the world faces today."[69] Not content even with this hyperbole, Gore upgraded global warming to a catastrophe on a par with genocide, claiming that it "threatens an environmental Holo-caust without precedent" and insisting that "evidence of an ecologi-cal *Kristallnacht* [a Nazi pogrom against the Jews] is as clear as the sound of glass shattering in Berlin."[70] Setting a standard for environ-mentalist chatter about the coming end times, Gore made a habit of attributing natural disasters to climate change, however dubious the connection. Thus, when the Red River flooded Grand Forks, North Dakota, in 1997, Gore claimed, with no evidence, that "global climate change" was responsible.[71]

Gore laid out apocalyptic scenarios in his 1992 book, *Earth in the Balance*, which called automobiles a "mortal threat" more dangerous than any "military enemy we are ever again likely to confront." The book was a bestseller, lauded by the increasingly radicalized environmental movement, which recognized that Gore had adopted much of its agenda. One environmental activist appreciatively noted that "the policies advocated by Gore in *Earth in the Balance* are largely consistent with those favored by the major organizations in the international environmental movement."[72]

Because Gore was "down" for the radical agenda, environmentalists overlooked the fact that he was hardly practicing what he preached. While hawking environmental catastrophe and the imperative of adopting environmentally conscious ways of living, Gore flew on environmentally reckless private jets and acquired mansions whose carbon footprint would match that of a small army.[73]

By his second term in the White House, Gore had established himself as the Paul Revere of the cause. In 1996, he produced and starred in a documentary film called *An Inconvenient Truth*. The film won him an Oscar and eventually a Peace Prize, from the left-wing Nobel committee, which he shared with the UN's IPCC. The film was also made into an opera performed at La Scala. Not surprisingly, *An Inconvenient Truth* became a staple of every progressively run classroom in America, despite the fact that it was filled with distortions and untenable claims, so much so that it was barred from public schools in Britain for that reason.[74]

Global-warming theorists like Gore concealed the shakiness of the empirical foundations of their claims by asserting that a "scientific consensus" supported their dire scenarios. There was no such consensus—although the honors and, more important, the funds heaped on those supporting the warming thesis certainly help to reduce the ranks of their critics. Ten years after the appearance of *Earth in the Balance*, however, the foundations of their claims began to crumble.

Global-warming activists had long cited a famous "hockey-stick" graph to make the case that man-made carbon emissions had contributed to the rise of global temperatures during the twentieth century. Designed in 1998 by climate scientist Michael Mann, the hockey stick tracked global temperatures over the last one thousand years. It purported to show that global temperatures had been constant for most of that time, represented as a flat line on a diagram, but began to accelerate sharply after the Industrial Revolution, forming a hockey-stick shape. The hockey-stick graph soon became the "seminal image of the climate scaremongering campaign," as one geologist put it.[75] But in 2003, Canadian statistician Stephen McIntyre exposed the hockey-stick diagram as deeply flawed. Working with colleague Ross McKitrick, an economist at the University of Guelph, McIntyre showed that Mann's hockey stick was really a "collation of errors, incorrect calculation, and other quality control defects" designed to prove a preconceived theory, namely that the Industrial Revolution had caused global warming.[76]

The artificial "consensus" on man-made global warming was dealt another devastating blow in 2006 when official temperature records released by the Climate Research Unit at the University of East Anglia in England showed that global warming was not actually occurring. In fact, for the years between 1998 and 2005, global average temperature not only did not increase, as environmentalists had claimed, but there was a slight decrease in global temperatures in that period.[77]

Worse yet, in November 2009, Russian hackers broke into computers at the Climate Research Unit at the University of East Anglia—the storehouse of the world's largest set of temperature data—and published 1,073 private e-mails and 72 documents that revealed a disturbing pattern on the part of the world's leading climatologists to cover up data and research that contradicted the theory of man-made global warming. The ensuing scandal, referred to in the press as "Climategate," has been called "one of the greatest in modern science."[78] There was good reason for this since it called into question the integrity of leading climate scientists and the reliability of the data that had been used for years to forge the so-called scientific consensus on global warming. Among those who had relied on its data was the UN's IPCC, which first transformed the global-warming agenda into an international concern.

The leaked trove of classified documents suggested nothing less than a conspiracy by the leading proponents of global warming to cover up information, to suppress evidence inconsistent with their theories, and to otherwise manipulate data when it contradicted the global-warming thesis. Most notoriously, in a 1999 e-mail exchange about charts showing the climate patterns of the last two millennia, Phil Jones, a longtime researcher at the Climate Research Unit, boasted that he had used a "trick" to "hide the decline" in global temperatures in the past fifteen years.[79] In another leaked e-mail, US climatologist Kevin Trenberth lamented that he and other global-warming proponents had been trying to show that global warming was real—the very negation of dispassionate scientific inquiry—but could not. "The fact is that we can't account for the lack of warming at the moment and it is a travesty that we can't," Trenberth wrote. Still other e-mails revealed that supporters of global warming had considered shunning the work of peer-reviewed journals and their scientific contributors simply because they published articles casting doubt on global-warming dogma.[80]

Climategate provoked an international backlash. In the scandal's wake, polls showed a sharp decline in the American public's belief that global warming represented an urgent concern and that human activities were primarily responsible for it.[81] But far from conceding defeat for their alarmist agendas, the global-warming advocates remained as aggressive as ever. Left-wing foundations were a major reason why. In 2007, for example, the Doris Duke Foundation created a $100 million program to find ways to reduce the threat of global warming.[82] In 2010, the Ford Foundation, which had been a staunch backer of environmental groups promoting the theory of man-made global warming, committed $85 million over five years to "combating climate change."[83]

The global-warming campaign has also been sponsored by smaller foundations like the Redwood, California–based Compton Foundation, which calls the United States "the largest national contributor to global climate change." The $64 million Compton Foundation has devoted a large share of its grants to funding environmental groups like EarthJustice, the Natural Resources Defense Council, the Sierra Club Foundation, the Tides Center, and other groups that have made the reduction of carbon emissions and global warming a central part of their platforms.[84]

Carbon is as central to the radicals' crusade for governmental control as is the prospect of a warming catastrophe. Massive state intervention can only be justified if global warming is seen as an apocalyptic threat, and only if something as ubiquitous as carbon, the most common element in life-forms, can be identified as its cause. As the late political scientist Aaron Wildavsky observed: "Warming (and warming alone), through its primary antidote of withdrawing carbon from production and consumption, is capable of realizing the environmentalist's dream of an egalitarian society based on rejection of economic growth in favor of a smaller population's eating lower on the food chain, consuming a lot less, and sharing a much lower level of resources much more equally."[85]

This political agenda explains why the network of environmentalist groups has championed ever more invasive regulations to combat global warming. A case in point is the so-called cap-and-trade program pushed by environmentalist groups like EarthJustice and the Natural Resources Defense Council, which was adopted by the Obama administration. Just as Obamacare greatly expanded government's reach into health care, "cap and trade" would extend the federal role into individuals' lives on the pretext of cutting carbon dioxide emissions. In a cap-and-trade scheme, the government would set a nationwide limit on carbon dioxide emissions and levy fines against companies that exceed the federal cap. Legislation very much along those lines was nearly enacted by Congress in 2009. Had it passed, this cap-and-trade bill would have imposed unprecedented regulation on American energy industries and individual citizens, one that would have raised the utility and gas taxes for the average American family by a staggering $500 per year as energy companies passed along the costs of the new regulations to consumers.

The supporters of cap and trade went much further. In the name of reducing greenhouse gases, the 2009 cap-and-trade bill proposed by the Obama administration contained regulations governing everything from lightbulbs to hot tubs. Even American buildings were not spared. On the grounds that buildings were major emitters of greenhouse gases, the cap-and-trade bill would have granted Washington power over local building codes—a spectacular federal power grab.[86] Cap and trade ultimately stalled in Congress due to Republican opposition, but the Obama administration's appetite for regulation was as strong as ever. In June 2011, for instance, the administration floated the idea of taxing automobile owners based on how many miles they drive, a bid to regulate one of Americans' most cherished freedoms.[87]

Attempts to regulate people's lives from their drive home to the moment they turn on the light switch would strike most Americans as oppressive. Yet "cap and trade" was placed on the nation's agenda and kept in play despite fierce opposition, thanks to the sponsorship of left-wing foundations. The Doris Duke Foundation's $100 million global-warming program included a mission that was designed specifically to research such policies. In 2000 and 2001, the Joyce Foundation, on whose board Barack Obama then sat, made a $1.1 million grant to establish the Chicago Climate Exchange (CCX), which describes itself as "North America's only cap and trade system for all six greenhouse gases, with global affiliates and projects worldwide." Maurice

Strong, the radical host of the 1992 Earth Summit, is one of CCX's nine directors.

Cap and trade has also been popular because many leaders of the environmental movement hope to profit from the program. Al Gore is an exemplary case. His Generation Investment Management, a carbon offset company, also exerts considerable influence over CCX and other carbon credit trading firms. (Maurice Strong is a longtime friend of Gore and remains a silent partner in Gore's company.) Gore has tried to atone for his energy-extravagant lifestyle by buying "carbon offsets" from the London-based Generation Investment Management, even though he is the company's chairman and stands to profit from such investments, which are in essence stocks in his own company.[88] Through this and other self-interested deals in the global-warming industry, Gore stands to become the world's leading "carbon billionaire."[89]

It is a sign of the influence of the environmentalist movement (and the profit-making potentials that government-subsidized "green" investments offer) that Republican administrations have also followed the drift toward intrusive regulation. In 2007, the Bush administration and the Democratic Congress passed the Energy Independence and Security Act. Among other provisions, the law called for phasing out traditional incandescent lightbulbs by the beginning of 2012 and replacing them with fluorescent ones. The most vigorous lobby for this law was a group called the Alliance to Save Energy. The group's president is Frances Beinecke, who is also president of the Natural Resources Defense Council. The alliance also counts a bipartisan collection of leading legislators among its honorary chairpeople. They include Democrats like Massachusetts representative Edward Markey, who would later sponsor the 2009 cap-and-trade bill, as well as Republican senators like Maine's Susan Collins and Indiana's Richard Lugar.[90]

Quite apart from their regulatory overreach, a striking flaw of cap-and-trade programs is that they have done little to reduce carbon emissions. In May 2010, New Jersey governor Chris Christie withdrew his state from the so-called Regional Greenhouse Gas Initiative, a cap-and-trade program covering ten northeastern states. The reason? Although the cap-and-trade program imposed some of the highest electricity rates in the country on New Jersey residents, it did little to curb greenhouse gases.[91]

Like other global-warming initiatives, cap and trade was being pushed with the greatest urgency at a time when the need for it was not obvious. According to recently released EPA data, tremendous strides have been made in reducing greenhouse gas emissions, all without the regulation imposed by cap and trade. The nation has reduced its emissions output to levels of the mid-1990s.[92] On a per capita basis, greenhouse gas emissions in the United States have declined by 16 percent over the last decade. That reduction is almost 50 percent better than what the fifteen richest nations in Europe achieved in the same time frame, even though Europe had a cap-and-trade program in place.[93]

While the Obama administration failed to deliver on cap-and-trade legislation, it did advance the environmental network's agenda. The Obama-era EPA declared carbon emissions and other greenhouse gases a threat to public health, as environmental groups had long urged. The administration also sank billions of taxpayer dollars into dubious green energy technology and tapped radical environmental activists to fill its environmental positions. Finally, it made climate change, and cap and trade, top domestic policy priorities, slighting more pressing economic concerns—like bringing down the 9 percent unemployment rate—in the process.

All this added up to a significant measure of the powerful influence of the modern and increasingly radical environmental movement. But even more telling was the way the Obama administration moved to enact these policies and regulations at a time when the environment, as measured by a number of different metrics, was in its best condition in decades. It is because of the radical agendas behind the modern environmental movement that its work is never done. And it is because of the enormous budgets of the left-wing foundation network that supports those agendas that it never has to be.

Just how large are those budgets? The net assets of the 553 left-wing, anticapitalist environmental groups total $9.5 billion. That is substantially more than the EPA's 2011 federal budget of $8.7 billion.[94] Indeed, if counted as a separate nation, the combined net assets of these 553 environmental groups would make it the eighty-first-largest in the world, just behind Bangladesh. Flush with nation-sized resources, these environmental groups have been able to overwhelm their free-market and nonradical environmental counterparts. There are 32 free-market and moderate environmental groups, and their net assets total $38.2 million—which is 249 times less than the financial resources of those on the environmental left. Smaller budgets have significantly constrained the influence of these groups. For instance, the 32 free-market and moderate environmental groups awarded total grants of $1.2 million, while the 553 left-wing environmental groups were able to make grants totaling nearly $555.4 million, a ratio of nearly 462 to 1.[95] Moreover, as mentioned in the introduction to this book, the federal government annually provides $568.9 million in grant money to 247 progressive environmental groups, while providing only $728,190 to 7 groups supporting free-market solutions to environmental problems.

Amid these staggering disparities, it is no surprise that environmental policy debates are increasingly conducted on the terms of the radicals, whose partisan lobbies—unlike those of energy producers and other corporate interests—speak in the name of the "public interest" and advocate in behalf of the public good. Conservative think tanks can speak with the same authority, but their voices are radically diminished by the scarcity of resources at their command. When it comes to the clash of ideologies in the area of green politics, the old-fashioned variety of "green" goes a long way.

8.

ONE NATION UNDER UNIONS

In February 2011, Wisconsin governor Scott Walker announced what he called a "budget repair" plan to avert his state's impending fiscal crisis and to bring its finances under control. It seemed like a modest proposal, since the reality of the crisis was beyond dispute. According to its Department of Administration, Wisconsin was facing a budget deficit of $137 million in 2011, and a looming $3.6 billion deficit between 2011 and 2013.

Driving these deficits were the unprecedented labor costs of government workers, whose unions had used collective-bargaining agreements (and campaign contributions) to negotiate salaries and benefits far in excess of what workers in the private sector received. For instance, while Wisconsin state employees paid almost nothing toward the cost of their pensions, the state's taxpayers had to contribute $190 million each year on their behalf.[1] This was in spite of the fact that state employees actually earned more on average than the private-sector workers whose taxes bankrolled their pensions.[2]

In a response notable for its restraint, Governor Walker's budget bill asked government employees to accept small cuts to their compensation. They were asked to contribute 5.8 percent toward their pension costs and 12.6 percent toward their health-care costs. Police officers, firefighters, and state troopers were exempt. As for other government workers, the contributions they were being asked to make were still far below the national average for government workers, and two-thirds or less than workers in the private sector.

To prevent a recurrence of the crisis, Governor Walker also sought to limit the scope of the collective-bargaining agreements by government unions that had produced the unsustainable pension and medical contracts in the first place. Government unions had a distinct advantage over private-sector unions in such negotiations. By using their treasuries to provide campaign funds to candidates, government unions had unparalleled leverage in negotiating deals with elected officials at the expense of taxpayers. The result was corrupting influence and a damaging blow to the democratic process.

Walker's budget repair bill aimed to restore at least a semblance of fairness to the process by limiting the scope of collective-bargaining agreements for some government workers. Under his plan, collective bargaining would be largely limited to wages. In addition, government workers would be asked to pay slightly more for their existing health-care and pension benefits. Union members would also be allowed to decide every year whether they wanted to belong to a union, and union dues would no longer be automatically deducted from state employees' paychecks. In light of the state's grave fiscal circumstances, Walker's bill seemed like a modest and reasonable measure to curb the runaway costs with which government unions had saddled the Badger State.

Nothing better illustrated the unions' sense of entitlement—or their power to thwart any attempt to modify those agreements even in the midst of a major fiscal crisis—than the furious backlash that greeted Governor Walker's bill. No sooner did Walker present his legislation than thousands of union members—among them teachers, prison guards, and nurses—flooded the state capital of Madison to protest. For nearly three weeks, their protests raged without interruption.

Teachers' unions were at the heart of the insurrection. In the Madison school district, second largest in the state, 40 percent of unionized teachers called in "sick" to take part in the demonstrations, forcing schools to close. Unions also mounted a destructive campaign of harassment and intimidation. Businesses that failed to back the unions' opposition to Walker's bill were threatened with public boycotts.[3] Walker was called a "fascist," as were other Republican lawmakers. One disgruntled teachers' union member sent death threats to fifteen Republican legislators in which she chillingly warned, "Please put your things in order because you will be killed and your families will also be killed due to your actions in the last 8 weeks."[4] Republican state senator Glenn Grothman received a note under his office door that read: "THE ONLY GOOD Republican is a DEAD Republican."[5] After Republicans circumvented a Democratic attempt to block a vote on the bill in March, an angry mob of five thousand union protesters vowed "class war" as they stormed the state capitol, broke windows, and barricaded themselves inside.[6] Damage to property in the capitol as a result of union-led protests came to nearly $8 million.[7]

Despite the antidemocratic extremism of the unions' campaign, the Democrats in the state legislature, dependent on union contributions, joined their attacks, providing a microcosm of the symbiotic partnership between government workers and Democrats that exists throughout the fifty states. Prominent Democratic legislators denounced Walker as a "dictator,"[8] and just as improbably branded his budget bill as an attack on democracy. Yet the legislators' own commitment to process was all but invisible as fourteen Senate Democrats fled the state in an attempt to prevent a vote on Walker's bill. Charging that Republicans had abused their power through the budget bill, Democrats also launched a recall effort to remove Walker and other Republican legislators from office—even though they had been elected in 2010 on a pledge to trim compensation for government workers.

The opposition mounted by government unions and their Democratic allies proved a powerful obstacle to reform. Passage of the bill was further delayed when a Wisconsin circuit court judge, whose son also happened to be a former political operative with the state affiliates of the AFL-CIO and the SEIU,[9] issued an injunction to prevent it from going into effect. The decision was later overturned by the Wisconsin Supreme Court. Not until the end of June 2011, five months after Governor Walker had unveiled the bill, did it finally go into effect. Even then, Democrats, urged on by unions, continued to maneuver to overturn the legislation and pressed for a recall of Walker and other Republicans.

In its struggles to contain the unsustainable and rapidly rising costs imposed by government unions, Wisconsin was not alone. All across the country, the salaries and pensions of state employees were straining government budgets to the breaking point. Decades of political mismanagement and fiscally irresponsible deals with government unions had led to massive debt. As of 2011, according to some estimates, state and local governments had approximately $3 trillion in unfunded pension liabilities.[10]

Daunting as these burdens were, they were only expected to increase in the years ahead. American taxpayers, meanwhile, had no reprieve for past agreements made between politicians and government unions. On the hook for budget-busting union contracts they did not ratify, taxpayers were forced to look on as state governments continued to hire union workers with money from "stimulus" funds provided by the Obama administration, even as private-sector businesses and households were downsizing in an economy sinking deeper into recession.

As the conflict was joined between Wisconsin's governor and the Left, President Obama weighed in early, characterizing the Walker reforms as an "assault" on the unions.[11] His reflexive support was inevitable given the key role the SEIU and other government unions had played in his election. The same symbiosis caused him to direct stimulus funds first and foremost to save union jobs at the state level. SEIU head (and Midwest Academy graduate) Andrew Stern provides a salient case of this dynamic at work.

Stern directed an $85 million SEIU campaign to elect Obama in 2008, and once in the White House, Obama reciprocated by giving Stern unprecedented access. In Obama's first year in office, Stern visited the White House twenty-two times, making him its most frequent visitor.[12] Patrick Gaspard, onetime political director for ACORN's New York office and onetime SEIU national political director, left the latter position to become the national political director of Obama's presidential campaign. After the 2008 election he was appointed director of the Office of Political Affairs in the White House, a position he left in 2011 to prepare for Obama's reelection bid as executive director of the Democratic National Committee.[13]

Obama's chief sponsors at the Midwest Academy and in the years after were the academy's founders, radicals Heather and Paul Booth, both of whom went on to prominent positions in the government unions that Obama rescued with taxpayer funds. Heather Booth first met Obama in the 1990s, when he was running voter registration projects on Chicago's South Side. She later became an influential organizer with the AFL-CIO, serving as assistant to former AFL-CIO president John Sweeney, head of the AFL-CIO's campaign for universal health care. Her husband, Paul, became a director of organizing at AFSCME, the third-largest government union after the SEIU.

Government unions were not always the preeminent political force they have become. Nor was the union agenda always focused on relentlessly expanding the state. In the years after World War II, when union influence was at its height, organized labor was dominated by industrial unions whose members were drawn from the private economy.[14] As a result, union members were "culturally conservative and economically pro-growth."[15] But as private workers invested in economic growth were replaced by workers dependent on taxpayer-provided jobs for wages and benefits, unions moved steadily to the left.

The growth of government unions was by no means inevitable. Until the 1950s government unions were a nonissue, not least for the labor movement itself.[16] Labor lawyer Ida Klaus noted in 1965 that "the subject of labor relations in public employment could not have meant less to more people, both in and out of government."[17] As late as 1960, there was not a single recognized union in the federal government.

The absence of government unions in the first half of the twentieth century had much to do with the fact that most politicians, and indeed most labor leaders, originally opposed collective bargaining in the public sector. President Franklin Roosevelt, although a supporter of private-sector unions, opposed unions for government workers. In 1937, Roosevelt insisted that "Meticulous attention should be paid to the special relations and obligations of public servants to the public itself and to the Government. . . . The process of collective bargaining, as usually understood, cannot be transplanted into the public service."[18] The ability government unions had to act politically represented an impossible conflict of interest. Government unions could raise slush funds for candidates and elect those who promised to raise their wages and provide them with lucrative benefit packages. The necessity of government unions was also not obvious since government workers, unlike those in the private sector, could vote to retire officials who treated them unfairly.

Roosevelt's objections to collective bargaining anticipated the angry crowds of union activists who mobbed the capitol to protest

Governor Walker's modest budget cuts, obstructed the legislature, and threatened to recall politicians who opposed their privileges. Roosevelt wrote that "[a] strike of public employees manifests nothing less than an intent on their part to obstruct the operations of government until their demands are satisfied. Such action looking toward the paralysis of government by those who have sworn to support it is unthinkable and intolerable."[19] His words could not have been more prescient.

Labor leaders like Samuel Gompers, founder of the American Federation of Labor, echoed Roosevelt's opposition. Gompers argued that there was no rationale for government unions because there was no parallel between profit-making companies and the state. Since governments did not make a profit, unions were not serving their intended purpose of bargaining for a fair wage between workers and owners.[20] George Meany, longtime president of the federation, believed it was "impossible to bargain collectively with the government."[21] The reasoning was straightforward: Because government was already a monopoly, protected from the forces of the economic marketplace, allowing government workers to organize and bargain collectively would make them virtually untouchable, giving them undue influence over politicians and unchecked power over taxpayers.[22] As a result, throughout the 1950s, the AFL-CIO did not support government unions and took a "hands-off" approach to their formation.[23]

Labor leaders' long-running opposition to government unions began to weaken in the late 1950s and 1960s, when the passage of collective-bargaining laws under Democratic administrations gave state workers powerful incentives to join unions. In 1957, the Democratic mayor of Philadelphia recognized the American Federation of State, County and Municipal Employees (AFSCME) as the exclusive bargaining agent for government employees in the city.[24] Democratic mayors in cities like New York followed suit. In 1959, Wisconsin, which was the birthplace of the AFSCME, passed the country's first state-level law establishing collective bargaining for government workers. As the 1950s gave way to the 1960s, the stage was set for the rise of government unions.

Between 1960 and 1980, the number of full-time unionized employees jumped from 10 percent to 36 percent of the government workforce.[25] AFSCME grew from 99,000 members in 1955 to just under 1 million members in 1980, and boasts 1.6 million today.[26] During the same period, the American Federation of Teachers (AFT) saw its membership swell from 40,000 to more than half a million members. Today, the AFT has 1.5 million members, making it larger than the biggest exclusively private-sector union, the United Food and Commercial Workers, which has 1.3 million members. And even the AFT pales in comparison to the largest government labor union in the United States, the National Education Association, which has 3.2 million members.[27] As private-sector unions have declined—thanks to the passage of laws ensuring fair employment practices including the health and safety of the workplace—government unions have grown exponentially. The Bureau of Labor Statistics reports that in 2009, for the first time ever, more public-sector employees (7.9 million) than private-sector employees (7.4 million) belonged to unions.

As a result of their massive growth, government unions have been able to wield disproportionate influence over American politics and public policy, through its favored instrument the Democratic Party. Critics have long warned that collective bargaining by government unions is inherently undemocratic, creating a system in which elected officials parcel out generous benefits and salaries to the same interests that help to elect them and keep them in power. Taxpayers, on the other hand, are forced to subsidize agreements in whose drafting they do not participate and whose terms are corrupted by the mutually self-interested alliance between unions and elected officials. Spectacular taxpayer-subsidized compensation has been the predictable result.

In the 1960s and 1970s, government employees were offered

generous pensions in exchange for accepting salaries that were at significantly lower historical levels than what they could earn for comparable work in the private sector. But while that disparity in earnings
has long since disappeared, the benefits packages have continued to
increase. As a consequence, federal employees now receive an average of $123,049 annually in pay and benefits—*twice* the average of
workers in the private sector.[28] State and local government salaries
are 34 percent higher than those for private-sector jobs, and the disparity is rising.

According to the US Bureau of Labor Statistics, from 1998 to
2008, public employee compensation grew by 28.6 percent, compared
with 19.3 percent for workers in the private economy. In 2009, a
recession year in which states faced record budget deficits, more than
half the states nevertheless awarded pay *raises* to state employees.[29]
Spurred on by generous stimulus grants from the Obama administration, states also went out of their way to hire even more government
workers. While the private sector has shed some eight million jobs
since 2008, local, state, and federal governments have added nearly
six hundred thousand.

Even as government workers have seen their pay rise in comparison to the private sector, they have not had to give up the generous
pensions that were once intended to compensate for the lower pay of
government work. In Wisconsin, for instance, the same public school
teachers who protested that Governor Walker's bill was an intolerable
assault on their livelihood paid next to nothing toward their retirement and health-care costs. For every dollar that teachers received
in salary, taxpayers paid 74.2 cents for their retirement and health-
care costs.[30] As a result, the average Wisconsin public school teacher
makes $95,000 a year in total compensation: $50,000 in wages and
$45,000 in benefits. By contrast, in Milwaukee, Wisconsin's largest
city, the average private-sector worker makes only $53,724 annually in
total compensation—wages and benefits combined.[31]

Wisconsin is hardly the only state where government unions have been able to negotiate unsustainably lavish pension and benefit packages, at taxpayers' expense. In fact, it is typical. Some 86 percent of state and local government workers across the country have access to employer-provided health insurance, compared to just 45 percent of private-sector workers. In many cases government employees pay little, if anything, toward the cost of their benefit plans. Thus, in New Jersey, 88 percent of public school teachers pay nothing toward their insurance premiums.[32] In California, state workers often retire at fifty-five years of age with pensions that exceed what they were paid during most of their working years.[33] In New York City, firefighters and police officers may retire after twenty years of service at half pay. The result is that, at a time when life expectancy is nearly eighty years, New York City is paying benefits to ten thousand retired cops who are less than fifty years old and are likely to live another thirty years.[34] In California, three thousand retired teachers and school administrators, many of whom stopped working as early as age fifty-five, will be collecting at least $100,000 a year in pensions for the rest of their lives.

Thanks to their sweetheart relations with elected officials, government unions have been able to create a socialist economy parasitic on the private sector, whose productive wealth sustains it. Buffalo, New York, had the same number of public workers in 2006 as it did in 1950—despite having lost half its population in the intervening decades with a commensurate decline in the need for public services.[35]

In the aftermath of the financial crash of 2008, the crippling costs of this socialist sector within the larger economy could no longer be ignored. Facing mounting pension liabilities for retired workers, many states teetered on the brink of bankruptcy. According to the Pew Center on the States, eighteen states face long-term pension liabilities in excess of $10 billion. In states like California and Illinois, the unfunded pension liabilities exceed $50 billion. If one adds retiree health-care costs to pension obligations, the unfunded liabilities of the states total $1 trillion.[36] Given the sheer magnitude of labor costs in state budgets, it is not surprising that, of the forty states that had a budget deficit in 2010, twenty-eight would have been able to balance their budgets if not for their exorbitant obligations to government workers.[37]

Cities and municipalities across the country struggled desperately to cope with the debts. San Jose mayor Chuck Reed declared a "fiscal emergency" in his city, warning that it no longer had the funds to support even basic public services, including police and firefighters.[38] In 2008, the city of Vallejo, California, was forced to declare bankruptcy largely because the payrolls for police and firefighters, and their pensions, consumed three-fourths of the city budget.

The chief reason that states and cities have been unable to turn back the tide of surging debt is that government unions have a lock on the Democratic Party and hold financial hammers over individual elected officials, enabling them to block meaningful cuts to state employee compensation.

During the Wisconsin budget battle, left-wing critics sought to make much of the fact that Wisconsin governor Scott Walker was supported by the millionaire Koch brothers, whose funding of libertarian causes made them a progressive target. But campaign finance filings show that Walker received just $43,000 from the Koch Industries political action committee during the 2010 election. By contrast, the Wisconsin Education Association Council—the state teachers' union—donated nearly $1.6 *million* to four Senate races opposing Walker and other Republicans in the 2010 election. The teachers' unions' anti-Walker war chest was further bolstered by support from two national government unions, AFSCME and the SEIU, which since 2008 gave more than $1.3 million to the Greater Wisconsin Committee, a group that supports Democratic Party candidates.

According to the Center for Responsive Politics, since 1989 unions have contributed over $509 million directly to political campaigns, a figure that does not include the amounts given through Section 527 organizations, political action committees, or other union adjuncts.

Unions' actual total political spending may be anywhere from ten to fifty times greater than these direct campaign contributions.

The SEIU reported spending over $85 million to support Barack Obama in the 2008 elections, a figure that did not include the equivalent cost of tens of thousands of campaign worker "volunteers" it provided to his campaign. The American Federation of State, County and Municipal Employees (AFSCME) spent $67 million on political activities in the same election year.[39] In the 2010 congressional elections, AFSCME was the biggest spender, investing $87.5 million in Democratic Party campaigns.[40] From 1989 to 2004, AFSCME was the biggest spender on federal elections in the entire country, giving nearly $40 million to candidates in federal elections, 98.5 percent of it to Democrats.[41] On average, 94 percent of government union contributions go to Democrats, cementing a relationship that has pushed the Democratic Party steadily to the left.[42]

The alliance between organized labor and the Democratic Party can be traced back to Franklin Roosevelt. Despite opposing government unions, Roosevelt signed the 1935 Wagner Act, which protected the rights of private-sector workers to organize and bargain collectively and made unions into a loyal Democratic constituency. The alliance was reinforced during the fight over the Taft-Hartley Act of 1947, a Republican effort to check union power. Democrats soon came to depend on labor unions for both funding and on-the-ground campaign organizing. By the 1950s and 1960s, "labor functioned as the most important nation-wide electoral organization for the Democratic Party," according to political scientist J. David Greenstone.[43] When private-sector unions began to decline in the latter part of the twentieth century, Democrats began to see government workers as a promising base of support. Jobs, expensive salaries, and benefits became the price of that support, as overburdened taxpayers were left to pick up the tab.

This cycle of political quid pro quos where Democrats go out of their way to support government unions, which in turn assure their reelection is now systemic. It was no coincidence that, of the fourteen Democrats who fled Wisconsin in order to prevent a vote on Governor Walker's budget repair bill, all were dependent on funding from government unions. In the previous two election cycles, one out of every five dollars raised by the fleeing Democratic senators came from government employees, such as teachers and firefighters and their unions. Among these senators, the largest recipient of union dollars, Spencer Coggs of Milwaukee, was a former treasurer of his AFSCME local. Despite his election to office, Coggs remains a member of the union because he is technically "on leave" from his municipal job. He is also active with two other unions.

Government unions' financial clout means that they are able to significantly dictate the content and conduct of public policy. One of the most striking examples of the damage that the influence of government unions have wrought is the parlous state of public education in America. Education experts point out that there is a strong correlation between the rise of teachers' unions and the decline in college aptitude test scores.[44] Tellingly, scores fell first and most rapidly where teachers' unions took hold.

Why that should be is not difficult to ascertain. Teachers' unions adversely distort the economics of education, making it difficult, if not virtually impossible, either to fire bad teachers or to reward good teachers with pay raises.[45] New York City, which has some of the worst public schools in the country, is a case in point. In New York, teachers earn tenure after only three years on the job, but proceedings to dismiss a bad teacher can take years and cost hundreds of thousands of dollars, since teachers are paid a full salary throughout despite not working.[46] As a result, it is rare for a teacher to be fired for incompetence. In addition, as law professors John O. McGinnis and Max Schanzenbach point out, union rules on teacher assignments make it more difficult to match teachers with the students for whom they would make the most difference. "In short," the professors conclude, "the teachers' unions make the public school rigid, unproductive, and hidebound at great monetary cost to taxpayers and at educational cost to the children that they are supposed to teach."[47]

With the complicity of Democratic legislators, teachers' unions have also succeeded in blocking educational reforms that could improve students' academic performance. In states like Minnesota, teachers' unions have made it impossible for their educational systems to take part in the Race to the Top program, a federal effort to spur reforms in state and local district K–12 education. Teachers' unions are also the chief obstacles to reforms like voucher programs, which offer promising low-income students in failing public schools a way to seek an alternative. In December 2009, for instance, teachers' unions used their influence over the Democratic Congress to eliminate the D.C. Opportunity Scholarship Program, a voucher program for low-income students in the District of Columbia. It was the first federally funded program providing K–12 education grants and enjoyed widespread support from D.C. parents, residents, and officials. But the teachers' unions viewed it as a threat to their dominance and demanded that it be ended. Democratic lawmakers complied, and the successful program was terminated.

For all that teachers' unions have done to prevent educational reforms, they have not been held accountable by the political class. There is no mystery in this. As Steven Brill has documented, teachers' unions have contributed $57 million over the last thirty years to federal campaigns. That is more than any other union or corporation.[48] An endorsement from the National Education Association helped Jimmy Carter win the presidency in 1976, support he repaid by creating a new federal bureaucracy—the Department of Education—in 1979. At the state level, the political contributions of teachers' unions are even larger. In Minnesota, for instance, the state affiliates of the National Education Association and the American Federation of Teachers give more money to politicians seeking statewide office than all other political organizations combined.[49]

Operating on a budget of $376.5 million (as of 2010), the NEA's political power is further amplified by its connection to the network of left-wing groups.[50] The NEA is a member of America Votes, the national coalition of progressive get-out-the-vote groups whose other members include ACORN, America Coming Together, the AFL-CIO, the AFSCME, the American Federation of Teachers, MoveOn .org, the SEIU, and the Sierra Club, among many others.[51]

The SEIU is another example of a government union that has come to exert a tremendous influence over public policy and Democratic politicians. Founded by a group of Chicago janitors and granted membership in the American Federation of Labor in 1921, the union today boasts that it is the country's fastest-growing union, so much so that it split from the umbrella of the AFL-CIO in 2005. In 2010 alone, the union took in $268 million in cash.[52] The SEIU's resources and reputation have earned it considerable political clout. As a candidate, Barack Obama acknowledged his debt to the union, asserting in a 2007 address to the SEIU political action committee that his career would not be where it is "if it hadn't been for an SEIU endorsement" back in 2004. In that same address, Obama presented himself as an effective member of the SEIU, urging attendees to "imagine having a president whose life work is your work."[53] In turn, the SEIU spent at a frenetic pace to assure Obama's election.

No sooner was Obama elected than he set about filling cabinet posts with SEIU officials. We have already noted that former SEIU political director Patrick Gaspard was made the White House political director and subsequently the executive director of the Democratic National Committee for Obama's reelection campaign. John Sullivan, the SEIU's associate general counsel, was appointed to a seat on the Federal Election Commission. Craig Becker, associate general counsel of both the SEIU and the AFL-CIO, was named to the National Labor Relations Board. Anna Burger, the SEIU's second-highest-ranking officer, was appointed to the president's Economic Recovery

Advisory Board. In February 2010, Obama appointed SEIU president Andy Stern to sit on a National Commission on Fiscal Responsibility and Reform, a particularly ironic choice given the SEIU's role in straining state and federal finances and opposing meaningful fiscal reform.[54]

As well as staffing his administration with SEIU members, Obama has also taken up much of the union's political agenda. He has supported the Employee Free Choice Act, which would eliminate secret ballot voting and thereby make it easier for unions to coerce workers into joining their ranks, and pushed ahead with the union's favored cause of universal health care. As the country's largest union of health-care workers—1.1 million SEIU members work in that industry—the SEIU would benefit more than most government unions from legislation that expanded government health insurance and with it the number of government workers, and would-be SEIU members, employed in the industry.

A left-wing advocacy campaign in which the SEIU played a critical part ultimately helped Obamacare to pass. Margarida Jorge, a former SEIU organizing director, served as a national field director for Health Care for America Now (HCAN), the leading coalition of left-wing advocacy groups in support of the legislation. SEIU was also a member of the HCAN coalition, which didn't prevent it from getting a special White House exemption for an SEIU affiliate in New York that found the coverage under the new law was too expensive.[55]

Health care was not the only issue on which the Obama administration bowed to union demands. The administration has also opposed free-trade agreements with Panama, Colombia, and South Korea because of union opposition. Most notoriously, the administration and fellow Democrats used taxpayer funds to bail out government unions amid the economic recession. In the 2009 "stimulus" bill and in other legislation, Democratic lawmakers sent more than $160 billion in federal cash to states, funds aimed in large part at preventing layoffs of government workers. At the same time, pro-union members of the administration engineered a government takeover of the struggling American auto industry, in effect a bailout of the United Auto Workers union. The administration's top official overseeing the auto industry bailout, Ron Bloom, a former United Steelworkers union adviser, even boasted, in reference to the bailout, "I did this all for the unions."[56]

Government unions are also active supporters and funders of a variety of other left-wing causes—including those unrelated to labor issues. The National Education Association, for example, has been an outspoken supporter of every left-wing cause from abortion rights to bilingual education to gay marriage. The union also spends millions funding left-wing advocacy groups such as ACORN, the Democracy Alliance, the League of United Latin American Citizens (LULAC), and the Mexican American Legal Defense and Educational Fund (MALDEF), among numerous others.[57] Approximately one-fourth of the SEIU's members are Hispanic immigrants, and the union has become a champion of amnesty for illegal aliens. In recent years, it has also become a patron of such left-wing causes as opposing the war in Iraq and supporting legislation to fight climate change.

Government unions remain separate from left-wing foundations, but their history and influence overlap. Like many foundations, unions were once supportive of capitalism and free markets, but shifted decisively to the left as government workers became the dominant union members and former 1960s radicals assumed positions of leadership. Like the foundations, government unions have become key members of the left-wing activist network, shaping public policy and funding a host of left-wing nonprofits. Their resulting influence has come to mirror and in some cases surpass those of megarich progressive foundations. As political entities, they are a dominant force in the Democratic Party and are in a position to directly shape the government policies that affect and increase their power, which in turn are the policies that increase the scope and power of government itself.

9.

A DISTURBING PROSPECT

F ollowing the Democrats' defeat in the 2004 presidential elections, George Soros and a network of activist billionaires resolved to put together a force that would change the political landscape and move the country permanently to the left. By August 2005, this "Democracy Alliance" had eighty members, each of whom pledged to donate at least $200,000 to a general fund that would then be channeled to progressive groups across the country.[1] At the end of its first year of operations, the Alliance had dispensed $50 million to left-wing groups.[2] By 2008, it was moving $80 million to over thirty-five groups, at least half of which had not even existed just a few years earlier.[3]

The alliance was determined to fund only organizations that were ideologically left-wing, and it was not interested in supporting self-styled centrist groups. At the heart of the Democracy Alliance venture was its funders' shared belief that if enough money was invested in progressive groups and a connected organizational infrastructure, the Left would finally succeed in capturing the commanding heights of government.

The success of this strategy was initially manifested in the target state of Colorado, then dominated by Republicans. In 2006, the Democracy Alliance started a chapter in Colorado with the aim of turning the red state blue. Within one election cycle it achieved its goal.

The Colorado Democracy Alliance was an umbrella association of thirty left-wing groups, led by millionaire activists like software entrepreneur Tim Gill and Pat Stryker, an heiress to a medical products company fortune. Armed with a budget of $16.5 million, the Colorado Democracy Alliance was able to create a potent ideological and political infrastructure of nonprofit, advocacy, and 527 groups— an "alternative political universe" in the words of the *Denver Post*, which came to be known as the "Colorado Model."[4]

The model had seven main components, each designed to win elections and establish left-wing political dominance. In describing the Colorado events, *Weekly Standard* editor Fred Barnes observed that to be successful on such an ambitious scale the Left had to have "the capacity to generate intellectual ammunition, to pursue investigations, to mobilize for elections, to fight media bias, to pursue strategic litigation, to train new leaders, and to sustain a presence in the new media."[5] Each of these components was created under the Colorado model.

For intellectual firepower, progressives set up a think tank called ProgressNowAction.org, a Colorado corollary to MoveOn.org. For media influence, left-wing activists created Colorado Media Matters, an in-state version of Media Matters.org, the left-wing attack site that poses as a media watchdog in order to tar opponents. Strategic investigations and litigation were carried out by Colorado Ethics Watch, a public-interest law firm, which targeted Republican legislators with

lawsuits and ethics complaints under the guise of providing governmental oversight. Groups like the Center for Progressive Leadership
Colorado trained aspiring political operatives and candidates, while
websites like ColoradoPols.com encouraged progressive activists to
publicize their message by taking advantage of social media and new
media technologies. Within months, the Colorado Democracy Alliance and its billionaire funders had put a synchronized, well-funded
political machine in place.

Its influence quickly proved decisive in shaping Colorado's elections. In October 2004, the GOP dominated politics at every level in
Colorado. Republicans held both US Senate seats, five of seven congressional seats, the governor's mansion, the secretary of state's and
treasurer's offices, and both houses of the state legislature.[6] Four years
later, each of these seats had fallen into Democratic hands. Although
registered Democrats were only the state's third-largest voting bloc
behind Independents and Republicans, by 2008 Democrats had overturned nearly a decade of Republican control to win the governor-
ship, both houses of the state legislature, a US Senate seat, and two
US House seats.[7] Elated by their success in Colorado, progressives
planned to export the model to states across the country. Their success inspired a book, aptly titled *The Blueprint: How Democrats Won
Colorado (and Why Republicans Everywhere Should Care)*.[8]

Electoral strategies like the Colorado model reinforce the Left's
dominance of another essential component of political success: election law. Encompassing everything from who is entitled to vote in
elections, to voting procedures and challenges of election results,
election law is increasingly shaped by progressive activists to provide
the Left with a critical advantage in close elections.

J. Christian Adams, an election lawyer who served in the Voting
Rights Section at the US Department of Justice, has documented how
millions of dollars from leftist foundations have established a permanent infrastructure of left-wing litigators and law firms designed to

alter election outcomes through policy advocacy and strategic litiga-
tion.[9] This infrastructure includes groups like Project Vote, DEMOS,
the Asian American Legal Defense Fund (AALDF), the Brennan
Center for Justice, the Mexican American Legal Defense Fund
(MALDEF), the NAACP Legal Defense Fund, the Advancement
Project, the National Association of Latino Elected and Appointed
Officials (NALEO), the League of Women Voters, the Asian Pacific
American Legal Center, and Common Cause.

Each of these groups works to shape election laws to favor Democrats and the Left. To that end, they bring lawsuits under federal
and state statutes ranging from the Voting Rights Act, Motor Voter
law, and the Help America Vote Act and launch media campaigns
to supplement those efforts. They dispatch teams of election observers in polling places around the nation and engage in grandstanding
about purported "voter intimidation," by which they mean attempts
to ascertain that a prospective voter is a legal citizen and a person
registered to vote. At the same time, they work to prevent states from
enforcing voter identification laws, cover up evidence of voter fraud,
and strategically oppose purging the voting rolls of dead or ineligible
voters when it could compromise victory for their favored, and invariably Democratic, candidates.

Under the Obama administration, the efforts of these left-wing
litigators and advocacy groups have been backed by the US government, which now acts as a training academy to replenish their ranks
and amplify their litigation. A case in point is the Voting Section
of the Civil Rights Division of the Department of Justice, which in
recent years has recruited lawyers from government unions like the
SEIU and left-wing law groups like the Advancement Project and
MALDEF. This synergy helps explain why, for instance, the Obama
Justice Department has blocked requirements in Georgia that voters
establish they are US citizens, and why it has conspicuously failed to
bring any lawsuits under federal law to ensure the voter rolls do not

include dead and ineligible felons. It also is why the administration turned a blind eye to an open-and-shut case of voter intimidation by dropping or reducing charges against a trio of armed New Black Panther thugs who had intimidated voters at polling stations in Philadelphia during the 2008 elections.

Even as the Left's ability to influence elections has grown, there remains no comparable infrastructure or coordination on the conservative side. Notwithstanding embryonic efforts such as "True the Vote," an organization created in 2009 to make sure that all voter applications are submitted by eligible citizens, and despite the hard work of some conservative public-interest lawyers, conservatives by and large have been absent from this critical battlefield.[10]

The events in Colorado and the Left's supremacy in the important arena of election law are a portent of possible political futures and also an emblematic expression of the themes of this book. The Left has created a powerful infrastructure inspired by a compelling narrative, rarely challenged, in which they are cast as "progressives," as noble advocates of the underdog "speaking truth to power," selflessly standing up for the economically disadvantaged and the politically disenfranchised. The reality, as we have seen, is quite different. While claiming the mantle of a for-the-people populism, progressives have operated as a moneyed elite, deploying the war chests of billionaires to redraw the political map to increase their power and expand the role of the state with negative consequences for working Americans and the poor. Yet, Republicans and conservatives continue to be stigmatized by Democratic politicians and their media sympathizers as the party of the rich.

In the world beyond the myth—in America's cultural mainstream—progressives *are* the power, shaping the purposes and pulling the purse strings of America's major philanthropic foundations, universities, and mainstream media institutions (network television, Public Broadcasting, and the metropolitan and national press). In government, progressives dominate America's major urban centers and the two most populated states—New York and California—which also happen to be the centers of American culture, media, and finance.

The views of these progressive elites are well to the left of the broad electorate, which is why at election time Democrats run against their core beliefs and present themselves as pragmatic and fiscally responsible, as believers in a middle ground between the private sector and government—which is the way that Barack Obama successfully sold his candidacy in the 2008 election. Such duplicity is a defining aspect of a much larger phenomenon: the disenfranchisement of the American people, which is the necessary consequence of the New Leviathan—the infrastructure of permanent foundations that the Left has created in its quest to reshape the cultural and political landscape.

We have seen how in areas and on issues crucial to the nation's self-definition and institutional future, a small group of individuals deploying the resources of these giant foundations have been able to shift the entire framework of the national policy debate on issues of critical importance. Thus the Ford Foundation was able to transform the American immigration debate and redefine the very notion of citizenship by sponsoring an institutional infrastructure and radical movement dedicated to undermining such traditional notions as assimilation and integration, and ultimately erasing the basic distinction between legal and illegal immigration. This transformation, underwritten by tens of millions in Ford Foundation grants, took place in just a few decades, as radical Latino "civil rights" groups waged a successful campaign to replace immigrants' traditional pursuit of assimilation with a cult of victimhood and racial separatism, while viewing the American experience, not as a new opportunity, but as a new form of persecution. Forty years after Ford began funding such groups, their influence has become so pervasive that a state like

Arizona, besieged by crimes committed by illegal immigrants, can find itself on trial and the target of a US Department of Justice lawsuit for enforcing the country's existing immigration laws.

Funding from the New Leviathan accomplished a similar transformation in the area of national security. In the anxious days of the Cold War, when America faced a nuclear enemy, progressive foundations led by the Ploughshares Fund sponsored an alarmist and defeatist "freeze" campaign to frighten Americans into ceding permanent military advantage to the Soviet Union and accepting a severe degradation of the country's defenses.

The Communist bloc's collapse ended the immediate threat of American retreat from global responsibility, but funding from left-wing foundations, including offshoots of the Ploughshares Fund, has kept the dream of diminishing America as a world power alive. During the Obama administration, its influence has succeeded in involving America in a war that has no visible national interest, in a country—Libya—that is not a security threat, with American troops being placed under foreign commanders, and the world's number one superpower taking a backseat to corrupt international agencies like the United Nations and hostile dictatorial alliances like the Arab League. Under Obama, progressives also succeeded in degrading America's deterrent by denying America's East European allies a nuclear shield.

The New Leviathan also spearheaded a momentous domestic transformation through the passage of Obama's universal health-care legislation. In 1994, a similar campaign was aborted when even a Democratic Congress failed to approve the radical health-care legislation proposed by First Lady Hillary Clinton. But not even public opinion constrained Democrats in 2009, after a war chest provided by the foundation network and by left-wing unions created an army of advocacy and pressure groups behind the campaign and enabled their candidate in the White House to push through the Patient Protection and Affordable Care Act despite overwhelming public disapproval. The new act represented the greatest expansion of government power in peacetime in American history and was seen by its progressive designers as a "non-reformist reform" and by its opponents as a game-changing step toward a socialist state.[11]

The New Leviathan that has emerged over the last half century through the efforts of the American Left is a permanent institutional network of unparalleled financial power. It is political in nature but operates outside the framework of a constitutional order in which the people are sovereign. Because of its enormous resources, this New Leviathan is able to steer the ship of state into uncharted waters, and to expand its power to the extent that it now threatens the individual liberties that are the heart of the American experiment.

Unlike legislators who are elected, the executives who run the New Leviathan are self-selecting and do not have to answer to voting constituencies. There are no shareholder-owners of foundations who can unseat boards that cease to reflect their wishes or—for that matter—the wishes of their founders.[12] They have no supporters on whom they depend. They are accountable to no one for the advocacy positions they sustain and for the agendas they advance, and ultimately for the directions in which they seek to point the American republic. The New Leviathan is self-sufficient and self-perpetuating. It is an aristocracy of wealth whose dimensions exceed any previous accumulations of financial power, whose influence already represents a massive disenfranchisement of the American people and whose agendas pose a disturbing prospect for the American future.

APPENDICES

The database for this book was prepared by Mike Bauer of DiscovertheNetworks.org. Profiles of all the major foundations referred to in this text can be found at Discover theNetworks.org and were compiled and written by Mike Bauer under the supervision of John Perazzo, its managing editor, and Peter Collier, its editor-in-chief.

APPENDIX I

Comparative Assets and Grant Expenditures of Conservative and Progressive Foundations

1. TOTAL ASSETS OF CONSERVATIVE AND PROGRESSIVE FOUNDATIONS COMPARED

The National Committee for Responsive Philanthropy and Think Progress—two progressive organizations—identified 86 conservative foundations, 82 of which currently do not have zero or negative assets.

As of 2010 the total asset value of those 82 conservative foundations was:

$10,288,081,969 ($10.29 billion).

DiscovertheNetworks.org has identified 122 major foundations as progressive, 115 of which currently do not have zero or negative assets. As of 2010, the total asset value of these 115 foundations was:

$104,555,636,781 ($104.56 billion).

This represents a total assets value for the Left that is over ten times (10.16×) larger than the total assets value of the Right.

2. AVERAGE ASSETS OF CONSERVATIVE AND PROGRESSIVE FOUNDATIONS COMPARED

For the 82 conservative foundations that had no zero or negative assets the National Committee for Responsive Philanthropy and Think Progress identified, the average assets value is currently:

$125,464,414 ($125.46 million).

For the 115 progressive foundations that had no zero or negative assets DiscovertheNetworks identified, the average assets value is:

$909,179,450 ($909.18 million).

This represents an average assets value for the Left that is over seven times (7.25×) larger than the average assets value of the Right.

3. TOTAL GRANTS AWARDED BY CONSERVATIVE AND PROGRESSIVE FOUNDATIONS COMPARED

Of the 82 conservative foundations that had no zero or negative assets identified by the National Committee for Responsive Philanthropy and Think Progress, the total grants awarded was:

$831,797,191 ($831.80 million).

Of the 115 progressive foundations that had no zero or negative assets identified by DTN, the total grants awarded figure was:

$8,807,988,218 ($8.81 billion).

This represents a total grants awarded figure by the Left that is over ten times (10.59×) larger than the total grants awarded by the Right.

4. AVERAGE GRANTS OF CONSERVATIVE AND PROGRESSIVE FOUNDATIONS COMPARED

Of the 82 conservative foundations that had no zero or negative assets identified by the National Committee for Responsive Philanthropy and Think Progress, the average grants awarded figure was:

$10,143,868 ($10.14 million).

Of the 115 progressive foundations that had no zero or negative assets identified by DTN, the average grants awarded figure was:

$76,591,202 ($76.59 million).

This represents an average grants awarded by the Left that is over seven times (7.55×) larger than the average grants awarded by the Right.

Progressive Foundations

Foundation	Assets	Grants Awarded	Year
Bill & Melinda Gates Foundation	33,498,185,159	3,626,100,000	2009
Ford Foundation	10,373,847,207	476,173,989	2009
Robert Wood Johnson Foundation	8,490,415,783	354,956,931	2009
William and Flora Hewlett Foundation	6,851,296,219	345,190,721	2009
W. K. Kellogg Foundation	6,371,046,123	305,000,000	2009
David and Lucile Packard Foundation	5,699,231,606	282,825,448	2009
John D. and Catherine T. MacArthur Foundation	5,237,796,060	234,719,855	2009
Andrew W. Mellon Foundation	5,051,529,429	216,162,235	2009
Rockefeller Foundation	3,317,100,678	145,129,900	2009
Annie E. Casey Foundation	2,564,720,003	150,343,185	2009
Carnegie Corporation of New York	2,432,582,536	112,195,444	2009
Simons Foundation	1,406,194,090	87,024,914	2009
Howard Heinz Endowments	1,363,037,029	55,124,695	2009
Open Society Institute	1,102,893,795	1,035,719,221	2009
Sandler Foundation	866,533,972	51,325,595	2009
Ahmanson Foundation	857,431,395	44,392,650	2009
Joyce Foundation	773,627,899	36,046,443	2009
Rockefeller Brothers Fund	729,263,381	31,188,924	2009
Surdna Foundation	693,515,303	38,678,619	2009
Morris and Gwendolyn Cafritz Foundation	590,983,904	21,624,544	2009

Foundation	Assets	Grants Awarded	Year
Vira I. Heinz Endowment	486,147,664	21,904,943	2005
Minneapolis Foundation	479,912,634	33,958,319	2010
Public Welfare Foundation	445,896,838	22,400,036	2009
Nathan Cummings Foundation	415,102,143	19,944,000	2009
Pew Charitable Trusts	350,837,431	106,223,642	2009
Verizon Foundation	241,741,456	56,289,332	2009
Geraldine R. Dodge Foundation	240,720,289	14,681,123	2009
Jenifer Altman Foundation	233,640,422	12,112,837	2009
William J. Clinton Foundation	181,936,614	4,046,086	2009
Tides Foundation	175,019,369	97,028,446	2009
Blue Moon Fund	173,631,303	9,735,736	2009
Educational Foundation of America	162,081,218	8,610,634	2009
United Nations Foundation	136,682,490	54,354,979	2009
Freddie Mac Foundation	133,953,554	13,119,576	2009
Bullitt Foundation	101,927,252	6,718,467	2009
Mertz Gilmore Foundation	101,021,755	6,066,405	2009
Flora Family Foundation	99,882,823	4,057,743	2009
Bauman Family Foundation	95,212,399	5,775,000	2010
Heinz Family Foundation	94,600,511	4,443,968	2009
Sierra Club	88,509,397	40,734,048	2009
J. M. Kaplan Fund	87,279,542	11,244,886	2009
Rockefeller Family Fund	87,257,641	8,884,650	2009
David Geffen Foundation	86,617,976	4,036,351	2009
Stanley Foundation	79,483,347	0	2009
Scherman Foundation	69,604,419	1,682,950	2009
Tides Center	69,556,930	5,959,805	2009
Energy Foundation	68,673,826	90,425,648	2009
AT&T Foundation	68,650,008	61,820,540	2009
Summit Charitable Foundation	68,269,520	6,681,134	2009
Columbia Foundation	67,970,254	2,543,274	2010

Foundation	Assets	Grants Awarded	Year
Compton Foundation	64,316,869	4,407,309	2009
Century Foundation	63,465,551	0	2010
Woods Fund of Chicago	56,844,180	2,693,760	2009
Prospect Hill Foundation	52,985,454	3,169,927	2009
Merck Family Fund	51,964,740	3,619,310	2009
Arca Foundation	48,011,069	1,872,793	2009
Town Creek Foundation	45,213,983	2,585,500	2009
Jessie Smith Noyes Foundation	44,534,986	2,780,520	2009
Foundation For Deep Ecology	43,216,776	1,167,854	2010
New World Foundation	40,675,611	9,151,838	2009
Ms. Foundation for Women	36,949,599	3,276,500	2010
Ploughshares Fund	35,741,105	5,236,650	2009
Schooner Foundation	33,351,026	3,456,397	2009
Schumann Center for Media and Democracy	32,781,435	2,890,280	2009
Allstate Foundation	31,544,604	18,344,750	2009
Alan B. Slifka Foundation	30,556,989	6,092,308	2009
Aetna Foundation	29,669,325	12,027,034	2009
Target Foundation	28,323,444	9,750,000	2010
New-Land Foundation	26,814,091	1,730,970	2009
Bank of America Foundation	25,110,853	190,668,042	2009
Funding Exchange	22,650,137	3,882,901	2009
Living Cities	22,219,372	16,728,332	2009
Lear Family Foundation	20,670,643	1,920,558	2009
Z. Smith Reynolds Foundation	18,380,219	20,774,269	2009
Wieboldt Foundation	17,864,007	753,714	2009
Glaser Progress Foundation	15,447,040	1,815,250	2009
Colombe Foundation	14,613,647	1,206,500	2010
Public Interest Projects	13,727,343	26,349,380	2009
Liberty Hill Foundation	13,100,108	4,896,583	2009

Foundation	Assets	Grants Awarded	Year
Stewart R. Mott Foundation	13,044,892	909,256	2008
Barbra Streisand Foundation	11,388,708	1,445,000	2009
Samuel Rubin Foundation	10,891,436	520,722	2010
American Express Foundation	8,212,520	7,739,700	2009
Turner Foundation	8,212,520	12,557,124	2005
Shefa Fund	7,173,516	4,216,198	2006
Jewish Funds for Justice	6,439,130	1,039,078	2009
Proteus Fund	5,402,326	6,088,118	2009
Ben & Jerry's Foundation	5,320,384	1,799,080	2009
Nuclear Age Peace Foundation	4,736,095	112,733	2009
Sara Lee Foundation	4,242,996	2,344,982	2009
ChevronTexaco Foundation	3,511,914	521,952	2009
Threshold Foundation	2,910,371	1,351,328	2009
Rosenberg Fund for Children	2,744,738	304,378	2009
Grassroots International	2,370,792	1,889,806	2009
National Comm. for Responsive Philanthropy	2,069,093	0	2009
Sunlight Foundation	2,066,772	2,640,282	2009
Righteous Persons Foundation	2,032,636	3,335,500	2009
PBS Foundation	1,838,189	2,777,352	2009
CarEth Foundation	1,836,013	0	2008
Peace Development Fund	1,328,101	277,775	2009
A. J. Muste Memorial Institute	1,253,123	842,790	2009
JEHT Foundation	962,818	0	2009
Three Rivers Community Foundation	920,674	145,886	2009
Alliance for Global Justice	898,823	305,448	2010
Stern Family Fund	806,158	311,500	2005
Steven and Michele Kirsch Foundation	666,488	40,698	2009
Beldon Fund	571,072	3,287,500	2009

Foundation	Assets	Grants Awarded	Year
Agape Foundation	364,139	497,786	2009
New York Times Company Foundation	308,902	1,545,535	2009
Neighborhood Funders Group	239,017	0	2009
Progress Unity Fund	213,523	198,481	2009
People's Rights Fund	79,201	245,130	2009
Interfaith Funders	40,930	0	2010
Changemakers	26,493	0	2009
Civil Justice Foundation	3,347	40,000	2010

Total Assets: $104,555,636,781

Total Grants Awarded: $8,807,988,218

Average Assets: $909,179,450

Average Grants Awarded: $76,591,202

Appendix III

Conservative Foundations

Foundation	Assets	Grants Awarded	Year
Walton Family Foundation	2,275,851,898	360,407,050	2009
John Templeton Foundation	1,689,804,911	59,804,795	2009
Anschutz Foundation	1,134,359,136	39,311,460	2009
Samuel Roberts Noble Foundation	928,531,577	6,526,670	2009
Lynde and Harry Bradley Foundation	622,913,819	44,367,300	2009
Smith Richardson Foundation	441,100,393	21,741,648	2009
F.M. Kirby Foundation	408,359,859	17,121,933	2009
Liberty Fund	265,825,617	0	2009
Sarah Scaife Foundation	243,990,427	14,099,500	2009
Charles G. Koch Charitable Foundation	206,497,763	15,551,465	2009
Gleason Family Foundation	158,749,761	6,010,384	2009
William H. Donner Foundation	121,881,454	4,634,145	2009
Searle Freedom Trust	121,297,567	12,365,616	2009
William E. Simon Foundation	107,777,054	10,283,535	2009
David H. Koch Charitable Foundation	95,264,998	0	2009
Richard and Helen DeVos Foundation	89,446,796	46,457,200	2009
Scaife Family Foundation	70,966,750	2,644,684	2009
Gilder Foundation	67,664,697	5,624,525	2009
Orville D. and Ruth A. Merillat Foundation	59,028,538	4,549,900	2010

Foundation	Assets	Grants Awarded	Year
Shelby Cullom Davis Foundation	57,170,564	1,415,135	2009
Randolph Foundation	57,143,420	2,407,900	2009
Donors Capital Fund	55,509,398	59,781,233	2009
Dick and Betsy DeVos Foundation	54,829,634	7,600,422	2009
Bodman Foundation	54,585,310	2,932,400	2009
Fairbrook Foundation	48,227,835	3,194,250	2009
Allegheny Foundation	47,138,307	4,067,000	2009
Dodge Jones Foundation and Subsidiary	45,159,300	12,756,250	2009
Thomas B. Fordham Foundation	44,795,429	275,000	2009
Rose-Marie and Jack R. Anderson Foundation	40,938,122	2,264,686	2009
Castle Rock Foundation	37,592,552	2,415,000	2009
Dr. P. Phillips Foundation	36,344,843	814,170	2010
Earhart Foundation	35,723,529	5,049,476	2009
Achelis Foundation	35,048,794	350,003	2009
Jaquelin Hume Foundation	32,266,903	6,785,917	2009
Newton D. and Rochelle F. Becker Foundation	31,827,949	1,240,777	2009
Roe Foundation	29,849,019	1,585,000	2009
Taube Family Foundation	26,500,285	1,262,885	2009
Huston Foundation	26,364,652	1,042,750	2009
Carthage Foundation	24,309,711	600,000	2009
Hickory Foundation	23,099,138	1,563,650	2009
William Rosenwald Family Fund	21,832,444	970,775	2009
Banbury Fund	19,708,778	960,740	2009
J.P. Humphreys Foundation	18,253,468	825,200	2010
Armstrong Foundation	17,769,361	666,590	2009
Vernon K. Krieble Foundation	17,634,064	245,000	2009
Chase Foundation of Virginia	17,078,294	756,000	2009

Foundation	Assets	Grants Awarded	Year
Newton and Rochelle Becker Charitable Trust	16,795,507	2,397,705	2009
J.B. Reynolds Foundation	15,816,617	750,000	2009
Richard D. and Lynette S. Merillat Foundation	15,368,036	843,500	2010
Donors Trust	13,780,991	12,641,403	2009
Philip M. McKenna Foundation	13,213,435	461,650	2009
Milliken Foundation	12,373,706	1,218,967	2009
E.A. Morris Charitable Foundation	12,077,661	607,000	2009
Brady Education Foundation	11,898,371	0	2009
Rodney Fund	10,261,947	1,112,750	2009
Grover Hermann Foundation	8,774,734	928,000	2009
Anchorage Charitable Fund	8,392,459	342,625	2010
Claude R. Lambe Charitable Foundation	7,349,000	2,819,461	2009
Alex C. Walker Educational & Charitable Foundation	7,296,665	354,000	2009
Ruth and Vernon Taylor Foundation	6,646,906	327,834	2010
Foundation for Partnership Trust	6,425,781	105,500	2001
Whitehead Foundation	6,106,515	2,898,371	2009
George E. Coleman Jr. Foundation	5,923,729	357,290	2009
Barbara and Barre Seid Foundation	5,313,087	1,728,965	2008
Foundation for Educational Choice	5,139,533	794,600	2009
Ceres Foundation	4,485,289	244,700	2009
Bill and Berniece Grewcock Foundation	4,158,493	0	2009
Lovett and Ruth Peters Foundation	3,932,494	1,624,000	2009
Aequus Institute	3,898,115	309,000	2009
Mark C. Pope III Foundation	3,676,707	72,414	2009
True Foundation	3,485,401	468,696	2009
Wilbur Foundation	2,477,714	115,000	2009

Foundation	Assets	Grants Awarded	Year
Curran Foundation	2,275,623	10,000	2009
Neal and Jane Freeman Foundation	1,646,258	80,000	2009
John M. Olin Foundation	1,121,088	1,225,000	2009
Charlotte and Walter Kohler Charitable Trust	876,745	821,041	2009
Gordon and Mary Cain Foundation	548,897	600,000	2009
John Locke Foundation	301,730	0	2010
Jean I. and Charles H. Brunie Foundation	152,179	0	2009
Windway Foundation	38,572	207,700	2009
Padden Family Foundation	36,866	0	2009
Saint Gerard Foundation	1,000	0	2009

Total Assets: $10,288,081,969

Total Grants Awarded: $831,797,191

Average Assets: $125,464,414

Average Grants Awarded: $10,143,868

Comparative Funding of Conservative and Progressive Immigration Groups

Note: "Progressive" refers to groups that support radical departures from traditional immigration policies and notions of sovereignty. These groups refer to illegal aliens as "undocumented immigrants" and support granting them rights traditionally reserved for legal citizens. "Conservative" refers to groups that support traditional immigration policies.

- Number of conservative groups focusing on immigration: **9**
- Total net assets of conservative immigration groups: **$15.05 million**
- Number of progressive groups focusing on immigration: **117**
- Total net assets of progressive immigration groups: **$194.67 million**

SUMMARY: Total net assets of progressive immigration groups are almost thirteen times (12.93×) greater than the total net assets of conservative immigration groups.

- Total annual revenues of the 9 conservative groups, which are against open borders and illegal immigration, are: **$13.80 million**
- Total annual revenues of the 117 progressive groups, which support open borders and illegal immigration, are: **$306.11 million**

SUMMARY: Total annual revenues of progressive immigration groups are over twenty-two times (22.19×) greater than the revenues available to conservative immigration groups.

APPENDIX V

Conservative Immigration Groups

Group	Net Assets	Annual Revenue	Year
Federation for American Immigration Reform	9,041,698	5,080,058	2009
NumbersUSA Foundation	3,225,021	3,859,543	2010
Center for Immigration Studies	1,651,355	1,766,533	2009
Americans for Immigration Control	358,950	1,323,279	2009
Americans for Better Immigration	336,658	2,497	2009
U.S. Border Control	306,951	369,950	2009
American Border Patrol	93,500	996,145	2009
Vdare Foundation (aka Lexington Research Inst.)	20,479	377,833	2009
U.S. Border Control Foundation	20,142	21,749	2007

Total Net Assets: $15,054,754

Total Annual Revenues: $13,797,587

Average Net Assets: $1,672,750

Average Annual Revenues: $1,533,065

APPENDIX VI

Progressive Immigration Groups

Groups	Net Assets	Annual Revenue	Year
National Council of La Raza	46,562,332	36,996,267	2009
Redlands Christian Migrant Association	23,647,481	61,072,478	2010
Comite de Bienestar	11,623,631	6,425,754	2009
Mexican American Legal Defense and Educational Fund	7,827,808	6,131,213	2009
Casa de Maryland	7,487,300	9,476,901	2009
Hispanic Federation	5,522,166	6,057,151	2009
Asian American Justice Center	4,895,674	6,328,094	2009
U.S. Committee for Refugees and Immigrants	4,891,542	24,124,720	2009
Spanish Catholic Center	4,237,973	5,270,354	2009
National Association of Latino Elected and Appointed Officials Educational Fund	4,198,043	6,544,704	2009
Catholic Legal Immigration Network	3,965,450	5,737,585	2009
National Immigration Forum	3,755,110	4,597,657	2009
LatinoJustice—PRLDEF	3,142,367	2,813,100	2010
California Rural Legal Assistance Foundation	3,031,314	2,119,781	2010
National Immigration Law Center	2,999,908	3,289,330	2009
Central American Resource Center of Southern California	2,786,969	1,296,087	2009
Latin American Youth Center	2,753,461	15,543,330	2009
Americas Voice Education Fund	2,740,900	3,598,063	2009

Groups	Net Assets	Annual Revenue	Year
Immigrant Legal Resource Center	2,724,497	2,812,915	2009
Make the Road New York	2,491,316	6,005,778	2009
Casa Latina	2,209,402	1,827,195	2009
American Immigration Council	2,009,142	2,080,097	2009
Center for New Community	1,644,776	1,176,381	2009
Asian American Legal Defense and Education Fund	1,620,784	1,868,558	2009
Mujeres Unidas y Activas	1,619,174	1,451,503	2009
Illinois Coalition for Immigrant and Refugee Rights	1,597,529	7,084,364	2009
Northwest Immigrant Rights Project	1,503,246	3,178,017	2009
New York Immigration Coalition	1,502,316	2,629,180	2009
National Day Laborer Organizing Network	1,348,515	878,037	2009
Coalition of Immokalee Workers	1,224,288	823,867	2009
Centro Campesino Farmworker Center	1,158,001	5,825,335	2009
Immigration Equality	1,102,839	1,300,929	2009
OneAmerica	1,092,221	1,415,135	2009
Farmworker Justice Fund	984,469	1,638,224	2009
New York State Defenders Association (Immigrant Defense Project)	982,158	2,073,082	2009
Grantmakers Concerned with Immigrants and Refugees	944,967	1,068,420	2009
Asian Law Caucus	916,747	1,982,664	2010
Massachusetts Immigrant and Refugee Advocacy Coalition	889,629	1,411,588	2009
National Lawyers Guild (National Immigration Project)	850,044	804,124	2009
Partnership for Immigrant Leadership and Action	802,158	876,867	2009
AnewAmerica Community Corporation	757,697	3,598,063	2009

Groups	Net Assets	Annual Revenue	Year
New Mexico Center on Law and Poverty	727,286	734,481	2009
Centro Romero	671,582	1,315,043	2009
Centro del Obrero Fronterizo— La Mujer Obrera	636,248	272,989	2009
Florence Immigrant and Refugee Rights Project	562,911	848,459	2009
Centro Campesino	546,613	511,927	2009
Asian Pacific American Legal Resource Center	530,377	832,558	2009
Mano a Mano Family Resource Center Foundation	527,955	511,502	2010
Equal Justice Center	526,903	700,464	2009
Florida Immigrant Advocacy Center	487,161	4,201,019	2009
Democracia Ahora	464,927	130,000	2009
Immigration Reform Law Institute	448,145	646,174	2009
Mississippi Immigrants Rights Alliance	425,397	701,501	2009
Florida Immigrant Coalition	421,095	786,786	2009
Workers Defense Project	382,555	552,542	2009
Las Americas Immigrant Advocacy Center	378,860	232,400	2010
Farmworker Association of Florida	376,246	888,387	2009
Tenants and Workers United— Inquilinos y Trabajodores Unidos	363,441	1,129,032	2009
Welcoming Center for New Pennsylvanians	354,979	1,341,433	2010
Working Hands Legal Clinic	351,451	843,167	2010
Hispanic Resource Center of Larchmont and Mamaroneck	351,386	421,793	2009
Refugee Womens Network	347,039	607,226	2009
United Farm Workers Foundation	332,870	223,912	2009
East Bay Sanctuary Covenant	317,202	271,770	2009

Groups	Net Assets	Annual Revenue	Year
Immigrant Law Center of Minnesota	300,905	764,840	2009
ImmigrationWorks Foundation	281,729	635,096	2009
Voto Latino	254,004	469,045	2009
Immigrant Welcome Center	224,600	58,928	2009
La Union del Pueblo Entero	217,223	912,122	2009
Fresno Center for New Americans	211,176	1,685,760	2009
Latino Union of Chicago	199,394	326,722	2009
Border Network for Human Rights	193,891	474,706	2009
Immigrants Rights Advocacy Center	183,503	1,049,036	2009
Institute for Family Development, Centro Familia	179,175	556,431	2009
Centro de los Derechos del Migrante	178,512	301,310	2009
El Puente Community Development Corporation	162,238	952,456	2009
Sunflower Community Action	161,273	416,024	2009
Libertys Promise	159,799	388,510	2009
Puente de la Costa Sur	158,240	931,993	2010
Main Street Project	157,235	555,575	2009
Ayuda	155,751	1,717,631	2009
U.S.-Mexico Border Philanthropy Partnership	137,849	681,042	2009
Refugee & Immigrant Center for Education & Legal Services	135,478	457,252	2009
National Alliance of Latin American and Caribbean Communities	134,499	18,491	2009
Latin American Coalition—Coalicion Latinoamericana	134,263	994,754	2010
League of United Latin American Citizens	131,032	668,255	2010
Just Neighbors Ministry	129,177	691,312	2009
Immigrants Assistance Center	126,947	294,708	2010
Global Workers Justice Alliance	126,258	357,582	2010

Groups	Net Assets	Annual Revenue	Year
La Escuelita	123,064	400,681	2008
Social and Economic Rights Action Center	122,856	225,267	2009
Coalition of African, Arab, Asian, European and Latino Immigrants of Illinois	107,104	589,642	2010
Workers Interfaith Network, Memphis	107,034	138,101	2009
Centro Hispano Cuzcatlan	101,132	230,528	2009
National Ethnic Coalition of Organizations Foundation	99,910	877,505	2009
Fund for Public Advocacy	99,836	188,478	2005
Capital Area Immigrants Rights Coalition	97,016	564,087	2009
Coalition for Humane Immigrant Rights of Los Angeles	91,874	1,621,247	2009
Farmworker Legal Services of New York	82,187	746,263	2009
National Immigration Forum Action Fund	72,095	424,727	2009
ALearn	65,869	136,097	2009
Cielo Project Radio Ranch	63,861	268,525	2009
Entre Hermanos	61,465	333,638	2009
Farmworker Health and Safety Institute	40,730	43,469	2009
Western North Carolina Workers Center	39,508	200,189	2009
Farm Labor Research Project	38,393	481,487	2009
National Network for Immigrant and Refugee Rights	32,029	245,938	2009
Northwest Workers Justice Project	30,806	177,130	2009
Metropolitan Community Development Corporation	28,285	108,538	2009
Center for Immigrant Democracy	26,937	1,194,081	2005

Groups	Net Assets	Annual Revenue	Year
Hispanic Advocacy and Community Empowerment through Research	26,019	121,095	2009
American Immigration Lawyers Association	25,618	69,796	2009
Mano a Mano Mexican Culture Without Borders	22,978	22,977	2009
Immigrant Workers Resource Center	17,796	100,118	2002
Latin American Legal Defense and Educational Fund	13,471	41,996	2010
Workers Interfaith Network, Minneapolis	12,152	182,639	2009
Immigrant Workers Citizenship Project	7,753	75,510	2009

Total Net Assets: $194,669,902

Total Annual Revenues: $306,106,787

Average Net Assets: $1,663,845

Average Annual Revenues: $2,616,297

The Ploughshares (Peace and Security Funders) Group of 64 Progressive Foundations Focused on National Security Issues

Foundation/Group	Net Assets	Grants Awarded	Annual Revenue	Year
Ford Foundation	10,880,830,407	464,331,181	1,217,104,175	2010
William and Flora Hewlett Foundation	6,851,296,219	345,190,721	73,267,564	2009
John D. and Catherine T. MacArthur Foundation	5,237,796,060	234,719,855	355,605,174	2009
Carnegie Corporation of New York	2,432,582,536	112,195,444	56,347,563	2009
Simons Foundation	1,406,194,090	87,024,914	403,002,102	2009
Open Society Institute	1,102,893,795	1,035,719,221	133,811,261	2009
Rockefeller Brothers Fund	729,263,381	31,188,924	1,560,335	2009
Public Welfare Foundation	445,896,838	22,400,036	20,633,576	2009
Park Foundation	320,897,293	17,719,762	6,782,236	2009
German Marshall Fund	185,886,321	8,615,293	23,501,298	2010
Tides Foundation	175,019,369	97,028,446	118,768,818	2009
Educational Foundation of America	162,081,218	8,610,634	2,225,946	2009
United Nations Foundation	136,682,490	54,354,979	105,050,738	2009
Mertz Gilmore Foundation	101,021,755	6,066,405	3,474,987	2009

Foundation/Group	Net Assets	Grants Awarded	Annual Revenue	Year
Flora Family Foundation	99,882,823	4,057,743	898,550	2009
Stanley Foundation	79,483,347	0	1,823,712	2009
Harry Frank Guggenheim Foundation	76,695,563	982,434	1,390,294	2009
Scherman Foundation	69,604,419	1,682,950	1,091,847	2009
Compton Foundation	64,316,869	4,407,309	1,457,413	2009
Prospect Hill Foundation	55,676,745	2,908,676	308,651	2010
Arca Foundation	48,011,069	1,872,793	7,407,714	2009
Town Creek Foundation	46,708,418	2,252,110	3,335,569	2010
Ploughshares Fund	33,784,853	6,505,050	6,029,323	2010
Schooner Foundation	33,351,026	3,456,397	1,493,259	2009
Alan B. Slifka Foundation	30,556,989	6,092,308	5,267,672	2009
New-Land Foundation	26,814,091	1,730,970	1,238,362	2009
David and Katherine Moore Family Foundation	18,271,854	954,500	398,270	2009
Secure World Foundation	18,046,098	0	1,223,910	2009
HKH Foundation	15,685,402	2,160,162	327,449	2009
Colombe Foundation	14,613,647	1,206,500	1,332,547	2010
New Cycle Foundation	13,233,291	583,500	464,602	2009
Stewart R. Mott Foundation	13,044,892	909,256	284,182	2008
Samuel Rubin Foundation	10,891,436	520,722	283,667	2010
Chino Cienega Foundation	6,912,470	297,300	264,159	2010

Foundation/Group	Net Assets	Grants Awarded	Annual Revenue	Year
Turner Foundation	5,780,751	9,769,365	12,542,068	2009
Proteus Fund	5,402,326	6,088,118	6,160,827	2009
Ben & Jerry's Foundation	5,320,384	1,799,080	2,104,796	2009
Livingry Foundation	4,912,543	95,500	82,456	2009
Steiner-King Foundation	4,267,946	418,802	302,190	2010
Agape Foundation	3,634,579	154,250	133,783	2010
Lydia B. Stokes Foundation	3,296,325	232,250	48,773	2010
Threshold Foundation	2,910,371	1,351,328	1,668,408	2009
CarEth Foundation	2,008,410	112,250	60,492	2009
Lippincott Foundation	1,927,879	99,000	44,558	2010
Janelia Foundation	1,761,363	87,000	298,566	2009
Kenbe Foundation	1,516,132	115,500	996,148	2009
Peace Development Fund	1,121,302	531,574	898,842	2010
Hunt Alternatives Fund	930,591	171,970	3,378,896	2009
Planethood Foundation	782,413	206,753	161,611	2009
A. J. Muste Memorial Institute	674,499	1,132,986	1,214,064	2010
Diana, Princess of Wales Memorial Fund	335,159	632,854	732,095	2002
Iara Lee and George Gund III Foundation	191,187	318,250	327,104	2009
Rational Games, Inc.	81,664	34,000	117,070	2010
Saga Foundation	30,505	115,100	152,312	2009
Joseph Rowntree Charitable Trust	0	5,752,351	5,731,566	2001
Cypress Fund for Peace and Security	0	0	0	2010

Berghof Foundation for Conflict Studies	Doesn't file a 990 form with the IRS	Located in Berlin, Germany
Charitable Foundation— Institute for Economics and Peace	Doesn't file a 990 form with the IRS	Located in Sydney, Australia
Connect U.S. Fund (A Project of the Tides Center)	Doesn't file a 990 form with the IRS	Located in Washington D.C.
Milton Lauenstein	Doesn't file a 990 form with the IRS	Individual Member
Peace, Conflict and Development Program Initiative	Doesn't file a 990 form with the IRS	Located in Ottawa, Canada
Rockefeller Financial Services	Doesn't file a 990 form with the IRS	Located in New York City
Wellspring Advisors, LLC	Doesn't file a 990 form with the IRS	Located in New York City
Working Assets	Doesn't file a 990 form with the IRS	Located in San Francisco

Total Net Assets: $30,990,813,403

Total Grants Awarded: $2,596,964,776

Total Annual Revenues: $2,594,613,550

Average Net Assets: $553,407,382

Average Grants Awarded: $46,374,371

Average Annual Revenues: $46,332,385

Comparative Funding of Conservative and Progressive Environmental Groups

Note: "Progressive" refers to groups that share "common" as-sumptions about business and the environment—that global warming—now "climate change"—is a fact of crisis propor-tions, that it is man-made, that businesses and corporations are principal environmental culprits, that government reg-ulation of business is the solution, that drastic revisions of American law are required, that litigation in behalf of green agendas is in order, that many natural resources—fossil fuels, land—must be put off limits to as great a degree as pos-sible, that human beings are toxic, and that "green" energy must replace other forms of energy as rapidly as possible. "Conservative" refers to groups that share preferences for property rights and free-market solutions to environmental problems, for preserving the rights of people to hunt and fish, who regard the issue of global warming as controversial and the theory of its human origins as questionable or at best un-resolved. These groups are advocates for clean coal mining, responsible drilling, and replanting of trees after logging. These groups do not oppose alternative energies but want to strike a balance with economic realities.

- Number of conservative environmental groups that promote market-friendly solutions: **32**
  - —Total net assets of conservative environmental groups: **$38.24 million**
- Number of progressive environmental groups that promote radical views that are anti-business: **552**
  - —Total net assets of progressive environmental groups: **$9.31 billion**

SUMMARY: The resources available to progressive environmental groups are over 243 times (243.49×) the resources available to conservative environmental groups.

- The grants awarded annually by the 32 conservative environmental groups total **$1.20 million**.
- The grants awarded annually by the 552 progressive environmental groups total **$553.70 million**.

SUMMARY: Progressive environmental groups spend over 460 times (460.34×) more on their causes than do the conservative environmental groups.

- The total annual revenues of the 32 conservative environmental groups are **$96.17 million**.
- The total annual revenues of the 552 progressive environmental groups are **$3.56 billion**.

SUMMARY: Total annual revenues of progressive environmental groups are over 37 times (37.05×) greater than the revenues available to conservative environmental groups.

Conservative Environmental Groups

Groups	Net Assets	Grants Awarded	Annual Revenue	Year
American Coalition for Clean Coal Electricity	9,183,016	0	53,733,277	2009
Keep America Beautiful	7,653,203	798,600	10,301,311	2009
Oregon Institute of Science and Medicine	4,303,197	0	489,226	2009
Mountain States Legal Foundation	4,226,140	0	2,295,025	2009
National Federal Lands Conference	3,549,776	0	64,189	2009
Political Economy Research Center	2,842,374	0	2,460,348	2009
Foundation for Research on Economics and the Environment	1,515,684	0	840,644	2009
Science & Environmental Policy Project	1,502,589	0	626,779	2009
Alaska Support Industry Alliance	740,484	0	522,683	2010
Institute for Energy Research	699,698	5,000	2,266,196	2009
Research Partnership to Secure Energy for America	584,106	85,000	15,762,634	2009
Committee for a Constructive Tomorrow	439,751	200,000	3,071,277	2009

Groups	Net Assets	Grants Awarded	Annual Revenue	Year
Public Lands Council	434,456	0	206,105	2010
Alliance for a Responsible CFC Policy	192,079	0	653,783	2009
Oregonians for Food and Shelter	154,879	0	427,554	2009
Doctors for Disaster Preparedness	102,021	0	55,337	2009
North Carolina Fisheries Association	76,018	0	223,025	2009
Oregonians in Action Education Fund	67,750	0	52,400	2009
Institute for Sustainable Forestry	43,648	0	60,333	2009
Oregonians in Action Legal Center	31,654	16,000	198,445	2009
Society for Environmental Truth	30,113	0	27,568	1999
Klamath Alliance for Resources and Environment	28,430	0	8,494	2009
Oregonians in Action	26,375	555	288,238	2009
Women In Mining	23,493	0	1,512	2010
South Texans Property Rights Association	19,292	0	159,990	2009
Women In Mining Education Foundation	13,766	0	9,111	2010
Council of Republicans for Environmental Advocacy	8,021	97,565	146,179	2005
Americans for Balanced Energy Choices	0	0	0	2008
Defenders of Property Rights	0	0	5,414	2007

Groups	Net Assets	Grants Awarded	Annual Revenue	Year
National Wetlands Coalition	0	0	42,250	2006
Blue Ribbon Coalition	−89,991	84	954,141	2009
National Wilderness Institute	−163,650	0	220,508	2003

Total Net Assets: $38,238,372

Total Grants Awarded: 1,202,804

Total Annual Revenues: $96,173,976

Average Net Assets: $1,194,949

Average Grants Awarded: 37,588

Average Annual Revenues:. $3,005,437

Progressive Environmental Groups

Groups	Net Assets	Grants Awarded	Annual Revenue	Year
Nature Conservancy	4,879,283,936	50,402,765	925,817,441	2010
Wildlife Conservation Society	631,569,794	11,495,091	197,345,941	2009
Conservation Fund	402,062,886	3,273,345	186,700,491	2009
ClimateWorks Foundation	348,718,398	92,782,494	60,272,759	2009
National Audubon Society	255,712,728	1,568,437	74,008,085	2009
World Wildlife Fund	238,133,260	52,100,176	177,738,454	2010
Conservation International	219,835,215	48,487,284	63,651,042	2010
Trust For Public Land	191,996,820	60,662,766	127,670,275	2010
Natural Resources Defense Council	181,427,464	0	96,971,952	2010
Aspen Institute	152,052,272	4,005,088	66,554,008	2009
Environmental Defense Fund	132,197,665	9,061,178	54,893,658	2010
Wildlands Conservancy	103,419,385	6,001,000	22,272,490	2009
Sierra Club Foundation	88,509,397	40,734,048	40,531,533	2009
Save the Redwoods League	86,397,122	2,882,236	8,488,400	2010
National Wildlife Federation Endowment	60,770,448	5,215,000	3,430,227	2010

Groups	Net Assets	Grants Awarded	Annual Revenue	Year
World Resources Institute	53,435,050	8,094,598	39,871,632	2010
Sierra Club	48,920,055	1,193,699	84,753,217	2009
Wilderness Society	46,523,153	900,327	23,008,956	2010
Global Green USA	41,075,226	209,250	3,872,324	2009
Resources for the Future	38,611,159	77,000	11,187,831	2009
Delaware Nature Society	38,350,688	0	2,075,643	2009
Urban Land Institute	35,076,680	253,411	49,145,315	2010
Resources Legacy Fund	35,008,209	10,548,008	21,832,121	2009
EarthJustice	32,377,514	89,160	23,143,420	2010
Union of Concerned Scientists	32,245,871	0	21,519,809	2009
Scenic Hudson	24,020,478	4,657,578	6,786,585	2010
Defenders of Wildlife	23,675,323	856,353	32,595,370	2010
Wildlands Support Fund	22,590,333	10,990,331	1,125,337	2009
Southern Environmental Law Center	22,589,875	37,500	13,126,546	2010
Woods Hole Research Center	22,570,799	2,391,901	19,462,864	2009
Ecotrust	22,401,950	1,232,379	15,173,919	2009
American Farmland Trust	20,049,808	0	9,771,008	2010
Oceana	19,062,372	50,000	13,079,625	2009
Alliance for Climate Protection	16,022,357	1,713,683	15,989,476	2009
Guanacaste Dry Forest Conservation Fund	15,854,969	384,903	1,206,183	2009
Ocean Conservancy	15,297,626	945,650	15,358,961	2009

Groups	Net Assets	Grants Awarded	Annual Revenue	Year
Adirondack Land Trust/ Nature Conservancy	14,807,221	0	2,027,281	2010
Organization for Tropical Studies	14,432,864	779,547	9,171,302	2010
Greenpeace Fund, Inc.	14,081,889	15,817,653	7,551,994	2009
Conservation Law Foundation	13,676,279	0	4,562,320	2009
Shorebank Enterprise Cascadia	12,449,403	0	6,212,643	2009
David Brower Center	11,922,862	0	413,149	2009
Rainforest Fund	11,671,472	1,204,243	76,797	2009
Environmental Law and Policy Center of the Midwest	10,895,016	148,175	6,758,809	2009
Acres Inc.	10,866,460	0	866,920	2009
Passaic River Coalition	10,596,683	0	805,972	2010
Allegheny Land Trust	10,472,612	0	1,098,866	2010
Penobscot River Restoration Trust	9,959,880	0	2,234,880	2009
Student Conservation Association	9,911,413	2,268,066	29,916,293	2009
300 Committee	9,897,113	400,000	697,503	2009
South Carolina Coastal Conservation League	9,420,526	11,134	3,169,604	2009
Pacific Forest Trust	9,302,664	0	1,325,319	2009
PRBO Conservation Science	8,890,417	0	5,520,183	2010
Environmental Defense Action Fund	8,140,207	2,258,000	10,086,663	2010
Earthwatch Institute	8,047,406	2,616,924	7,956,446	2009
Land Institute	8,004,652	29,654	2,586,137	2010
Land Trust Alliance	7,978,772	1,680,693	9,586,693	2009

Groups	Net Assets	Grants Awarded	Annual Revenue	Year
American Rivers	7,914,312	2,230,705	12,105,943	2010
Alaska Conservation Foundation	7,906,612	4,120,455	6,649,809	2010
Rocky Mountain Institute	7,685,049	0	13,104,464	2010
NatureServe	7,524,843	0	9,940,117	2009
Save the Bay	7,497,116	0	3,423,572	2010
Audubon Nature Institute	7,333,618	3,478,681	25,326,607	2009
Environmental Stewardship Foundation	7,110,330	243,278	353,275	2009
CERES	7,017,870	0	9,559,268	2009
Farm and Wilderness Foundation	6,611,321	0	3,622,479	2009
Coalition for Buzzards Bay	6,550,264	0	5,337,329	2009
Earth Island Institute	6,498,989	1,408,665	11,188,273	2009
Energy Action Coalition	6,498,989	1,408,665	11,188,273	2009
Center for Biological Diversity	6,462,365	68,557	9,178,681	2008
Greater Yellowstone Coalition	6,293,689	169,352	2,346,450	2010
Environmental Law Institute	6,237,426	0	5,111,200	2009
League of Conservation Voters, Inc.	6,044,600	2,679,775	14,312,581	2009
League of Conservation Voters Education Fund	6,009,631	5,639,171	8,993,753	2009
Trust for Conservation Innovation	5,847,165	223,536	8,262,039	2009
Back Country Land Trust	5,611,295	11,000	204,354	2010

Groups	Net Assets	Grants Awarded	Annual Revenue	Year
Ground Water Protection Council	5,496,785	0	1,583,076	2009
Southern Utah Wilderness Alliance	5,476,386	0	1,746,205	2009
Institute for Agriculture and Trade Policy	5,342,435	123,894	2,124,605	2009
Green for All	5,301,037	110,000	7,381,949	2009
Global Greengrants Fund	5,292,374	5,799,917	8,441,206	2010
Hillside Trust	5,260,557	0	82,972	2009
Yampa Valley Land Trust	4,992,878	0	3,497,062	2009
Clean Air Task Force	4,935,629	1,329,650	4,815,649	2009
Connecticut Fund for the Environment	4,859,739	0	2,370,583	2009
Rainforest Alliance	4,510,417	1,761,627	32,810,981	2009
Strategies for the Global Environment	4,479,269	0	1,423,685	2010
North Cascades Institute	4,334,278	0	2,107,513	2009
Citizens for Pennsylvania's Future	4,194,037	0	3,566,889	2010
Forest Trends Association	4,128,379	126,415	6,618,050	2009
Green Corps	3,925,172	46,097	1,550,667	2010
Amazon Conservation Team	3,826,653	2,709,390	2,898,514	2009
Wildlands Conservancy, Inc.	3,796,541	0	3,833,472	2009
EarthRights International	3,775,036	43,861	2,141,615	2010
Earth Day Network	3,772,477	39,605	4,550,337	2009
SeaWeb	3,706,649	1,219,575	2,665,207	2009

Groups	Net Assets	Grants Awarded	Annual Revenue	Year
Environmental Working Group	3,599,736	0	3,489,108	2009
Amazon Conservation Association	3,480,484	1,949,773	2,900,166	2009
Mountain Institute	3,471,083	1,248,605	3,157,550	2009
Island Press— Center for Resource Economics	3,445,905	0	5,249,636	2009
Carbonfund.org Foundation	3,417,165	0	2,347,541	2009
Monteverde Conservation League US	3,386,762	1,445	190,544	2009
Health Care Without Harm	3,249,552	2,225,750	4,574,286	2009
Environment California	3,071,514	2,991,467	2,991,467	2009
Meridian Institute	3,071,071	0	10,265,871	2009
Sustainability Institute	3,057,797	598,218	2,569,788	2009
Accokeek Foundation	3,005,242	0	1,127,561	2010
Adirondack Council	2,914,402	0	1,582,958	2010
Land Partners Through Stewardship	2,896,518	0	661,579	2009
Keystone Center	2,896,003	0	7,487,586	2009
Environmental and Energy Study Institute	2,870,006	0	991,078	2009
Environment America Research and Policy Center	2,841,444	1,021,750	4,491,964	2009
O2 for Life	2,807,889	0	78,606	2009
Conservation Alliance	2,806,821	904,615	2,122,434	2010
Northeast-Midwest Institute	2,793,995	0	1,860,307	2009
League to Save Lake Tahoe	2,758,029	0	2,512,339	2009

Groups	Net Assets	Grants Awarded	Annual Revenue	Year
Rose Foundation for Communities and the Environment	2,680,346	2,769,451	2,832,572	2009
Pacific Environment	2,672,333	807,500	2,678,572	2010
Sustainable Conservation	2,652,652	84,590	2,094,883	2009
Social and Environmental Entrepreneurs	2,432,812	68,195	3,279,853	2009
BRING Recycling	2,410,048	0	1,296,731	2010
Funders Network for Smart Growth and Livable Communities	2,391,332	0	2,548,447	2010
Center on Race, Poverty and the Environment	2,333,915	102,111	1,397,697	2009
Grist Magazine	2,327,538	0	2,581,640	2009
Fresh Energy	2,323,902	0	2,341,383	2009
Save San Francisco Bay Association	2,269,609	107,327	2,597,574	2009
Friends of the Earth	2,266,982	162,000	4,880,379	2009
International Rivers Network	2,142,792	105,727	2,411,664	2009
National Religious Partnership for the Environment	2,134,702	666,053	1,304,684	2010
Center for Rural Affairs	2,074,339	105,373	3,362,444	2009
Kentucky Coalition	2,068,885	13,333	2,051,394	2009
Upstate Forever	2,042,872	0	1,322,692	2009
Northeast Wilderness Trust	2,027,183	0	301,769	2009
Public Citizen Texas	1,990,811	20,000	3,122,568	2010
Sightline Institute	1,966,015	0	1,055,538	2009

Groups	Net Assets	Grants Awarded	Annual Revenue	Year
Theodore Roosevelt Conservation Partnership	1,952,953	0	4,908,097	2009
ICLEI—Local Governments for Sustainability USA	1,939,115	120,016	4,553,618	2009
Quivira Coalition	1,927,723	61,325	614,665	2009
International Wilderness Leadership Wild Foundation	1,910,049	1,068,338	4,117,777	2009
Coalition for Clean Air	1,881,512	0	440,611	2009
Marine Conservation Biology Institute	1,881,351	263,315	1,362,225	2009
Bridging the Gap	1,859,336	44,000	1,231,744	2010
Appalachia Ohio Alliance	1,809,009	301	570,308	2009
Stockholm Environment Institute U.S.	1,805,570	0	3,697,633	2009
Green Building Alliance	1,800,573	307,327	1,498,063	2009
Alliance to Save Energy	1,756,114	0	12,130,202	2009
Group for the East End	1,730,431	0	1,343,221	2009
Vermont Natural Resources Council	1,716,458	0	967,052	2010
EcoLogic Development Fund	1,687,500	0	1,955,104	2009
Minnesota Center for Environmental Advocacy	1,680,111	90,000	1,100,842	2010
James River Association	1,644,510	0	1,504,052	2009
Washington Environmental Council	1,626,788	0	1,555,039	2010

Groups	Net Assets	Grants Awarded	Annual Revenue	Year
Consultative Group on Biological Diversity	1,600,798	0	1,600,798	2009
Environment Northeast	1,582,089	22,500	1,605,340	2009
Clean Air-Cool Planet	1,577,957	0	3,088,587	2009
Center for Neighborhood Technology	1,564,673	115,522	3,806,642	2009
North Carolina Conservation Network	1,539,870	30,000	1,219,201	2009
Adopt-A-Stream Foundation	1,534,602	0	452,158	2010
National Center for Appropriate Technology	1,519,652	0	5,300,469	2009
Bay Institute of San Francisco	1,517,128	0	1,644,307	2009
Pinelands Preservation Alliance	1,486,394	0	745,313	2009
Jackson Hole Conservation Alliance	1,485,156	0	712,500	2010
Pacific Institute for Studies in Development, Environment and Security	1,473,246	0	2,643,908	2009
Belgrade Regional Conservation Alliance	1,470,657	0	447,538	2009
Clean Water Fund	1,463,797	59,555	4,085,662	2009
Alaska Wilderness League	1,451,801	0	3,547,710	2009
U.S. Climate Action Network	1,432,499	763,000	2,544,399	2009
Southern Alliance for Clean Energy	1,412,285	0	3,477,277	2009

Groups	Net Assets	Grants Awarded	Annual Revenue	Year
Rainforest Action Network	1,407,280	179,347	4,486,840	2010
Foundations of Success	1,388,168	0	1,007,847	2009
1Sky Education Fund	1,385,556	0	1,398,850	2010
Center for Energy Efficiency and Renewable Technologies	1,363,599	2,250	3,134,391	2009
Center for International Environmental Law	1,355,985	79,014	2,099,352	2010
Communities for a Better Environment	1,350,493	0	2,052,349	2009
Environmental Defense Center	1,317,463	0	1,036,532	2009
Riverkeeper	1,316,763	0	2,585,567	2010
West Harlem Environmental Action	1,307,105	0	1,992,754	2009
Regeneration Project	1,304,142	357,994	1,566,011	2009
Alliance for the Great Lakes	1,268,452	0	1,749,987	2010
Center for Whole Communities	1,229,295	0	802,576	2010
Environmental Law Alliance Worldwide	1,208,601	280,439	1,216,847	2009
Clean Wisconsin	1,203,436	0	1,736,280	2009
Earth Conservation Corps	1,186,604	0	1,669,659	2009
Sustainable Northwest	1,186,571	0	1,819,247	2010
Conservation Biology Institute	1,181,596	9,500	2,802,487	2009
Environmental Health Coalition	1,144,455	0	1,946,061	2010

Groups	Net Assets	Grants Awarded	Annual Revenue	Year
Environmental Grantmakers Association	1,141,189	0	1,224,521	2009
Oregon Natural Desert Association	1,138,905	0	1,499,802	2010
West Michigan Environmental Action Council	1,138,423	0	390,306	2010
Environmental Investigation Agency	1,137,218	106,887	1,734,120	2009
Adirondack Mountain Club	1,131,860	0	3,205,855	2009
Washington Toxics Coalition	1,124,624	238,000	1,181,141	2009
Western Environmental Law Center	1,122,755	57,822	2,198,310	2009
National Wildlife Federation Action Fund	1,120,831	17,500	1,574,784	2009
Alabama Forest Resources Center	1,112,638	0	9,859,700	2009
Earth Force	1,109,251	0	1,657,507	2009
Colorado Environmental Coalition	1,084,771	0	1,279,573	2009
Restore America's Estuaries	1,056,917	1,183,835	1,183,835	2009
Global Exchange	1,023,872	138,219	4,772,257	2009
River Network	1,022,405	142,140	2,041,802	2010
Active Transportation Alliance	1,021,266	0	3,574,030	2009
California League of Conservation Voters	1,014,331	0	3,458,792	2009

Groups	Net Assets	Grants Awarded	Annual Revenue	Year
Clean Ocean Action	1,000,373	0	732,511	2009
Environmental Integrity Project	993,244	91,000	2,467,173	2009
Midwest Energy Efficiency Alliance	991,054	0	14,923,934	2010
Conservation Northwest	975,851	7,726	1,792,860	2010
Resource Innovation Group	974,558	0	850,549	2009
Energy Consumers Alliance of New England	973,279	0	2,458,827	2010
Physicians for Social Responsibility	968,717	94,386	2,949,036	2009
Living Planet	967,507	0	2,898,723	2009
Great Plains Institute for Sustainable Development	965,278	0	862,044	2010
People for Puget Sound	963,802	0	1,908,445	2010
Agricultural Stewardship Association	957,163	0	942,363	2010
Environment California Research and Policy Center	954,319	0	440,183	2009
Bronx River Alliance	949,299	0	1,605,101	2009
Forest Ethics	948,421	0	2,456,273	2009
Acterra: Action for a Sustainable Earth	928,493	482,000	2,552,991	2010
World Media Foundation— Living on Earth	918,922	0	2,131,718	2009

Groups	Net Assets	Grants Awarded	Annual Revenue	Year
Midwest Environmental Advocates	906,269	1,500	538,063	2010
Institute for Governance and Sustainable Development	903,310	0	2,568,537	2010
William C. Anderson Wilderness and Wildlife Preservation Society	901,770	17,750	58,140	2009
Minnesota Environmental Initiative	900,416	0	2,102,585	2009
PennEnvironment Research and Policy Center	865,584	0	608,366	2009
Los Angeles and San Gabriel Rivers Watershed Council	860,851	0	3,167,254	2010
Community Environmental Legal Defense Fund	847,352	0	570,004	2009
Center for Climate Strategies	844,456	159,959	5,891,870	2009
Society of Environmental Journalists	835,295	0	559,726	2009
Local Government Commission	831,004	0	1,989,563	2009
World Land Trust—US	821,827	1,540,942	1,995,936	2009
Environmental Advocates of New York	814,061	0	934,160	2009
1,000 Friends of Minnesota (aka Envision Minnesota)	794,958	327,000	931,006	2009

Groups	Net Assets	Grants Awarded	Annual Revenue	Year
Climate Solutions	793,017	0	1,707,155	2009
Center for the Study of Carbon Dioxide and Global Change	792,017	31,000	1,552,628	2009
Environmental Support Center	788,615	101,278	679,120	2009
Rachel's Network	782,529	0	823,051	2009
Cascadia Region Green Building Council	781,733	0	2,172,092	2009
National Wildlife Refuge Association	781,042	0	1,353,472	2010
Oregon Environmental Council	773,827	0	897,174	2010
Baykeeper	764,431	0	832,079	2010
Earth Policy Institute	752,429	0	726,664	2009
Alabama Forestry Foundation	745,215	3,000	202,489	2009
National Center for Conservation Science and Policy	740,519	0	943,101	2009
Cazenovia Preservation Foundation	723,466	0	98,151	2009
Rainforest Café Friends of the Future Foundation	715,145	185,951	157,537	2009
Access Fund	704,059	43,281	1,273,699	2009
Clark Fork Coalition	688,554	0	618,313	2008
Puget Soundkeeper Alliance	682,799	0	482,058	2009
WildAid	678,610	0	2,079,021	2009
EarthShare	660,260	10,440,503	12,527,810	2010
Beyond Pesticides	644,793	4,403	866,694	2009

Groups	Net Assets	Grants Awarded	Annual Revenue	Year
Missouri Coalition for the Environment Foundation	613,777	106,011	662,385	2009
California Coastkeeper Alliance	608,017	0	367,827	2010
Earth School Educational Foundation	600,090	0	362,224	2009
Natural Capital Institute	599,667	0	2,991,022	2009
Orange County Coastkeeper	594,180	0	1,011,333	2009
Amazon Center for Environmental Education Research Foundation	591,431	0	334,838	2009
Ag Innovations Network	587,328	240,000	1,916,423	2009
Work Environment Council of New Jersey	585,239	0	631,368	2009
Environment Ohio Research and Policy Center	558,736	0	155,725	2010
Southeast Alaska Conservation Council	557,049	50,000	1,046,994	2009
Dogwood Alliance	549,040	0	550,425	2009
International Food and Agricultural Trade Policy Council	546,058	0	803,595	2009
Tamarisk Coalition	537,959	0	1,024,879	2009
Sierra Nevada Alliance	533,958	636,893	839,770	2010
Center for Clean Air Policy	529,257	0	4,604,393	2009

Groups	Net Assets	Grants Awarded	Annual Revenue	Year
Environment Maryland Research and Policy Center	519,495	0	458,045	2010
Chesapeake Climate Action Network	516,278	0	1,002,103	2010
Silicon Valley Leadership Group Sustainable Valley Foundation	511,333	318,000	960,699	2009
Affordable Comfort	510,286	0	2,245,274	2010
Environmental Coalition of South Seattle	495,883	0	816,069	2009
Facing the Future: People and the Planet	493,796	0	569,320	2009
Waterkeeper Alliance	492,204	183,846	3,393,479	2010
California Wilderness Coalition	484,117	500	587,730	2009
Environmental League of Massachusetts	481,982	0	612,230	2010
Climate Group	476,233	0	3,643,374	2009
Appalachian Voices	474,191	0	1,120,614	2009
Northern Alaska Environmental Center	473,714	0	689,526	2009
Organic Center for Education and Promotion	472,704	0	632,455	2009
Coalition to Restore Coastal Louisiana	466,685	0	718,438	2009
River Alliance of Wisconsin	457,225	6,530	695,345	2010
Second Nature	447,777	0	1,427,177	2009
Model Forest Policy Program	442,910	0	443,002	2010

Groups	Net Assets	Grants Awarded	Annual Revenue	Year
Raritan Baykeeper	432,451	0	644,093	2009
Metropolitan Waterfront Alliance	428,842	0	809,020	2009
Green Foothills Foundation	427,524	0	452,453	2010
Wild Earth Society	423,865	48,713	574,784	2009
U.S. Green Building Council	420,965	0	1,319,017	2009
Amazon Watch	420,318	100,965	1,100,184	2009
Friends of Milwaukee's River	412,450	0	235,352	2010
East Michigan Environmental Action Council	411,847	0	365,959	2010
Santa Monica Baykeeper	411,225	0	789,421	2009
Rainforest Foundation	407,432	327,074	530,140	2009
Institute for Social and Environmental Transition	405,597	0	2,073,941	2009
Great Lakes Aquatic Habitat Network and Fund—Freshwater Future	400,399	293,899	885,292	2010
What Is Missing? Foundation	400,235	25,000	275,596	2009
Western Organization of Resource Councils Education Project	396,487	1,704,498	1,833,790	2010
Association of New Jersey Environmental Commissions	385,866	0	823,579	2009
Houston Wilderness	384,864	0	720,677	2010

Groups	Net Assets	Grants Awarded	Annual Revenue	Year
Silicon Valley Toxics Coalition	363,644	0	607,031	2009
Sitka Conservation Society	362,511	9,999	286,222	2009
Prairie Rivers Network	361,417	0	497,329	2009
Climate Policy Initiative	360,757	0	1,000,000	2009
GreenSpace Alliance	359,010	0	514,345	2010
Crag Law Center	355,012	0	345,396	2009
Trustees for Alaska	346,113	0	830,612	2009
Texas Conservation Alliance	342,217	0	334,182	2008
Delaware Riverkeeper Network	342,119	0	1,077,844	2009
Biomass Energy Resource Center	340,990	0	1,561,299	2009
Clean Energy Group	336,449	0	595,697	2010
Occidental Arts and Ecology Center	324,050	6,144	1,165,844	2009
Business Council for Sustainable Development	322,312	0	1,133,554	2009
Potomac Riverkeeper	319,455	0	526,487	2009
Front Range Economic Strategy Center	318,525	0	777,840	2009
Thorne Ecological Institute	317,660	0	391,312	2009
Michigan Land Use Institute	316,319	0	1,201,459	2009
Blue Ridge Environmental Defense League	316,187	2,400	267,811	2009
San Diego Coastkeeper	314,907	0	1,308,664	2009

Groups	Net Assets	Grants Awarded	Annual Revenue	Year
California League of Conservation Voters Education Fund	310,862	0	711,327	2009
Youth for Environmental Sanity	310,781	158,643	944,436	2010
Virginia League of Conservation Voters Education Fund	310,607	0	254,469	2009
Earthworks	309,922	148,900	1,438,657	2009
Air Alliance Houston	307,155	0	413,687	2009
Defenders of Wildlife Action Fund	304,977	8,700	1,225,290	2010
Endangered Species Media Project	302,583	0	94,760	2009
Ohio Valley Environmental Coalition	301,366	68,343	651,084	2009
Ohio Environmental Council	297,983	0	1,480,278	2009
National Caucus of Environmental Legislators	296,845	0	474,249	2008
Architecture 2030	295,344	0	621,410	2009
New Energy Economy	293,356	0	346,403	2010
Gifford Pinchot Task Force	290,933	0	544,514	2009
Innovation Center for Energy and Transportation	290,000	180,000	601,568	2009
Georgia River Network	285,083	117,600	386,974	2009
Southwest Network for Environmental and Economic Justice	282,081	0	286,959	2009

Groups	Net Assets	Grants Awarded	Annual Revenue	Year
Dovetail Partners	281,414	0	256,572	2009
Friends of the Riverfront	280,109	0	292,483	2009
Friends of the Forest Preserves	278,209	0	562,870	2009
Save the Rainforest	276,085	0	357,795	2010
Alaska Conservation Alliance	268,526	0	675,168	2009
Natural Resources Council of America	265,660	49,008	84,125	2008
Tennessee Clean Water Network	262,342	0	143,350	2009
Women's Environment and Development Organization	260,372	0	1,840,543	2009
Sky Island Alliance	257,508	0	902,665	2009
Evangelical Environmental Network	255,433	0	611,886	2010
Craighead Environmental Research Institute	245,300	102,843	384,859	2009
Clean Air Watch	243,882	0	216,916	2009
Climate Law and Policy Project	239,562	0	8,408	2008
Northeast States for Coordinated Air Use Management	233,607	0	7,112,198	2009
Earth Ministry	231,718	0	192,524	2009
Montana Environmental Information Center	229,817	0	504,057	2009
Ecologic Institute	229,624	0	366,509	2009

Groups	Net Assets	Grants Awarded	Annual Revenue	Year
Greenaction for Health and Environmental Justice	229,520	0	201,907	2009
Coalition for a Livable Future	224,245	0	362,763	2009
Cleveland National Forest Foundation	223,567	0	49,110	2010
1,000 Friends of Oregon	222,499	0	1,096,117	2010
Maryland League of Conservation Voters Education Fund	215,602	0	215,326	2009
EcoAmerica	213,169	0	1,682,551	2009
Two Rivers Institute	210,323	0	135,361	2008
Izaak Walton League of America	210,241	0	33,257	2009
Environment Oregon Research and Policy Center	205,352	28,893	156,544	2009
Will Steger Foundation	204,642	0	448,733	2010
Energy Programs Consortium	204,544	0	905,453	2009
1% for the Planet	203,448	0	830,852	2009
Baton Rouge Economic and Agricultural Development Alliance	196,486	0	336,974	2009
Environmental Federation of Oregon	193,041	497,349	753,493	2010
Southeast Energy Efficiency Alliance	190,446	0	452,666	2009
Columbia Riverkeeper	187,495	0	357,662	2009
International Union for Conservation of Nature and Natural Resources	187,113	1,055,435	653,963	2009

Groups	Net Assets	Grants Awarded	Annual Revenue	Year
Committee for the Great Salt Pond	184,854	0	151,079	2009
Lake Worth Lagoon Environmental Defense Fund	184,731	0	156,506	2009
Northeast States Center for a Clean Air Future	182,942	0	912,164	2009
Kentucky Environmental Foundation	180,777	0	590,757	2009
Chesapeake Research Consortium	180,520	1,974,347	3,135,340	2009
Flint River Watershed Coalition	180,167	0	259,652	2009
Salt Pond Coalition	179,457	0	128,477	2010
Baton Rouge Green	178,767	0	422,654	2009
Earth Sangha	174,609	0	192,940	2009
Renewable Energy Alaska Project	174,239	0	253,539	2008
Clean Water Network	168,942	0	222,009	2009
Friends of the Bay	165,002	0	160,039	2009
Indigenous Environmental Network	161,001	338,678	672,467	2007
Lands Council	159,865	0	474,223	2009
Earthteam	147,117	0	373,036	2010
San Francisco Community Power Cooperative	146,991	0	678,003	2009
Citizens League for Environmental Action Now	140,770	0	57,965	2009

Groups	Net Assets	Grants Awarded	Annual Revenue	Year
White River Partnership	140,371	0	200,919	2009
Utah Rivers Council	139,174	0	189,826	2009
Amigos de Bolsa Chica	138,690	0	49,580	2009
1,000 Friends of New Mexico	136,648	196,702	236,804	2008
Futurewise	133,888	0	684,282	2009
Indiana Recycling Coalition	131,991	0	250,256	2009
Action Pajaro Valley	131,173	0	51,771	2010
Rainforest2Reef	127,836	0	515,974	2009
Rainforest Nations Conservation Alliance	126,738	0	2,005,640	2009
Utah Environmental Congress	122,826	0	159,403	2009
Vermont Public Interest Research Group Education Fund	120,188	0	474,718	2009
Shark River Cleanup Coalition	119,607	0	13,554	2009
Kootenai Environmental Alliance	117,269	0	179,241	2009
Foundation for Sustainable Development	117,090	85,000	210,500	2009
Health In Harmony	116,979	182,715	327,687	2009
PCL Foundation	116,569	0	413,908	2009
China-U.S. Energy Efficiency Alliance	115,152	0	155,738	2009
East Coast Greenway Alliance	114,962	0	441,828	2009
Tree Musketeers	114,868	0	408,436	2009
ExLoco	112,361	0	292,626	2009

Groups	Net Assets	Grants Awarded	Annual Revenue	Year
Environmental Action Committee of West Marin	111,964	0	177,865	2008
Bootstraps to Share of Tucson	111,712	0	141,779	2009
Alaska Center for the Environment	110,492	0	1,292,609	2009
Coalition for Rainforest Nations Secretariat	109,224	0	404,829	2009
Planning and Conservation League	108,505	0	576,627	2009
Alabama Rivers Alliance	106,858	0	177,598	2009
Western North Carolina Alliance	105,987	0	315,610	2009
CEIBA Foundation for Tropical Conservation	105,711	0	393,783	2009
Green Media Toolshed	103,916	0	623,416	2009
Klamath Riverkeeper	103,230	0	137,991	2010
Rock Creek Alliance	102,569	65,519	167,918	2009
Marion Institute	101,128	0	1,913,658	2009
Tri-Valley Communities Against a Radioactive Environment	98,876	0	264,109	2009
A Rocha USA	98,748	284,323	377,499	2009
Oregon Shores Conservation Coalition	96,646	0	189,650	2009
Alliance for International Reforestation	94,775	0	94,576	2009
Earth Friends	94,676	0	193	2009
Prairie Stewardship Network	93,243	0	232,108	2009

Groups	Net Assets	Grants Awarded	Annual Revenue	Year
Citizens Environmental Coalition Educational Fund	92,755	0	166,641	2009
Aspen Global Change Institute	92,091	0	381,496	2009
Texas Rice Industry Coalition for the Environment	88,089	0	226,980	2009
Improving Kids Environment	88,064	0	504,834	2010
Great Basin Resource Watch	86,600	0	131,528	2009
Rivers Coalition Defense Fund	84,952	0	36,517	2010
Friends of the Cedar River Watershed	84,864	0	250,014	2008
Citizens for a Healthy Bay	84,740	0	412,719	2009
New Jersey Highlands Coalition	84,468	0	315,519	2010
Louisiana Environmental Action Network	79,740	0	380,898	2009
International Biochar Initiative	79,587	0	587,060	2010
Dakota Rural Action	79,063	0	390,436	2009
Ancient Forest International	76,650	5,000	18,109	2008
West Virginia Rivers Coalition	76,525	24,762	166,998	2009
Dairy Industry Environmental Coalition	69,896	0	1,110,797	2009

Groups	Net Assets	Grants Awarded	Annual Revenue	Year
Clean Water for North Carolina	69,519	0	146,219	2009
Securing America's Future Energy Foundation	68,974	293,726	3,793,309	2009
Washington Citizens for Resource Conservation	67,450	0	128,829	2009
Rainforest International	67,367	0	109,642	2009
Little Village Environmental Justice Organization	67,155	0	268,501	2009
Center for Resource Solutions	66,887	0	2,040,375	2009
1Sky	66,613	50,000	19,012	2010
Vermont Sustainable Jobs Fund	65,137	277,781	793,135	2009
State Environmental Leadership Program	64,049	235,414	144,852	2009
Alabama Clean Water Partnership	61,532	0	675,135	2009
Jackson-Macon Conservation Alliance	61,231	10,000	69,960	2009
Womens Health and Environmental Network	57,327	0	119,284	2009
Idaho Smart Growth	56,864	0	101,813	2009
Environmental Stewardship	54,649	0	120,049	2009
Rivers Alliance of Connecticut	54,551	42,895	108,947	2009
Alabama Coastal Foundation	53,740	0	115,001	2009

Groups	Net Assets	Grants Awarded	Annual Revenue	Year
Rainforest Partnership	52,492	0	83,652	2009
Urban Agenda	51,179	0	397,367	2009
New Mexico Recycling Coalition	50,620	0	131,549	2009
KAHEA: The Hawaiian Environmental Alliance	49,776	0	164,535	2010
Altamaha Riverkeeper	48,952	0	266,200	2009
Civic Engagement Fund	47,531	175,000	72	2009
Land Empowerment Animals People	47,296	309,600	512,582	2009
Sustainable Obtainable Solutions	46,492	0	121,653	2009
EcoAdapt	46,470	0	48,306	2008
Community In-Power and Development Association	45,498	320,000	491,000	2009
Presbyterians for Earth Care	45,207	0	23,767	2009
Conservation Action Fund for Education	43,992	0	54,471	2009
Croton Watershed Clean Water Coalition	43,762	0	171,550	2009
Focus the Nation	43,077	0	211,182	2010
Green House Network	43,077	0	211,182	2010
Alabama Environmental Council	42,898	0	189,732	2009
Alaska Marine Conservation	42,031	42,000	674,104	2009
Resurrection Bay Conservation Alliance	41,542	0	79,261	2009
Massachusetts Rivers Alliance	40,470	0	95,625	2009

Groups	Net Assets	Grants Awarded	Annual Revenue	Year
Quaker Earthcare Witness	39,539	3,561	105,250	2010
Environmental Federation of New York	39,352	954,736	1,182,543	2010
Bay Area Environmental Research Institute	37,551	0	4,534,133	2009
Carolinas Clean Air Coalition	37,498	0	160,615	2009
Sustainable Biodiesel Alliance	36,589	0	231,022	2009
Las Lianas Resource Center for Science Culture and Environment	35,973	36,418	64,759	2009
Orion Society	32,724	0	1,459,455	2009
Bonobo Conservation Initiative	32,221	0	477,923	2009
Baltimore Harbor Waterkeeper	31,480	0	39,298	2009
Rainforest Conservation Fund	29,620	23,700	77,031	2009
EarthReports	28,871	0	181,902	2009
Climate Cycle	28,172	0	104,912	2009
A World Institute for a Sustainable Humanity	26,976	0	166,407	2010
Kudzu Coalition	25,358	0	33,690	2009
Androscoggin River Alliance	25,246	0	45,057	2009
Sierra Madre Alliance	24,554	92,233	214,144	2009
High Road for Human Rights Education Project	24,408	0	328,077	2009

Groups	Net Assets	Grants Awarded	Annual Revenue	Year
Cayuga Lake Watershed Network	24,305	0	78,353	2009
Arizona League of Conservation Voters Education Fund	24,001	0	77,024	2009
Central Oregon Landwatch	22,235	0	132,138	2009
Sustainable Seattle	21,616	14,761	122,423	2009
Climate Lab	21,140	0	90,083	2009
Blaine County Citizens for Smart Growth	19,817	278	64,790	2010
Friends of the Earth Action	19,388	0	196,056	2009
Trout Unlimited	18,881	11,560	21,300	2009
Environment New Jersey Research and Policy Center	18,507	1,547	202,066	2009
Redefining Progress	17,814	1,069,774	1,318,374	2008
Climate Institute	17,799	0	253,754	2009
New Voice of Business	17,257	0	166,214	2009
Connecticut Coalition for Environmental Justice	17,131	0	333,532	2009
Wild Fund	16,094	45,167	103,281	2009
Oregon Toxics Alliance	15,441	0	80,443	2009
Advocates for Community Empowerment	12,201	0	28,602	2008
Coalition for Affordable Housing and the Environment	11,990	0	32,889	2010
Institute for Sustainability Education and Ecology	11,961	0	106,080	2009

Groups	Net Assets	Grants Awarded	Annual Revenue	Year
Governors' Biofuels Coalition	11,878	0	203,956	2009
1,000 Friends of Connecticut	11,663	0	98,023	2009
Kentucky Resources Council	11,420	5,000	241,124	2010
Friends of the Nature Conservancy of Canada	10,618	2,134,233	1,464,657	2010
Sustainable Travel International	9,892	0	1,088,699	2009
Artists Alliance of North Florida, Floridas Eden	8,585	0	125,967	2009
Alaska Community Action on Toxics	8,103	0	870,057	2009
Skylands CLEAN	7,509	0	63,019	2009
Envirolution	6,782	0	49,901	2009
Pace Environmental Litigation Clinic	5,920	0	10,035	2010
Massachusetts Watershed Coalition	4,193	0	41,270	2009
Southeast Environmental Task Force	3,579	0	42,915	2009
Iowa Environmental Council	2,929	0	494,190	2009
United Growth for Kent County	2,252	0	3,097	2010
Greater Cincinnati Earth Coalition	2,203	0	2,347	2009
GIS Institute	2,133	0	33,080	2009
Land Is Life	945	222,210	324,889	2009
Rainforest Defense Fund	945	222,210	324,889	2009

Groups	Net Assets	Grants Awarded	Annual Revenue	Year
Amazon Alliance for Indigenous and Traditional Peoples of the Amazon Basin	0	0	198,941	2010
American Lands Alliance	0	0	4,452	2009
Association for the Protection of the Adirondacks	0	0	493,179	2010
Conservation and Preservation Charities of America	0	2,266,827	2,548,811	2010
Grand River Partners	0	0	244,414	2009
Maderas Rainforest Conservancy	−1,776	0	135,009	2009
Save America's Forests Fund	−1,925	59,463	90,635	2009
Sustainable Silicon Valley	−4,387	0	248,441	2010
Build it Green	−8,148	0	2,103,011	2009
Global Justice Ecology Project	−9,072	4,704	189,924	2010
Arizona Wilderness Coalition	−10,922	0	265,154	2010
Greenpeace, Inc.	−16,197	0	26,043,420	2009
Ohio League of Conservation Voters Education Fund	−26,173	0	165,000	2009
Well Network	−31,255	0	394,851	2009
Citizens Environmental Coalition	−43,071	0	128,555	2009
Women's Environmental Institute	−46,316	0	226,677	2009

Groups	Net Assets	Grants Awarded	Annual Revenue	Year
Alliance for Affordable Energy	−47,742	0	530,747	2009
Awareness Society	−53,113	78,853	1,570,206	2010
Neighborhood Network Research Center	−82,074	0	474,221	2008
Californians Against Waste	−130,855	0	180,176	2009
Earth Action Network	−259,600	0	689,593	2010
Climate Registry	−360,917	0	2,712,669	2010
Climate Central	−473,105	0	766,698	2009
Alliance to Protect Nantucket Sound	−568,413	0	1,379,747	2009
Clean Water Action	−1,465,075	0	9,685,616	2009
Blue Planet Run Foundation	−2,811,737	326,939	660,214	2009
National Wildlife Federation	−20,769,974	4,007,437	98,426,951	2010

Total Net Assets: **$9,310,833,507**

Total Grants Awarded: **$553,696,966**

Total Annual Revenues: **$3,562,921,349**

Average Net Assets: **$16,867,452**

Average Grants Awarded: **$1,003,074**

Average Annual Revenues: **$6,454,568**

APPENDIX XI

Comparative Government Funding of Conservative and Progressive Immigration Groups

- Number of conservative immigration groups that receive federal grants, which are against open borders and illegal immigration: **1**
  —Total net assets of government funded conservative immigration groups: **$28,531**
- Number of progressive immigration groups that receive federal grants, which support open borders and illegal immigration: **111**
  —Total net assets of progressive immigration groups that the government funds: **$334.5 million**

SUMMARY: Total net assets of progressive immigration groups that the government funds are over 11,722 times more than the total net assets of conservative immigration groups that the government funds.

- Total federal grants received by the 1 conservative immigration group: **$18,094**
- Total federal grants received by the 111 progressive immigration groups: **$325.3 million**

SUMMARY: The government funds progressive immigration groups over 17,976 times more than it funds conservative immigration groups.

Government Funding of Conservative Immigration Groups

Group	Net Assets	Federal Grants Received	Annual Revenue	Year
National Policy Institute	28,531	18,094	78,831	2009
American Border Patrol	93,500	0	996,145	2009
Americans for Better Immigration	336,658	0	2,497	2009
Americans for Immigration Control	−153,124	0	1,299,877	2010
Center for Immigration Studies	1,651,355	0	1,766,533	2009
English First	336,429	0	73,581	2009
English First Foundation	23,309	0	36,305	2009
Federation for American Immigration Reform	9,041,698	0	5,080,058	2009
New Century Foundation	1,651,391	0	1,185,513	2010
NumbersUSA Foundation	3,225,021	0	3,859,543	2010
U.S. Border Control	306,951	0	369,950	2009
U.S. Border Control Foundation	20,142	0	21,749	2007
U.S. English	250,618	0	3,023,018	2009
U.S. English Foundation	241,008	0	517,049	2009

Group	Net Assets	Federal Grants Received	Annual Revenue	Year
Lexington Research Institute (aka Vdare Foundation)	20,479	0	377,833	2009

Total Net Assets: $17,073,966

Total Federal Grants Received: $18,094

Total Annual Revenues: $18,688,482

Average Net Assets: $1,138,264

Average Federal Grants Received: $1,206

Average Annual Revenues: $1,245,899

Government Funding of Progressive
Immigration Groups

Groups	Net Assets	Federal Grants Received	Annual Revenue	Year
Redlands Christian Migrant Association	23,647,481	58,303,251	61,072,478	2010
Church World Service (Immigration and Refugee Program)	10,057,302	35,567,657	82,412,807	2010
American Bar Association Fund for Justice and Education	13,045,692	34,955,262	51,389,525	2009
World Relief	20,599,131	32,701,335	56,683,191	2010
U.S. Committee for Refugees and Immigrants	4,891,542	22,875,403	24,124,720	2009
Northwest Justice Project	3,475,812	19,037,773	19,574,388	2010
Latin American Youth Center	2,071,891	9,573,975	14,613,180	2010
Bronx Defenders	3,472,415	9,139,650	10,351,256	2010
Community Action Agency of Southern New Mexico	1,579,947	9,048,786	9,280,775	2010
Heartland Alliance for Human Needs and Human Rights	13,866,331	7,091,370	13,537,188	2010

Groups	Net Assets	Federal Grants Received	Annual Revenue	Year
Catholic Council for the Spanish Speaking of the Diocese of Stockton	999,979	6,883,572	7,780,263	2010
Illinois Coalition for Immigrant and Refugee Rights	2,105,550	6,317,555	8,358,006	2010
Urban Justice Center	11,793,687	5,582,986	9,116,463	2010
Asian Americans for Community Involvement	6,953,212	5,475,850	12,435,958	2010
National Council of La Raza	46,562,332	5,136,535	36,996,267	2009
Casa de Maryland	12,815,589	4,966,948	11,916,615	2010
Legal Services of South Central Michigan	1,762,594	4,633,647	5,668,579	2009
Urban League, Minneapolis	6,544,110	3,367,046	4,954,185	2009
Comite de Bienestar	11,623,631	3,306,460	6,425,754	2009
Centro Campesino Farmworker Center	1,158,001	3,020,555	5,825,335	2009
Spanish Catholic Center	2,814,924	2,367,209	4,468,978	2010
Americas Promise—The Alliance for Youth	26,495,452	2,068,616	11,237,114	2009
Make the Road New York	2,491,316	1,928,863	6,005,778	2009
California Rural Legal Assistance Foundation	3,031,314	1,805,661	2,119,781	2010
Hispanic Federation	5,174,349	1,776,887	4,645,692	2010
Florida Immigrant Advocacy Center	487,161	1,668,450	4,201,019	2009

Groups	Net Assets	Federal Grants Received	Annual Revenue	Year
Michigan Nonprofit Association (Michigan Participation Project)	3,897,612	1,611,031	7,494,079	2010
Asian Law Caucus	916,747	1,478,405	1,982,664	2010
San Francisco Bar Association Volunteer Legal Services Program	1,543,817	1,457,109	3,741,592	2009
New York State Defenders Association (Immigrant Defense Project)	820,868	1,315,879	2,026,336	2010
Casa Latina	2,209,402	1,262,332	1,827,195	2009
Neighborhood Development Center	8,285,670	1,004,047	4,091,022	2009
Welcoming Center for New Pennsylvanians	354,979	924,959	1,341,433	2010
Pacific News Service	3,111,402	900,000	11,266,846	2009
East Bay Community Law Center	4,146,681	885,362	3,084,359	2010
Fresno Center for New Americans	130,618	838,237	1,501,379	2010
Northwest Immigrant Rights Project	1,503,246	816,608	3,178,017	2009
Tahirih Justice Center	1,092,374	805,228	1,797,120	2009
Mattie Rhodes Center	1,654,407	726,041	1,943,575	2009
Immigrants Rights Advocacy Center	183,503	722,275	1,049,036	2008
Farmworker Legal Services of New York	82,187	715,169	746,263	2009
Migration Policy Institute	7,452,930	665,126	3,539,796	2010
Migizi Communications	878,129	655,412	1,131,189	2009

Groups	Net Assets	Federal Grants Received	Annual Revenue	Year
Farmworker Justice Fund	984,469	504,784	1,638,224	2009
Legal Aid Justice Center	2,069,457	501,778	4,410,131	2010
Farmworker Association of Florida	376,246	461,355	888,387	2009
Puente de la Costa Sur	158,240	437,944	931,993	2010
OneAmerica	1,290,334	423,886	2,149,571	2010
El Puente Community Development Corporation	162,238	410,796	952,456	2009
Ayuda	155,751	363,294	1,717,631	2009
Catholic Legal Immigration Network	3,965,450	344,945	5,737,585	2009
Centro Romero	671,582	343,250	1,315,043	2009
AnewAmerica Community Corporation	757,697	326,353	1,390,759	2009
Southwest Public Workers Union	359,041	320,927	474,906	2009
Immigrant Law Center of Minnesota	897,319	295,482	1,631,734	2010
Centro Legal de la Raza	126,219	294,263	1,635,354	2010
Legal Services for Children	996,484	292,368	1,844,642	2010
New York Immigration Coalition	1,573,646	255,268	2,294,592	2010
Refugee Women's Network	409,806	245,000	425,927	2010
MADRE	1,769,723	230,406	1,910,770	2009
Mano a Mano Family Resource Center Foundation	527,955	216,416	511,502	2010

Groups	Net Assets	Federal Grants Received	Annual Revenue	Year
Central American Resource Center of Southern California	2,786,969	199,414	1,296,087	2009
New Mexico Center on Law and Poverty	760,425	184,747	702,840	2010
Nebraska Appleseed Center for Law in the Public Interest	570,871	183,350	909,423	2009
Marion County Commission on Youth	528,285	177,211	869,578	2009
Institute for Family Development, Centro Familia	2,021	176,535	181,869	2010
Northwest Workers Justice Project	30,806	168,947	177,130	2009
Organization of the NorthEast	533,453	164,341	959,480	2010
Mujeres Unidas y Activas	1,619,174	153,507	1,451,503	2009
Cielo Project Radio Ranch	63,861	149,237	268,525	2009
Just Neighbors Ministry	129,177	136,010	691,312	2009
West Town Leadership United	11,286	131,672	197,068	2010
Lawyers' Committee for Civil Rights of the San Francisco Bay Area	2,146,371	121,375	2,278,872	2010
Immigrant Legal Resource Center	2,724,497	108,180	2,812,915	2009
Refugee & Immigrant Center for Education & Legal Services	135,478	107,266	457,252	2009
Housing Preservation Project	718,731	106,524	913,289	2009

Groups	Net Assets	Federal Grants Received	Annual Revenue	Year
La Escuelita	123,064	100,439	400,681	2008
Latin American Coalition—Coalicion Latinoamericana	134,263	90,250	994,754	2010
National Immigration Law Center	4,725,938	83,005	5,817,845	2010
Centro del Obrero Fronterizo—La Mujer Obrera	636,248	82,823	272,989	2009
Hispanic Advocacy and Community Empowerment through Research	26,019	77,892	121,095	2009
Centro de los Derechos del Migrante	178,512	77,886	301,310	2009
Immigrant Workers Citizenship Project	7,753	74,022	75,510	2009
Entre Hermanos	61,465	72,843	333,638	2009
United Farm Workers Foundation	332,870	70,000	223,912	2009
Legal Services of North Carolina	681,395	60,076	310,076	2009
Grantmakers Without Borders	16,112	58,385	226,182	2009
Carnegie Endowment for International Peace	224,284,273	55,000	16,570,518	2010
East L.A. Community Corporation	6,590,146	51,817	2,795,526	2010
Coalition of African, Arab, Asian, European and Latino Immigrants of Illinois	107,104	43,614	589,642	2010
Mississippi Immigrants Rights Alliance	159,835	38,570	416,996	2010

Groups	Net Assets	Federal Grants Received	Annual Revenue	Year
La Union del Pueblo Entero	217,223	38,530	912,122	2009
Metropolitan Community Development Corporation	28,285	34,938	108,538	2009
Zocalo	411,591	32,972	381,141	2009
Colorado Progressive Coalition	161,173	30,000	792,583	2010
Appleseed Foundation	1,885,552	27,475	1,776,757	2010
Las Americas Immigrant Advocacy Center	378,860	26,120	232,400	2010
National Organizers Alliance	175,964	25,571	37,349	2010
Public Policy and Education Fund of New York	120,017	25,250	1,384,743	2009
People Escaping Poverty Project	7,676	23,268	146,939	2009
Mission Asset Fund	1,192,688	20,000	382,838	2009
National Day Laborer Organizing Network	1,318,058	19,700	1,230,215	2010
LatinoJustice— PRLDEF	1,680,380	16,699	2,813,100	2010
Organizing Apprenticeship Project	257,276	13,970	428,736	2009
Latin American Legal Defense and Educational Fund	13,471	9,371	41,996	2010
National Network for Immigrant and Refugee Rights	32,029	9,224	245,938	2009

Groups	Net Assets	Federal Grants Received	Annual Revenue	Year
National Association of Latino Elected and Appointed Officials Educational Fund	4,198,043	5,500	6,544,704	2009
Mano a Mano Mexican Culture Without Borders	22,978	4,620	97,442	2009
Interfaith Funders	40,930	2,900	77,863	2010
Hispanic Resource Center of Larchmont and Mamaroneck	351,386	2,401	421,793	2009
Arab American Action Network	186,413	1,855	449,946	2009
Latino Union of Chicago	199,394	1,569	326,722	2009

Total Net Assets: $334,458,490

Total Federal Grants Received: $325,274,908

Total Annual Revenues: $614,679,567

Average Net Assets: $3,013,140

Average Federal Grants Received: $2,930,405

Average Annual Revenues: $5,537,654

Comparative Government Funding of Conservative and Progressive Environmental Groups

- Number of federally funded conservative environmental groups that promote market-friendly solutions: **7**
  —Total net assets of conservative environmental groups that the government funds: **$359,324**
- Number of federally funded progressive environmental groups that promote radical antibusiness views: **246**
  —Total net assets of progressive environmental groups that the government funds: **$8.75 billion**

SUMMARY: **Total net assets of progressive environmental groups that the government funds are over 24,350 times more than the total net assets of conservative environmental groups that the government funds.**

- Total federal grants received by the 7 conservative environmental groups: **$728,118**
- Total federal grants received by the 247 progressive environmental groups: **$568.5 million**

SUMMARY: **The government funds progressive environmental groups over 780 times more than they fund conservative environmental groups.**

Government Funding of Conservative Environmental Groups

Group	Net Assets	Federal Grants Received	Annual Revenue	Year
American Recreation Coalition	−37,759	423,240	728,268	2009
Oregonians in Action	26,375	197,547	288,238	2009
Oregonians for Food and Shelter	154,879	53,580	427,554	2009
Doctors for Disaster Preparedness	90,665	35,123	58,633	2010
Oregonians in Action Education Center	67,750	11,175	52,400	2009
Institute for Sustainable Forestry	43,648	6,978	60,333	2009
Women In Mining Education Foundation	13,766	475	9,111	2010
Alaska Support Industry Alliance	740,484	0	522,683	2010
Alliance for a Responsible CFC Policy	192,079	0	653,783	2009
American Coalition for Clean Coal Electricity	9,183,016	0	53,733,277	2009
American Council on Science and Health	3,006,728	0	2,364,878	2010
Americans for Balanced Energy Choices	0	0	0	2008
Blue Ribbon Coalition	−89,991	0	954,141	2009

Group	Net Assets	Federal Grants Received	Annual Revenue	Year
Center for Consumer Freedom	1,289,224	0	8,052,437	2009
Committee for a Constructive Tomorrow	439,751	0	3,071,277	2009
Defenders of Property Rights	0	0	5,414	2007
Foundation for Research on Economics and the Environment	1,515,684	0	840,644	2009
Hill Country Alliance	113,061	0	175,561	2009
Institute for Energy Research	699,698	0	2,266,196	2009
Keep America Beautiful	7,653,203	0	10,301,311	2009
Klamath Alliance for Resources and Environment	25,599	0	27,288	2010
Mountain States Legal Foundation	4,648,588	0	2,411,521	2010
National Federal Lands Conference	4,066,277	0	127,026	2010
North Carolina Fisheries Association	66,049	0	212,813	2010
Oregon Institute of Science and Medicine	4,303,197	0	489,226	2009
Oregonians in Action Fund	933,678	0	11,406	2010
Oregonians in Action Legal Center	31,654	0	198,445	2009
Political Economy Research Center	2,842,374	0	2,460,348	2009
Public Lands Council	434,456	0	206,105	2010
Science & Environmental Policy Project	1,584,123	0	251,584	2010

Group	Net Assets	Federal Grants Received	Annual Revenue	Year
South Texans Property Rights Association	33,408	0	190,021	2010
Taxpayers for Common Sense	589,184	0	1,094,592	2009
Women In Mining—California	35,848	0	8,943	2010
Women In Mining National	23,492	0	1,512	2010

Total Net Assets: $44,720,188

Total Federal Grants Received: $728,118

Total Annual Revenues: $92,256,969

Average Net Assets: $1,315,300

Average Federal Grants Received: $21,415

Average Annual Revenues: $2,713,440

Government Funding of Progressive Environmental Groups

Groups	Net Assets	Federal Grants Received	Annual Revenue	Year
Nature Conservancy	4,879,283,936	122,450,349	925,817,441	2010
Wildlife Conservation Society	631,569,794	71,458,821	197,345,941	2009
Winrock International	59,554,956	47,414,980	58,766,249	2008
World Wildlife Fund	238,133,260	40,436,468	177,738,454	2010
Conservation Fund	402,062,886	30,762,978	186,700,491	2009
Internews Network	629,989	30,745,460	33,098,734	2009
Structured Employment Economic Development Corporation	5,370,722	28,081,802	46,754,751	2009
Trust For Public Land	191,996,820	26,298,567	127,670,275	2010
Conservation International	219,835,215	15,578,864	63,651,042	2010
Midwest Energy Efficiency Alliance	991,054	13,242,210	14,923,934	2010
Institute for Sustainable Communities	3,674,329	10,931,006	14,030,981	2010
Rainforest Alliance	4,510,417	7,539,848	32,810,981	2009
National Audubon Society	255,712,728	7,054,069	74,008,085	2009
Points of Light Institute	4,336,733	6,434,238	31,234,333	2009

Groups	Net Assets	Federal Grants Received	Annual Revenue	Year
Bay Area Environmental Research Institute	37,551	4,483,180	4,534,133	2009
World Resources Institute	53,435,050	4,397,908	39,871,632	2010
NatureServe	7,524,843	4,282,176	9,940,117	2009
Woods Hole Research Center	22,570,799	4,077,719	19,462,864	2009
American Rivers	7,914,312	3,688,003	12,105,943	2010
Chesapeake Research Consortium	180,520	2,953,366	3,135,340	2009
Alliance to Save Energy	1,756,114	2,853,092	12,130,202	2009
Environmental Defense Fund	132,197,665	2,756,786	54,893,658	2010
Los Angeles and San Gabriel Rivers Watershed Council	860,851	2,604,941	3,167,254	2010
Community Partners	14,825,480	2,542,393	14,671,638	2010
Shorebank Enterprise Cascadia	12,449,403	2,537,209	6,212,643	2009
Resources for the Future	38,611,159	1,830,065	11,187,831	2009
California Rural Legal Assistance Foundation	3,031,314	1,805,661	2,119,781	2010
Restore America's Estuaries	1,056,917	1,773,596	1,183,835	2009
Save the Bay	7,497,116	1,765,906	3,423,572	2010
Land Trust Alliance	7,978,772	1,738,950	9,586,693	2009
Global Rights	3,157,908	1,718,890	7,116,215	2009
International Center	2,692,128	1,667,769	2,214,321	2009
Minnesota Environmental Initiative	900,416	1,443,348	2,102,585	2009

Groups	Net Assets	Federal Grants Received	Annual Revenue	Year
Women's Environment and Development Organization	260,372	1,415,975	1,840,543	2009
Active Transportation Alliance	1,021,266	1,410,704	3,574,030	2009
Northeast States for Coordinated Air Use Management	233,607	1,409,994	7,112,198	2009
Mountain Institute	3,471,083	1,386,453	3,157,550	2009
Forest Trends Association	4,128,379	1,281,127	6,618,050	2009
Ecotrust	22,401,950	1,260,640	15,173,919	2009
Earth Day Network	3,772,477	1,250,500	4,550,337	2009
Local Government Commission	831,004	1,202,226	1,989,563	2009
American Farmland Trust	20,049,808	1,166,726	9,771,008	2010
Organization for Tropical Studies	14,432,864	1,085,911	9,171,302	2010
Biomass Energy Resource Center	340,990	997,499	1,561,299	2009
Regional Plan Association	2,843,111	981,025	4,535,205	2010
Reconnecting America	1,626,055	929,836	4,740,666	2009
Northeast-Midwest Institute	2,793,995	903,829	1,860,307	2009
Environmental Law Institute	6,237,426	899,795	5,111,200	2009
Southeast Alaska Conservation Council	557,049	825,433	1,046,994	2009
Earth Conservation Corps	1,186,604	821,312	1,669,659	2009
Accokeek Foundation	3,005,242	805,768	1,127,561	2010

Groups	Net Assets	Federal Grants Received	Annual Revenue	Year
Stockholm Environment Institute U.S.	1,805,570	770,512	3,697,633	2009
East Meets West Foundation	9,901,208	758,751	11,991,847	2009
Allegheny Land Trust	10,472,612	753,630	1,098,866	2010
Kingsley Association	12,000,671	719,082	1,277,670	2010
Farmworker Legal Services of New York	82,187	715,169	746,263	2009
Joint Venture—Silicon Valley Network	474,193	699,317	1,671,364	2009
World Media Foundation— Living on Earth	918,922	695,977	2,131,718	2009
Ground Water Protection Council	5,496,785	688,929	1,583,076	2009
Rose Foundation for Communities and the Environment	2,680,346	672,417	2,832,572	2009
Global Philanthropy Partnership	250,047	665,807	1,160,807	2009
Bay Institute of San Francisco	1,517,128	654,644	1,644,307	2009
Living Planet	967,507	650,273	2,898,723	2009
Institute for Governance and Sustainable Development	903,310	647,575	2,568,537	2010
International Humanities Center	919,415	645,128	6,235,623	2008
Adirondack Land Trust/ Nature Conservancy	14,807,221	619,183	2,027,281	2010
Earth Island Institute	6,498,989	598,738	11,188,273	2009
Energy Action Coalition	6,498,989	598,738	11,188,273	2009

Groups	Net Assets	Federal Grants Received	Annual Revenue	Year
Natural Resources Defense Council	181,427,464	576,466	96,971,952	2010
TransForm	2,029,002	573,764	2,377,507	2009
Res Publica	146,976	558,224	1,555,736	2009
ICLEI—Local Governments for Sustainability USA	1,939,115	554,551	4,553,618	2009
Save San Francisco Bay Association	2,269,609	549,882	2,597,574	2009
Farmworker Justice Fund	984,469	504,784	1,638,224	2009
National Geographic Society	724,542,997	504,780	445,138,171	2009
Passaic River Coalition	10,596,683	491,281	805,972	2010
Improving Kids Environment	88,064	479,149	504,834	2010
Earth Force	1,109,251	477,995	1,657,507	2009
Alaska Center for the Environment	110,492	474,420	1,292,609	2009
Amazon Conservation Association	3,480,484	471,069	2,900,166	2009
West Harlem Environmental Action	1,307,105	464,887	1,992,754	2009
Farmworker Association of Florida	376,246	461,355	888,387	2009
Green Building Alliance	1,800,573	456,646	1,498,063	2009
James River Association	1,644,510	452,048	1,504,052	2009
Agricultural Stewardship Association	957,163	446,568	942,363	2010
Bronx River Alliance	949,299	445,842	1,605,101	2009
Sierra Nevada Alliance	533,958	445,181	839,770	2010

Groups	Net Assets	Federal Grants Received	Annual Revenue	Year
Environmental Coalition of South Seattle	495,883	426,441	816,069	2009
Smart Growth America	4,264,895	411,653	3,464,934	2010
Connecticut Fund for the Environment	4,859,739	407,886	2,370,583	2009
Dairy Center for Strategic Innovation and Collaboration	25,863	400,470	400,470	2009
Environmental Health Coalition	1,144,455	399,795	1,946,061	2010
Alabama Clean Water Partnership	61,532	396,931	675,135	2009
Adopt-A-Stream Foundation	1,534,602	396,645	452,158	2010
Penobscot River Restoration Trust	9,959,880	358,718	2,234,880	2009
National Wildlife Federation	-20,769,974	352,211	98,426,951	2010
Inuit Circumpolar Conference	623,518	350,000	1,503,442	2009
River Alliance of Wisconsin	457,225	341,131	695,345	2010
San Diego Coastkeeper	314,907	337,136	1,308,664	2009
Healthy African American Families	0	336,147	340,175	2008
National Wildlife Refuge Association	781,042	319,727	1,353,472	2010
Trust for Conservation Innovation	5,847,165	315,118	8,262,039	2009
Defenders of Wildlife	23,675,323	292,750	32,595,370	2010
Upstate Forever	2,042,872	290,212	1,322,692	2009

Groups	Net Assets	Federal Grants Received	Annual Revenue	Year
Southern Alliance for Clean Energy	1,412,285	287,655	3,477,277	2009
Sustainable Conservation	2,652,652	285,227	2,094,883	2009
Pacific News Service	1,400,921	284,298	5,470,919	2009
Work Environment Council of New Jersey	585,239	263,807	631,368	2009
Energy Programs Consortium	204,544	256,854	905,453	2009
Appalachia Ohio Alliance	1,809,009	253,105	570,308	2009
Baton Rouge Economic and Agricultural Development Alliance	196,486	250,087	336,974	2009
Santa Monica Baykeeper	411,225	243,423	789,421	2009
Ocean Conservancy	15,297,626	241,149	15,358,961	2009
North Cascades Institute	4,334,278	237,677	2,107,513	2009
Rainforest2Reef	127,836	228,391	515,974	2009
Salzburg Global Seminar	10,482,781	226,199	5,829,387	2009
Sustainable Silicon Valley	-4,387	221,328	248,441	2010
Center for A New American Dream	488,093	208,501	502,792	2009
Institute for Social and Environmental Transition	405,597	207,184	2,073,941	2009
Delaware Nature Society	38,350,688	204,094	2,075,643	2009
Audubon Nature Institute	7,333,618	197,617	25,326,607	2009
Bridging the Gap	1,859,336	183,270	1,231,744	2010

Groups	Net Assets	Federal Grants Received	Annual Revenue	Year
Climate Central	−473,105	182,099	766,698	2009
Dovetail Partners	281,414	178,530	256,572	2009
Yampa Valley Land Trust	4,992,878	177,341	3,497,062	2009
San Francisco Community Power Cooperative	146,991	176,757	678,003	2009
Sustainable Northwest	1,186,571	176,624	1,819,247	2010
Resource Innovation Group	974,558	172,922	850,549	2009
Affordable Comfort	510,286	172,500	2,245,274	2010
Coalition for Utah's Future	1,603,103	170,000	1,220,264	2009
Build it Green	−8,148	166,034	2,103,011	2009
Organization of the NorthEast	533,453	164,341	959,480	2010
Thorne Ecological Institute	317,660	163,931	391,312	2009
Climate Institute	17,799	158,250	253,754	2009
River Network	1,022,405	155,613	2,041,802	2010
California Wilderness Coalition	484,117	154,326	587,730	2009
Center for Neighborhood Technology	1,564,673	148,244	3,806,642	2009
West Michigan Environmental Action Council	1,138,423	148,100	390,306	2010
Model Forest Policy Program	442,910	142,999	443,002	2010
WildAid	678,610	140,056	2,079,021	2009
Maderas Rainforest Conservancy	−1,776	134,509	135,009	2009

Groups	Net Assets	Federal Grants Received	Annual Revenue	Year
Delaware Riverkeeper Network	342,119	132,511	1,077,844	2009
On the Commons	1,151,778	131,705	582,969	2009
Two Rivers Institute	210,323	127,296	135,361	2008
Women's Environmental Institute	−46,316	124,588	226,677	2009
Pacific Environment	2,672,333	123,353	2,678,572	2010
Social and Environmental Entrepreneurs	2,432,812	119,894	3,279,853	2009
Quivira Coalition	1,927,723	117,285	614,665	2009
Indiana Recycling Coalition	131,991	116,739	250,256	2009
Lake Worth Lagoon Environmental Defense Fund	184,731	111,405	156,506	2009
Concerned Citizens of Tillery	6,388	110,511	189,646	2009
Friends of the Earth Action	19,388	109,745	196,056	2009
Friends of the Cedar River Watershed	84,864	108,923	250,014	2008
Environmental Law Alliance Worldwide	1,208,601	107,350	1,216,847	2009
White River Partnership	140,371	104,474	200,919	2009
Center for Clean Air Policy	529,257	101,993	4,604,393	2009
Belgrade Regional Conservation Alliance	1,470,657	100,346	447,538	2009
Sustainable Obtainable Solutions	46,492	100,008	121,653	2009
Wildlands Conservancy, Inc.	3,796,541	99,891	3,833,472	2009

Groups	Net Assets	Federal Grants Received	Annual Revenue	Year
Environmental Stewardship	54,649	87,225	120,049	2009
Friends of the Riverfront	280,109	84,913	292,483	2009
Tamarisk Coalition	537,959	83,190	1,024,879	2009
Clean Energy Group	336,449	82,500	595,697	2010
Cascadia Region Green Building Council	781,733	81,516	2,172,092	2009
Puget Soundkeeper Alliance	682,799	80,899	482,058	2009
Friends of the Forest Preserves	278,209	77,500	562,870	2009
Artists Alliance of North Florida, Florida's Eden	8,585	72,644	125,967	2009
Coalition to Restore Coastal Louisiana	466,685	72,509	718,438	2009
Occidental Arts and Ecology Center	324,050	70,256	1,165,844	2009
Supportive Housing Network of New York	1,321,317	68,317	1,127,662	2009
Michigan Land Use Institute	316,319	68,058	1,201,459	2009
Baton Rouge Green	178,767	63,407	422,654	2009
Oregon Environmental Council	773,827	61,943	897,174	2010
Washington Toxics Coalition	1,124,624	60,928	1,181,141	2009
Center for Resource Solutions	66,887	58,500	2,040,375	2009
Grand River Partners	0	56,404	244,414	2009
Garrison Institute	110,137	49,743	3,123,372	2009

Groups	Net Assets	Federal Grants Received	Annual Revenue	Year
Guanacaste Dry Forest Conservation Fund	15,854,969	47,507	1,206,183	2009
Center for Energy Efficiency and Renewable Technologies	1,363,599	47,500	3,134,391	2009
Tree Musketeers	114,868	43,965	408,436	2009
Volunteer Center of Silicon Valley	−35,043	41,679	56,913	2010
Flint River Watershed Coalition	180,167	41,197	259,652	2009
Global Green USA	41,075,226	40,351	3,872,324	2009
Energy Consumers Alliance of New England	973,279	38,525	2,458,827	2010
Planning and Conservation League	108,505	38,249	576,627	2009
China-U.S. Energy Efficiency Alliance	115,152	37,500	155,738	2009
National Center for Conservation Science and Policy	740,519	37,050	943,101	2009
Communities for a Better Environment	1,350,493	34,309	2,052,349	2009
Action Pajaro Valley	131,173	33,841	51,771	2010
Sustainable Seattle	21,616	33,135	122,423	2009
Facing the Future: People and the Planet	493,796	31,294	569,320	2009
Global Justice Ecology Project	−9,072	30,644	189,924	2010
East Coast Greenway Alliance	114,962	28,881	441,828	2009
GIS Institute	2,133	28,577	33,080	2009

Groups	Net Assets	Federal Grants Received	Annual Revenue	Year
Western North Carolina Alliance	105,987	26,895	315,610	2009
Aspen Institute	152,052,272	26,402	66,554,008	2009
Bootstraps to Share of Tucson	111,712	26,381	141,779	2009
Alabama Coastal Foundation	53,740	25,056	115,001	2009
SeaWeb	3,706,649	25,000	2,665,207	2009
Land Empowerment Animals People	47,296	25,000	512,582	2009
International Food and Agricultural Trade Policy Council	546,058	23,370	803,595	2009
Scenic Hudson	24,020,478	23,190	6,786,585	2010
Orange County Coastkeeper	594,180	22,307	1,011,333	2009
Clark Fork Coalition	688,554	21,865	618,313	2008
New Mexico Recycling Coalition	50,620	21,610	131,549	2009
Earth Ministry	231,718	21,199	192,524	2009
PCL Foundation	116,569	20,749	413,908	2009
Environmental League of Massachusetts	481,982	20,000	612,230	2010
Hillside Trust	5,260,557	19,672	82,972	2009
State Environmental Leadership Program	64,049	17,761	144,852	2009
A World Institute for a Sustainable Humanity	26,976	17,500	166,407	2010
Metropolitan Waterfront Alliance	428,842	17,228	809,020	2009
Jackson Hole Conservation Alliance	1,421,062	17,227	553,588	2009

Groups	Net Assets	Federal Grants Received	Annual Revenue	Year
Vermont Sustainable Jobs Fund	65,137	15,697	793,135	2009
Keystone Center	2,896,003	15,200	7,487,586	2009
Environmental and Energy Study Institute	2,870,006	15,000	991,078	2009
Connecticut Coalition for Environmental Justice	17,131	14,076	333,532	2009
Organizing Apprenticeship Project	257,276	13,970	428,736	2009
Envirolution	6,782	13,168	49,901	2009
Coalition for a Livable Future	224,245	12,774	362,763	2009
EarthReports	28,871	12,280	181,902	2009
Will Steger Foundation	204,642	12,039	448,733	2010
Clean Water Network	168,942	11,565	222,009	2009
West Virginia Rivers Coalition	76,525	10,684	166,998	2009
Renewable Energy Alaska Project	174,239	10,309	253,539	2008
Futurewise	133,888	10,000	684,282	2009
Southeast Environmental Task Force	3,579	10,000	42,915	2009
Oregon Clean Water Action Project	−1,388	8,031	8,129	2009
Innovation Center for Energy and Transportation	290,000	8,000	601,568	2009
Oregon Shores Conservation Coalition	96,646	5,814	189,650	2009

Groups	Net Assets	Federal Grants Received	Annual Revenue	Year
Alliance for Affordable Energy	−47,742	5,390	530,747	2009
Global Urban Development	8,033	5,000	108,000	2009
Commonwealth Foundation	40,396	4,999	191,044	2009
Columbia Riverkeeper	187,495	4,803	357,662	2009
Montezuma Valley Historical Society	99,478	4,800	69,977	2008
Land Partners Through Stewardship	2,896,518	4,050	661,579	2009
Earth Sangha	174,609	3,811	192,940	2009
Advocates for Community Empowerment	12,201	3,556	28,602	2008
Presbyterians for Earth Care	45,207	1,983	23,767	2009
International Indian Treaty Council	3,926	1,750	328,617	2009
Quaker Earthcare Witness	39,539	1,623	105,250	2010
Northeast States Center for a Clean Air Future	182,942	1,404	912,164	2009
Community Network for Appropriate Technologies	9,924	1,266	26,738	2010
Rivers Alliance of Connecticut	54,551	1,208	108,947	2009
Environmental Action Committee of West Marin	111,964	1,006	177,865	2008
Back Country Land Trust	5,611,295	1,000	204,354	2010

Total Net Assets: $8,749,604,236

Total Federal Grants Received: $568,451,487

Total Annual Revenues: $3,331,671,845

Average Net Assets: $35,567,497

Average Federal Grants Received: $2,310,778

Average Annual Revenues: $13,543,381

NOTES

Chapter 1. The New Leviathan

1. http://academic.csuohio.edu/kneuendorf/content/cpuca/gorespch.htm.
2. Edward L. Ayers, *The Promise of the New South: Life After Reconstruction* (Oxford University Press, 2007), p. 38.
3. Jean Edward Smith, *FDR* (Random House, 2008), p. x.
4. Kenneth Morris, *Jimmy Carter, American Moralist* (University of Georgia Press, 1997), pp. 114–15.
5. Ibid., p. 187.
6. http://www.huffingtonpost.com/2010/05/17/photos-al-goree-new-8875_n_579286.html.
7. http://www.telegraph.co.uk/earth/energy/6401195/Al-Gore-could-become-worlds-first-carbon-billionaire.html.
8. http://washingtonexaminer.com/blogs/beltway-confidential/democrats-party-rich.
9. Ibid.
10. Christopher Caldwell, "The Ideological Divide," *New York Times Book Review*, October 24, 2010.
11. Charles Gasparino, *Bought and Paid For: The Unholy Alliance Between Barack Obama and Wall Street* (Sentinel HC, 2010), pp. 30–31.
12. Ibid., p. 40.
13. Matt Bai, *The Argument: Billionaires, Bloggers and the Battle to Remake Democratic Politics* (Penguin Press, 2007), p. 26.
14. Ibid., p. 25.
15. David Callahan, *Fortunes of Change: The Ruse of the Liberal Rich and the Remaking of America* (John Wiley and Sons, 2010).
16. http://www.washingtonpost.com/wp-dyn/content/article/2005/08/06/AR2005080600848_pf.html.
17. http://www.nytimes.com/2005/11/28/opinion/28miller.html.
18. http://www.commonwealinstitute.org/archive/1-billion-for-ideas-conservative-think-tanks-in-the-1990s.
19. The report identifies 82 conservative foundations, but 7 of the foundations named had zero or negative assets in 2009. For up-to-date charts of both conservative and progressive foundations, see Appendices I to III of this volume. The original NCRP report listed 79 conservative foundations but by 2009, 4 of these had zero or negative assets.
20. See Appendix II.
21. http://www.rightweb.irc-online.org/profile/Scaife_Foundations.

22. http://www.bradleyfdn.org/pdfs/Reports2009/2009FinancialStatements.pdf.
23. http://www.gatesfoundation.org/about/Pages/foundation-fact-sheet.aspx.
24. http://www.tides.org/fileadmin/user/pdf/TidesFoundation_AnnualReport_ 2001-2002.pdf p. 2.
25. http://www.discoverthenetworks.org/Articles/Tides%20Foundation%20 and%20Tides%20Center1.htm.
26. http://www.discoverthenetworks.org/funderProfile.asp?fndid=5184.
27. http://www.capitalresearch.org/pubs/pdf/v1285956045.pdf.
28. http://www.tides.org/about/history/.
29. http://www.discoverthenetworks.org/printfunderProfile.asp?fndid=5184.
30. http://www.washingtonpost.com/wp-srv/politics/special/clinton/stories/ scaifemain050299.htm.
31. The numbers refer to the tax code provision under which these groups are classified.
32. See Appendix IV.
33. See Appendix VIII.
34. David Horowitz and Richard Poe, *The Shadow Party* (Thomas Nelson, 2007).
35. Ibid., p. 208.
36. http://online.wsj.com/article/SB10001424052702303348504575184591934009422.html.
37. http://nrd.nationalreview.com/article/?q=ZGFmMDY4NzdkMmIwZTQ1Mz U2ZDA4NGZhNzJlNGU2MTE=.
38. http://www.akdart.com/edu31.html; http://www.akdart.com/edu32.html; http://www.akdart.com/edu33.html.
39. http://archive.frontpagemag.com/readArticle.aspx?ARTID=10240.
40. See Appendix XVI.
41. See Appendix XIV.
42. See Appendix XI.

Chapter 2. The Making of a President

1. http://fightthesmears.com/.
2. Stanley Kurtz, *Radical-in-Chief: Barack Obama and the Untold Story of American Socialism* (Simon and Schuster, 2010).
3. http://www.discoverthenetworks.org/printgroupProfile.asp?grpid=6782.
4. Matthew Vadum, *Subversion, Inc.: How Obama's ACORN Red Shirts Are Still Terrorizing and Ripping Off the American Taxpayers* (WND Books, 2011).
5. http://www.discoverthenetworks.org/individualProfile.asp?indid=2314.
6. David Remnick, *The Bridge: The Life and Rise of Barack Obama* (Random House, 2010), p. 121.
7. Ibid.
8. Quoted in Arthur MacEwan, *Neo-Liberalism or Democracy?: Economic*

Strategy, Markets, and Alternatives for the 21st Century (Zed Books, 1999), p. 15.
9. Ellen Reese, *Backlash Against Welfare Mothers: Past and Present* (University of California Press, 2005), p. 113.
10. http://www.commondreams.org/headline/2010/03/24-4.
11. David Horowitz, *Barack Obama's Rules for Revolution*, pamphlet, 2010.
12. Kurtz, *Radical-in-Chief*, p. 177.
13. http://www.discoverthenetworks.org/printgroupProfile.asp?grpid=7492.
14. http://www.discoverthenetworks.org/printgroupProfile.asp?grpid=7004.
15. Ibid.
16. Timothy Walch, *Immigrant America: European Ethnicity in the United States* (Taylor and Francis, 1994), p. 190.
17. http://www.discoverthenetworks.org/printgroupProfile.asp?grpid=6725.
18. Ibid.
19. Kurtz, *Radical-in-Chief*, p. 249.
20. Ibid. pp. 227–28.
21. http://projectvote.org/our-board.html.
22. Ibid.
23. http://www.nationalreview.com/articles/225898/planting-seeds-disaster/stanley-kurtz.
24. Kurtz, *Radical-in-Chief*, p. 230.
25. Heidi J. Swarts, *Organizing Urban America: Secular and Faith-based Progressive Movements (Social Movements, Protest and Contention)* (University of Minnesota Press, 2008), p. 84.
26. http://www.discoverthenetworks.org/individualProfile.asp?indid=1773.
27. http://anitamoncrief.blogspot.com/2008/12/great-acorn-bank-heist-part-two.html.
28. http://www.pittsburghlive.com/x/pittsburghtrib/news/election/s_584284.html.
29. Kurtz, *Radical-in-Chief*, pp. 182–83.
30. Ibid., p. 189.
31. David Freddoso, *The Case Against Barack Obama: The Unlikely Rise and Unexamined Agenda of the Media's Favorite Candidate* (Regnery Publishing, 2008), p. 129.
32. Amy B. Dean, David B. Reynolds, and Harold Meyerson, *A New New Deal: How Regional Activism Will Reshape the American Labor Movement* (Cornell University Press, 2010), p. 207.
33. http://fightthesmears.com/articles/28/KurtzSmears.html.
34. Freddoso, *The Case Against Barack Obama*, p. 130.
35. Jerome Corsi, *The Obama Nation: Leftist Politics and the Cult of Personality* (Simon and Schuster, 2008), p. 145.
36. http://blog.washingtonpost.com/fact-checker/2008/02/obamas_weatherman_connection.html.

37. http://www.newyorker.com/online/blogs/tny/2008/11/mr-ayerss-neighborhood.html.

38. Edward McClelland, *Young Mr. Obama: Chicago and the Making of a Black President* (Bloomsbury Publishing USA, 2010), p. 96.

39. http://www.discoverthenetworks.org/Articles/chicannenbergchallengeredo 1031.html.

40. http://www.nationalreview.com/articles/225971/wright-101/stanley-kurtz.

41. Ibid.

42. http://frontpagemag.com/2009/11/18/michael-klonsky/.

43. McClelland, *Young Mr. Obama*, p. 96.

44. http://www.nationalreview.com/articles/print/226071.

45. http://online.wsj.com/article/SB122212856075765367.html.

46. McClelland, *Young Mr. Obama*, p. 98.

47. http://blog.washingtonpost.com/fact-checker/2008/02/obamas_weatherman_connection.html.

48. Kurtz, *Radical-in-Chief*, pp. 280–81.

49. Ibid.

50. http://www.discoverthenetworks.org/funderprofile.asp?fndid=5340& category=79.

51. http://www.americanthinker.com/2008/07/obama_and_the_woods_fund_of_ch.html.

52. Pamela Geller, Robert Spencer, and John Bolton, *The Post-American Presidency: The Obama Administration's War on America* (Simon and Schuster, 2010), p. 84.

53. http://biggovernment.com/centralillinois912project/2010/03/13/the-star-players-in-the-shorebank-story/.

54. William Ayers, *A Kind and Just Parent: The Children of Juvenile Court* (Beacon Press, 1998).

55. http://michellemalkin.com/2008/10/19/oh-these-are-the-people-in-your-neighborhood/.

56. Ibid.

57. http://www.discoverthenetworks.org/funderprofile.asp?fndid=5310& category=79.

58. McClelland, *Young Mr. Obama*, p. 96.

59. Ibid.

60. http://www.city-journal.org/html/13_2_acorns_nutty_regime.html.

61. http://www.usatoday.com/news/nation/2009-09-23-acorn_N.htm.

62. John Fund, *Stealing Elections: How Voter Fraud Threatens Our Democracy* (Encounter Books, 2008), p. 63.

63. Peter Schweizer, *Architects of Ruin: How Big Government Liberals Wrecked the Global Economy—and How They Will Do It Again If No One Stops Them* (HarperCollins, 2010), p. 35.

64. Fund, *Stealing Elections*, p. 28.

65. McClelland, *Young Mr. Obama*, p. 77.
66. http://online.wsj.com/article/SB124182750646102435.html.
67. Fund, *Stealing Elections*, p. 60.
68. http://fightthesmears.com/articles/20/acornrumor.html.
69. Ibid.
70. Robert Fisher, *The People Shall Rule: ACORN, Community Organizing, and the Struggle for Economic Justice* (Vanderbilt University Press, 2009), p. 34.

Chapter 3. The Progressive Money Machine

1. Stanley Kurtz, *Radical-in-Chief: Barack Obama and the Untold Story of American Socialism* (Simon and Schuster 2010), p. 280.
2. http://www.discoverthenetworks.org/funderProfile.asp?fndid=5340.
3. Joseph Charles Kiger, *Philanthropists & Foundation Globalization* (Transaction Publishers, 2008), p. 152.
4. William Baker, *Endless Money: The Moral Hazards of Socialism* (John Wiley and Sons, 2009), p. 176.
5. http://www.discoverthenetworks.org/funderProfile.asp?fndid=5213.
6. Ibid.
7. http://www.discoverthenetworks.org/groupProfile.asp?grpid=6991.
8. http://www.discoverthenetworks.org/groupProfile.asp?grpid=6714.
9. http://www.discoverthenetworks.org/funderProfile.asp?fndid=5213.
10. Kiger, *Philanthropists & Foundation Globalization*, p. 121.
11. Waldermar Nielsen, *Golden Donors: A New Anatomy of the Great Foundations* (Transaction Publishers, 2002), pp. 103–110.
12. Ibid.
13. Ibid.
14. Ibid.
15. http://www.americasfuture.net/1996/dec96/96-1208c.html.
16. http://www.slate.com/id/85794/.
17. Roger D. Silk, James W. Lintott, Christine M. Silk, *Creating a Private Foundation: The Essential Guide for Donors and Their Advisers* (Bloomberg Press, 2003), p. 59.
18. http://www.capitalresearch.org/pubs/pdf/FW0105.pdf.
19. Ibid.
20. http://www.earthcharterinaction.org/content/pages/Council.html#16.
21. http://www.discoverthenetworks.org/funderprofile.asp?fndid=5322&category=79.
22. http://www.capitalresearch.org/pubs/pdf/FW0105.pdf.
23. Ibid.
24. http://www.sandiego.edu/peacestudies/ or http://en.wikipedia.org/wiki/Joan_Kroc (Under Philanthropy).

25. http://fumento.com/military/defense.html; http://www.discoverthenetworks
    .org/groupProfile.asp?grpid=6631.
26. http://www.campus-watch.org/blog/2010/01/tariq-ramadan-may-return-to-
    usa-notre-dame-says.
27. http://archive.frontpagemag.com/readArticle.aspx?ARTID=11367; http://
    archive.frontpagemag.com/readArticle.aspx?ARTID=34496; http://archive
    .frontpagemag.com/readArticle.aspx?ARTID=11367.
28. Ibid.
29. Ibid.
30. http://nlpc.org/stories/2010/07/29/john-kerry%E2%80%99s-yacht-another-
    tax-rich-republicans.
31. http://www.acene.org/8901.html?°session°id°key°=°session°id°val°.
32. http://archive.frontpagemag.com/readArticle.aspx?ARTID=34036.
33. http://archive.frontpagemag.com/readArticle.aspx?ARTID=11366.
34. Ibid.
35. Ibid.
36. Eric Thomas Chester, *Covert Network: Progressives, the International
    Rescue Committee, and the CIA* (M.E. Sharpe, 1995), p. 43.
37. David Halberstam, "The Very Expensive Education of McGeorge Bundy,"
    Harper's, July 1969.
38. Alfred Regnery, *Upstream: The Ascendance of American Conservatism*
    (Simon and Schuster, 2008), p. 201.
39. http://www.dareassociation.org/Papers/2008_JPTC_V24.01_05.pdf.
40. Vincent Cannato, *The Ungovernable City* (Basic Books, 2002), pp. 340–51.
41. Ibid.
42. Peter B. Levy, *The New Left and Labor in the 1960s* (University of Illinois
    Press, 1994), p. 80.
43. Noliwe Rooks, *White Money/Black Power: The Surprising History of African
    American Studies and the Crisis of Race in Higher Education* (Beacon Press,
    2007), pp. 88–89.
44. Juan Sepúlveda, *The Life and Times of Willie Velásquez* (Arte Publico Press,
    2003), p. 89.
45. http://articles.cnn.com/2008-10-09/politics/acorn.fraud.claims_1_acorn-
    officials-voter-fraud-voter-registration?_s=PM:POLITICS.
46. Regnery, *Upstream*, p. 200; http://www.city-journal.org/html/6_4_a1.html.
47. Robert Grimm, *Notable American Philanthropists: Biographies of Giving
    and Volunteering* (Greenwood Publishing Group, 2002), p. 97.
48. For a description of some of the radical beneficiaries of Ford funds see: http://
    discoverthenetworks.org/funderProfile.asp?fndid=5176.
49. http://blog.nj.com/njv_guest_blog/2007/10/history_matters_because_it_can
    .html.
50. http://www.blackpast.org/?q=primary/moynihan-report-1965.

51. http://blog.nj.com/njv_guest_blog/2007/10/history_matters_because_it_can .html.
52. Alvin S. Felzenberg, *Governor Tom Kean: From the New Jersey Statehouse to the 9-11 Commission* (Rutgers University Press, 2006), pp. 91–92.
53. Steven Teles, *The Rise of the Conservative Legal Movement: The Battle for Control of the Law* (Princeton University Press, 2010), p. 46.
54. Ibid.
55. Teles, *Rise of the Conservative Legal Movement*, p. 49.
56. Ibid.
57. http://www.irs.gov/charities/charitable/article/0,,id=96099,00.html.
58. Ibid.
59. http://www.featuregroup.com/fgarchive/jta.org/jta.org2/index.html.
60. Mark Sidel, *More Secure, Less Free?: Antiterrorism Policy & Civil Liberties After September 11* (University of Michigan Press, 2007), p. 122.
61. http://www.ngo-monitor.org/article.php?id=984.
62. Author interview.
63. Interview with William Schambra.
64. See Appendix I.
65. See Appendices IV and VII.

Chapter 4. Deconstructing the American Identity

1. http://www.discoverthenetworks.org/Articles/nclr5.html.
2. http://archive.frontpagemag.com/readArticle.aspx?ARTID=14499.
3. Julie Leininger Pycior, *LBJ and Mexican Americans: The Paradox of Power* (University of Texas Press, 1997), p. 211.
4. Linda Chavez, *Out of the Barrio: Toward a New Politics of Hispanic Assimilation* (Basic Books, 1992), p. 81.
5. Hugh Davis Graham, *Civil Rights in the United States* (Penn State Press, 2004), p. 78.
6. http://www.discoverthenetworks.org/printgroupProfile.asp?grpid=153.
7. Vicki Ruíz and Virginia Sánchez Korrol, *Latinas in the United States: A Historical Encyclopedia*, Volume 1 (Indiana University Press, 2006), p. 514.
8. http://www.nclr.org/index.php/support_us/corporate_partner_opportunities/.
9. Deidre Martinez, *Who Speaks for Hispanics?: Hispanic Interest Groups in Washington* (SUNY Press, 2009), p. 27.
10. http://www.discoverthenetworks.org/Articles/1995%20January%20Vol.3,%20 No.1.pdf.
11. Michelle Malkin, *Invasion: How America Still Welcomes Terrorists, Criminals, and Other Foreign Menaces to Our Shores* (Regnery Publishing, 2004), p. 83.

12. http://www.cis.org/node/1046.
13. Patrick J. Buchanan, *State of Emergency: The Third World Invasion and Conquest of America* (Macmillan, 2007), p. 25.
14. Samuel P. Huntington, *Who Are We?: The Challenges to America's National Identity* (Simon and Schuster, 2004), p. 246.
15. http://www.wecanstopthehate.org/site/why_this_matters.
16. http://denbeste.nu/external/idealogical_war.pdf.
17. http://www.foxnews.com/politics/2010/04/29/border-states-dealing-illegal-immigrant-crime-data-suggests/#ixzz1DftxnnoA.
18. http://michellemalkin.com/2010/03/29/the-death-of-an-arizona-rancher/.
19. http://www.cbsnews.com/stories/2010/04/15/politics/main6399651.shtml.
20. http://www.politico.com/news/stories/0410/36365.html.
21. http://www.nytimes.com/2010/04/24/us/politics/24immig.html.
22. http://www.lvrj.com/blogs/mitchell/Can_Supremacy_Clause_apply_to_unenforced_federal_law.html.
23. Chavez, *Out of the Barrio*, p. 80.
24. Otis Graham, *Immigration Reform and America's Unchosen Future* (AuthorHouse, 2008), p. 247; http://archive.frontpagemag.com/readArticle.aspx?ARTID=14499.
25. Richard A. Buitron, *The Quest for Tejano Identity in San Antonio, Texas, 1913–2000* (Psychology Press, 2004), p. 76.
26. http://www.discoverthenetworks.org/printgroupProfile.asp?grpid=6807.
27. http://www.judicialwatch.org/files/documents/2009/SotomayorPRLDEFreport.pdf.
28. http://www.discoverthenetworks.org/Articles/Sotomayor%20Claims%20Little%20Involvement%20with.html.
29. http://www.nationalreview.com/articles/227625/how-sotomayor-misspoke/rich-lowry.
30. http://online.wsj.com/article/SB10001424052748704709304576124502622737210.html?mod=WSJ_Opinion_LEFTThirdBucket.
31. Ibid.
32. See Appendix VI.
33. See Appendix V.
34. See Appendix XIV.
35. David Horowitz and Jacob Laksin, *One-Party Classroom: How Radical Professors at America's Top Colleges Indoctrinate Students and Undermine our Democracy* (Random House, 2009), pp. 51–52.
36. Noliwe M. Rooks, *White Money/Black Power: The Surprising History of African American Studies and the Crisis of Race in Higher Education* (Beacon Press, 2007), p. 20.
37. John J. Miller, *The Unmaking of Americans: How Multiculturalism Has Undermined the Assimilation Ethic* (Simon and Schuster, 1998), p. 129.

38. Ibid., 76.
39. Arthur Meier Schlesinger, *Reflections on a Multicultural Society* (W. W. Norton & Company, 1998).

Chapter 5. Redefining National Security

1. http://www.discoverthenetworks.org/groupprofile.asp?grpid=7156& category=79.
2. http://www.nytimes.com/2006/11/01/obituaries/01lilienthal.html.
3. Paul Hollander, *Political Pilgrims: Western Intellectuals in Search of the Good Society* (Transaction Publishers, 1981).
4. Paul Hollander, *The Survival of the Adversary Culture: Social Criticism and Political Escapism in American Society* (Transaction Publishers, 1988), p. 68.
5. Ibid.
6. http://www.ploughshares.org/grant_search?DateApproved_TurnedDown [min]=1984&DateApproved_TurnedDown[max]=1985&keyword_ op=any&keyword=.
7. http://www.capitalresearch.org/pubs/pdf/v1249061645.pdf.
8. http://www.ploughshares.org/about-us/board.
9. http://www.capitalresearch.org/pubs/pdf/v1249061645.pdf.
10. http://www.ploughshares.org/our-impact.
11. http://www.discoverthenetworks.org/groupProfile.asp?grpid=6190.
12. http://www.discoverthenetworks.org/groupProfile.asp?grpid=6895.
13. http://www.discoverthenetworks.org/groupProfile.asp?grpid=6935.
14. http://www.winwithoutwar.org/pages/about.
15. http://www.ploughshares.org/expert/205.
16. http://www.ploughshares.org/sites/default/files/resources/040107_WMDIraq EvidenceImplications.pdf.
17. http://blog.foreignpolicy.com/posts/2007/09/14/north_korea_syria_nuclear_ ties_deja_vu_all_over_again.
18. Ibid.
19. http://www.csmonitor.com/USA/Foreign-Policy/2008/0425/p02s02-usfp .html.
20. http://politics.foxnews.mobi/quickPage.html?page=23888&content=4981678 8&pageNum=-1.
21. http://www.nytimes.com/2006/11/01/obituaries/01lilienthal.html.
22. http://www.ploughshares.org/grant_search?page=8&DateApproved_Turned Down[min]=1981&DateApproved_TurnedDown[max]=&keyword_op=any& keyword=.
23. http://www.discoverthenetworks.org/printgroupProfile.asp?grpid=6519.
24. http://www.peaceandsecurity.org/373/32385.html. Fifty-six of these groups filed 990s with the IRS from which the dollar figures are taken. Seven

of them did not file 990s. Two of them did but are defunct and were not included in the above figure. One member is an individual whose tax return is not public and was not included in the above figure.

25. http://www.policyexperts.org/organizations/organizations_results.cfm?Organ ization=&Head=&rdoSearchType=COUNTRY&AllPriorityIssues=national+ security&Country=ALL&State=ALL&Org=AllOrg&Tax=ALL&Search= Verify%3E&Submit=Submit.
26. See Appendix VII.
27. http://www.peaceandsecurity.org/394/32511.html.
28. http://findarticles.com/p/articles/mi_m1571/is_31_16/ai_64566664/.
29. Richard Ericson and Kevin Haggerty, *The New Politics of Surveillance and Visibility* (University of Toronto Press, 2006), p. 168.
30. http://www.capitalresearch.org/pubs/pdf/v1249061645.pdf.
31. http://www.aei.org/article/101705.
32. http://www.globalsecurity.org/military/world/war/libya-civil-war-nfz.htm.
33. http://www.defensenews.com/story.php?i=6208477&c=MID&s=TOP.
34. http://blogs.abcnews.com/politicalpunch/2011/03/defense-secretary-libya-did-not-pose-threat-to-us-was-not-vital-national-interest-to-intervene.html.
35. http://www.un.org/en/documents/charter/chapter1.shtml.
36. George Soros, *The Age of Fallibility: Consequences of the War on Terror* (Public Affairs, 2006), pp. 141–42.
37. http://www.stanleyfoundation.org/publications/pab/LuckPAB808.pdf.
38. http://www.stanleyfoundation.org/history.cfm.
39. http://www.stanleyfoundation.org/articles.cfm?id=23.
40. http://www.stanleyfoundation.org/history.cfm.
41. http://www.stanleyfoundation.org/publications/pab/LuckPAB808.pdf.
42. http://www.stanleyfoundation.org/publications/report/UNND808.pdf.
43. http://www.whitehouse.gov/the-press-office/2011/03/28/remarks-president-address-nation-libya.
44. http://www.chicagotribune.com/news/columnists/ct-oped-0403-chapman-20110403,0,4286197.column.
45. http://www.responsibilitytoprotect.org/index.php/crises/37-the-crisis-in-darfur/277-exactly-142-days-after-bush-said-the-word-darfur-he-added-a-more-important-word-genocide-but-does-the-policy-match-the-sentiment.
46. http://www.tnr.com/article/against-the-current/85621/libya-iraq-muammar-qaddafi.
47. http://www.martinkramer.org/sandbox/2008/03/speaking-truth-to-power/.
48. http://www.nationalaffairs.com/publications/detail/legalism-in-wartime.
49. http://www.mlive.com/news/ann-arbor/index.ssf/2009/06/aclu_washtenaw_chapter_invites.html.
50. http://www.theacru.org/VadumACLU.pdf.
51. Horowitz, *Unholy Alliance: Radical Islam and the American Left* (Regnery Publishing, 2004), p. 204.

52. Robert Spencer, *Onward Muslim Soldiers: How Jihad Still Threatens America and the West* (Regnery Publishing, 2003), p. 22.

53. http://cltampa.com/tampa/the-al-arian-factor/Content?oid=2012793.

54. David E. Bernstein, *You Can't Say That!: The Growing Threat to Civil Liberties from Antidiscrimination Laws* (Cato Institute, 2003), p. 152.

55. http://www.aclu.org/organization-news-and-highlights/ford-foundation-gives-7-million-aclu-endowment-campaign.

56. http://www.foxnews.com/story/0,2933,364763,00.html.

57. http://articles.latimes.com/2009/oct/21/opinion/la-oew-mcneil-sanchez21-2009oct21.

58. http://www.bordc.org/list.php?sortChrono=1.

59. http://www.discoverthenetworks.org/groupProfile.asp?grpid=6756.

60. http://www.bordc.org/newsletter/2011/04/#lead; http://www.bordc.org/list.php; http://antemedius.com/content/your-town-can-demand-justice-more-powerfully-you-can (5th paragraph).

61. http://blog.timesunion.com/capitol/archives/56454/patriot-act-vote-surprises-republicans-with-27-voting-against-extension-including-chris-gibson/.

62. http://www.huffingtonpost.com/2011/02/08/house-rejects-extensions-patriot-act_n_820554.html.

63. http://content.usatoday.com/communities/ondeadline/post/2011/05/senate-votes-to-extend-patriot-act-anti-terror-provisions/1.

64. http://abcnews.go.com/US/PollVault/story?id=833703.

65. http://query.nytimes.com/gst/fullpage.html?res=9A0DEED7123EF930A1575BC0A9609C8B63.

66. http://www.fas.org/irp/congress/2007_cr/fisa011707.html.

67. http://online.wsj.com/public/resources/documents/UnclassifiedReportPSP.pdf.

68. http://online.wsj.com/public/resources/documents/UnclassifiedReportPSP.pdf.

69. For an extensive list of these organizations and their agendas, see http://www.discoverthenetworks.org/viewGroups.asp?catid=95.

70. http://www.weeklystandard.com/blogs/aclu-blow-military-commissions.

71. http://www.nytimes.com/2009/11/14/us/14terror.html?pagewanted=all.

72. http://www.discoverthenetworks.org/printgroupProfile.asp?grpid=6707.

73. Andrew McCarthy, *How the Obama Administration Has Politicized Justice* (Encounter Books), 2010.

74. Marc Thiessen, *Courting Disaster: How the CIA Kept America Safe and How Barack Obama Is Inviting the Next Attack* (Regnery Publishing, 2010), p. 32.

75. http://blog.american.com/?p=14632.

76. http://www.nationalaffairs.com/publications/detail/legalism-in-wartime.

77. http://archive.frontpagemag.com/readArticle.aspx?ARTID=14166.

78. David Horowitz, *Unholy Alliance,* p. 179; Gunter Lewy, *The Cause That*

Failed: Communism in American Political Life (Oxford University Press, 1990), p. 289.

79. Thiessen, *Courting Disaster*, pp. 240–42.
80. Ibid.
81. http://www.weeklystandard.com/blogs/gitmo-recidivism-rate-soars_521965.html.
82. http://abcnews.go.com/Blotter/aclu-sues-us-government-awlakis-hit-list-designation/story?id=11316084&page=2.
83. http://www.nydailynews.com/ny_local/2010/07/15/2010-07-15_lynn_stewart_80yearold_radical_lawyer_sentenced_to_10_years_in_prison_for_aiding.html.
84. http://old.nationalreview.com/york/york200502170843.asp.
85. Ibid.http://old.nationalreview.com/york/york200502170843.asp.

Chapter 6. Socialism by Stealth

1. http://thehill.com/homenews/house/70557-hoyer-dems-need-to-focus-on-economy-to-avoid-mid-term-losses.
2. http://people-press.org/2009/01/22/economy-jobs-trump-all-other-policy-priorities-in-2009/.
3. https://www.1healthrecord.org/sub.aspx?id=804.
4. http://www.youtube.com/watch?v=_cqN4NIEtOY.
5. http://online.wsj.com/article/SB100014240529702042514045743421700728 65070.html.
6. http://blog.heritage.org/2009/08/21/is-healthcare-a-%E2%80%98right%E2%80%99/.
7. http://online.wsj.com/article/SB100014240529702042514045743421700728 65070.html.
8. http://healthcare.procon.org/view.source.php?sourceID=009592.
9. David Gratzer, *The Cure: How Capitalism Can Save American Health Care* (Encounter Books, 2006).
10. http://www.trumanlibrary.org/anniversaries/healthprogram.htm.
11. http://www.theDailyBeast.com/newsweek/2009/07/17/the-cause-of-my-life.html.
12. Sally Pipes, *The Truth About ObamaCare* (Regnery Gateway, 2010), p. 25.
13. Jonathan Gruber, *Public Finance and Public Policy* (Macmillan, 2004) p. 422.
14. Ibid.
15. http://online.wsj.com/article/SB124268737705832167.html.
16. https://www.cia.gov/library/publications/the-world-factbook/geos/us.html.
17. http://www.nationalaffairs.com/publications/detail/how-to-fix-medicaid
18. Nancy J. Niles, *Governing Health: The Politics of Health Policy* (JHU Press 2006), p. 273.

19. http://m.rockfound.org/uploads/files/ebafb89b-2d68-45c0-885e-74d40e8c55d9.pdf.
20. http://www.tides.org/fileadmin/user/pdf/TheRightToTheCity.pdf.
21. http://www.discoverthenetworks.org/viewSubCategory.asp?id=1237.
22. http://www.discoverthenetworks.org/funderprofile.asp?fndid=5211& category=79.
23. http://www.pharmalot.com/2011/04/foundations-conflicts-of-interest-and-drugmakers/.
24. David Brock, *The Seduction of Hillary Rodham Clinton* (Simon and Schuster, 1998), p. 349.
25. http://cppp.usc.edu/doc/RP15.pdf.
26. Ibid.
27. http://www.discoverthenetworks.org/funderProfile.asp?fndid=5202.
28. http://www.discoverthenetworks.org/funderProfile.asp?fndid=5268.
29. http://cppp.usc.edu/doc/RP15.pdf.
30. http://www.npr.org/news/national/election2000/coverage/issues/healthcare .html.
31. http://www.issues2000.org/Al_Gore_Health_Care.htm.
32. http://www.capitalresearch.org/pubs/pdf/v1280761786.pdf.
33. Stanley Kurtz, *Radical-in-Chief: Barack Obama and the Untold Story of American Socialism* (Simon and Schuster 2010), p. 55.
34. http://www.capitalresearch.org/pubs/pdf/v1280761786.pdf
35. Kurtz, *Radical-in-Chief,* p. 55.
36. http://www.capitalresearch.org/pubs/pdf/v1280761786.pdf.
37. http://www.discoverthenetworks.org/printgroupProfile.asp?grpid=7559.
38. http://www.familiesusa.org/issues/uninsured/hccu/about-hccu.html.
39. http://www.familiesusa.org/issues/uninsured/hccu/hccu-agreement.pdf.
40. http://www.discoverthenetworks.org/printgroupProfile.asp?grpid=7643.
41. http://online.wsj.com/article/SB10001424052748704041504575045704570299768 3276.html?mod=rss_Today%27s_Most_Popular.
42. http://www.nationalcenter.org/PR-PfizerJJ042310.html.
43. http://www.discoverthenetworks.org/printgroupProfile.asp?grpid=6535.
44. Alan Marcus and Hamilton Cravens, *Health Care Policy in Contemporary America* (Penn State Press, 1997), p. 79.
45. Marie Gottschalk, *The Shadow Welfare State: Labor, Business, and the Politics of Health-Care in the United States* (Cornell University Press, 2000), p. 139.
46. http://www.nytimes.com/2005/12/28/opinion/28fitch.html.
47. Matthew Crenson and Benjamin Ginsberg, *Downsizing Democracy: How America Sidelined Its Citizens and Privatized Its Public* (The Johns Hopkins University Press, 2002), p. 134.
48. http://www.nationalaffairs.com/publications/detail/the-trouble-with-public-sector-unions.

49. Ibid.

50. http://www.nytimes.com/2007/01/26/us/26labor.html.

51. http://www.heritage.org/Research/Reports/2009/09/Why-Organized-Labor-Supports-Government-Health-Care.

52. Ibid.

53. http://blog.aflcio.org/2006/06/12/we-need-universal-health-care/.

54. http://www.aflcio.org/aboutus/thisistheaflcio/ecouncil/ec03062007.cfm.

55. http://www.opensecrets.org/lobby/clientsum.php?lname=AFL-CIO&year=2008.

56. SEIU 990 IRS form for 2009.

57. http://nlpc.org/stories/2010/01/13/top-ten-union-corruption-stories-year.

58. http://www.cbsnews.com/stories/2011/04/27/opinion/main20057833.shtml.

59. http://www.seiu.org/2007/11/nfib-joins-aarp-business-roundtable-and-seiu.php.

60. http://www-static-w2-md.aarp.org/issues/dividedwefail/get_involved/congressional_pledge.html; http://www.minoritynurse.com/asian-american-nurses/boomer-chief.

61. Saul Alinsky, *Rules for Radicals: A Practical Primer for Realistic Radicals* (Random House Digital, Inc., 1989).

62. Timothy Carney, *Obamanomics: How Barack Obama Is Bankrupting You and Enriching His Wall Street Friends, Corporate Lobbyists, and Union Bosses* (Regnery Publishing, 2009), p. 71.

63. http://www.discoverthenetworks.org/printgroupProfile.asp?grpid=6434.

64. http://www.communitychange.org/our-projects/hrop.

65. http://www.discoverthenetworks.org/individualProfile.asp?indid=2423.

66. Thomas Massaro, *United States Welfare Policy: A Catholic Response* (Georgetown University Press, 2007), p. 158.

67. http://www.denverpost.com/news/ci_14689452?source=pkg.

68. http://www.discoverthenetworks.org/printgroupProfile.asp?grpid=6434.

69. http://www.keywiki.org/index.php/Heather_Booth#cite_note-13.

70. http://www.communitychange.org/who-we-are/our-board.

71. http://nation.foxnews.com/george-soros/2009/08/11/soros-gives-5-million-liberal-health-care-group.

72. http://www.discoverthenetworks.org/funderProfile.asp?fndid=5184.

73. http://www.politico.com/blogs/thecrypt/0708/Elizabeth_Edwards_headlines_40M_health_care_campaign.html.

74. http://www.nytimes.com/2010/06/07/health/policy/07campaign.html.

75. http://blog.healthcareforamericanow.org/2009/06/01/82-million-and-united-for-health-care/.

76. Ibid.

77. Rick Sanchez, *Conventional Idiocy: Why the New America Is Sick of Old Politics* (Penguin, 2010).

78. http://www.nytimes.com/2009/08/07/opinion/07krugman.html?adxnnl=1&adxnnlx=1302894195-FZ9aCGeL/6CMW+DJduI9zA.

79. Michelle Malkin, *Culture of Corruption: Obama and His Team of Tax Cheats, Crooks, and Cronies* (Regnery Publishing, 2010), p. 176.
80. http://healthcareforamericanow.org/site/content/about_us/.
81. http://www.quinnipiac.edu/x1295.xml?ReleaseID=1382.
82. Pipes, *The Truth About ObamaCare*, p. 9.
83. Richard Wolfe, *Revival: The Struggle for Survival Inside the Obama White House* (Crown, 2010).
84. http://www.dailykos.com/story/2010/03/23/849637/-BEST-PHOTO-DIARY-EVER!-:%29-Bring-tissue.
85. Pipes, *The Truth About ObamaCare*, p. 28.

Chapter 7. Controlled Environments

1. http://www.politicalaffairs.net/epa-moves-to-regulate-carbon-dioxide-holds-atlanta-hearing/.
2. Roy Spencer, *Climate Confusion: How Global Warming Hysteria Leads to Bad Science, Pandering Politicians and Misguided Policies That Hurt the Poor* (Encounter Books, 2010), p. 81.
3. http://earthjustice.org/news/press/2008/six-easy-things-the-obama-administration-can-do-to-heal-our-environment.
4. http://www.time.com/time/health/article/0,8599,1880897,00.html.
5. Riley Dunlap and Angela Mertig, *American Environmentalism: The U.S. Environmental Movement, 1970–1990* (Taylor & Francis, 1992), p. 14.
6. Rich Trzupek, *How the EPA's Green Tyranny Is Stifling America* (Encounter Books, 2011).
7. Ibid.
8. http://www.time.com/time/magazine/article/0,9171,488848,00.html.
9. Gregg Easterbrook, *The Progress Paradox: How Life Gets Better While People Feel Worse* (Random House Digital, Inc., 2004), p. 43.
10. http://www.discoverthenetworks.org/Articles/ENVIRONMENTAL%20DEFENSE%20-%20verified.html.
11. Douglas Bevington, *The Rebirth of Environmentalism: Grassroots Activism from the Spotted Owl to the Polar Bear* (Island Press 2009), p. 20.
12. John Berlau, *Eco-freaks: Environmentalism Is Hazardous to Your Health!* (Thomas Nelson Inc., 2006), p. 35.
13. Ibid., p. 38.
14. http://www.acsh.org/healthissues/newsID.442/healthissue_detail.asp.
15. http://malaria.jhsph.edu/about_malaria/.
16. http://www.acsh.org/healthissues/newsID.442/healthissue_detail.asp.
17. http://www.discoverthenetworks.org/funderprofile.asp?fndid=5310&category=79.
18. http://www.edf.org/pressrelease.cfm?contentID=9290.
19. http://www.politico.com/news/stories/0111/46973.html.

20. http://www.discoverthenetworks.org/Articles/nrdcactivitiesand.html.
21. John Adams, Patricia Adams, and George Black, *A Force for Nature: The Story of NRDC and Its Fight to Save Our Planet* (Chronicle Books, 2010).
22. NRDC 990 IRS form; http://www.discoverthenetworks.org/Articles/nrdcactivitiesand.html.
23. Adams et al., *A Force for Nature.*
24. http://www.nrdc.org/about/.
25. http://www.nrdc.org/about/who_we_are.asp.
26. Doug Bandow, *The Politics of Envy: Statism as Theology* (Transaction Publishers 1994), p. 78.
27. Ibid.
28. Ibid.
29. Ben Bolch and Harold Lyons, *Apocalypse Not: Science, Economics, and Environmentalism* (Cato Institute, 1993), p. 40.
30. http://www.epa.gov/oppsrrd1/REDs/factsheets/0032fact.pdf.
31. http://activistcash.com/organization_overview.cfm/o/19-natural-resources-defense-council.
32. Adams et al., *A Force for Nature.*
33. http://activistcash.com/organization_overview.cfm/o/19-natural-resources-defense-council.
34. http://www.discoverthenetworks.org/Articles/nrdcactivitiesand.html.
35. http://switchboard.nrdc.org/blogs/fbeinecke/obama_presents_nrdc_founder_jo.html.
36. http://blogs.forbes.com/henrymiller/2011/07/12/fear-mongering-junk-science-and-nrdc/.
37. Bevington, *Rebirth of Environmentalism*, p. 22.
38. Arthur Herman, *The Idea of Decline in Western History* (Simon and Schuster, 2007).
39. Robert Gottlieb, *Forcing the Spring: The Transformation of the American Environmental Movement* (Island Press, 2005), p. 145.
40. Ibid.
41. Murray Bookchin, Dave Foreman, and Steve Chase, *Defending the Earth: A Dialogue Between Murray Bookchin and Dave Foreman* (South End Press), 1991, p. 59.
42. http://www.discoverthenetworks.org/Articles/nrdcactivitiesand.html.
43. http://www.discoverthenetworks.org/individualProfile.asp?indid=2364.
44. http://www.aei.org/speech/100219.
45. http://washingtonexaminer.com/blogs/examiner-opinion-zone/2009/02/green-jobs-scam-and-confusion.
46. http://www.juandemariana.org/pdf/090327-employment-public-aid-renewable.pdf.
47. http://www.aei.org/speech/100219.
48. Ibid.

49. Michael Mayerfeld Bell, Michael Bell, and Michael S. Carolan, *An Invitation to Environmental Sociology* (Pine Forge Press, 2008), p. 256.
50. Paula Young Lee, *Meat, Modernity, and the Rise of the Slaughterhouse* (University Press of New England, 2008), p. 259.
51. http://www.discoverthenetworks.org/printgroupProfile.asp?grpid=7570.
52. http://www.discoverthenetworks.org/printgroupProfile.asp?grpid=6903.
53. http://www.opensecrets.org/lobby/clientsum.php?id=D000047849&year=2011.
54. http://www.discoverthenetworks.org/groupProfile.asp?grpid=7562.
55. http://www.discoverthenetworks.org/printgroupProfile.asp?grpid=6527.
56. http://www.discoverthenetworks.org/printgroupProfile.asp?grpid=7554.
57. http://www.nationalreview.com/corner/186715/more-candor-please/stephen-spruiell.
58. Van Jones, *The Green Collar Economy* (HarperOne, 2009), p. 98.
59. http://www.discoverthenetworks.org/printgroupProfile.asp?grpid=7554
60. Ian Rowlands, *The Politics of Global Atmospheric Change* (Manchester University Press ND, 1995), p. 69.
61. http://denisdutton.com/cooling_world.htm.
62. Roy Spencer, *Climate Confusion: How Global Warming Hysteria Leads to Bad Science, Pandering Politicians, and Misguided Policies That Hurt the Poor* (Encounter Books, 2010), p. 26.
63. http://www.telegraph.co.uk/comment/personal-view/3624242/There-IS-a-problem-with-global-warming...-it-stopped-in-1998.html.
64. Ibid.
65. http://www.dailymail.co.uk/news/article-1250872/Climategate-U-turn-Astonishment-scientist-centre-global-warming-email-row-admits-data-organised.html.
66. Christopher Booker, *The Real Global Warming Disaster: Is the Obsession with "Climate Change" Turning Out to Be the Most Costly Scientific Blunder in History?* (Continuum Publishing Group, December 1, 2009), p. 53.
67. http://www.discoverthenetworks.org/individualProfile.asp?indid=2461.
68. Booker, *Real Global Warming Disaster*, p. 39.
69. http://www.nationalaffairs.com/doclib/20080709_19941141howmuchdoes globalwarmingmatterwilfredbeckerman.pdf.
70. Bob Zelnick, *Gore: A Political Life* (Regnery Publishing, 2000), p. 183.
71. Ibid., p. 331.
72. Frederick Buttel, "Rethinking International Environmental Policy in the Late Twentieth Century," in *Environmental Justice: Issues, Policies and Solutions*, ed. Bunyan Bryant (Island Press, 1995), p. 188.
73. Ian Murray, *The Really Inconvenient Truths: Seven Environmental Catastrophes Liberals Don't Want You to Know About—Because They Helped Cause Them* (Regnery Publishing, 2008), p. 15.
74. http://scienceandpublicpolicy.org/images/stories/press_releases/

monckton-response-to-gore-errors.pdf; http://www.telegraph.co.uk/earth/
environment/climatechange/7309204/UKIP-would-ban-Al-Gore-film-in-
schools.html.

75. http://www.telegraph.co.uk/comment/personal-view/3624242/There-IS-
a-problem-with-global-warming...-it-stopped-in-1998.html; http://www
.bibliotecapleyades.net/archivos_pdf/globalwarmingemperor_noclothes.pdf.

76. Julie Kerr Casper, *Global Warming Cycles: Ice Ages and Glacial Retreat*
(Facts on File Publishing, 2009), p. 23.

77. http://www.telegraph.co.uk/comment/personal-view/3624242/There-IS-a-
problem-with-global-warming...-it-stopped-in-1998.html.

78. http://blogs.news.com.au/heraldsun/andrewbolt/index.php/heraldsun/
comments/hadley_hacked/.

79. http://www.discoverthenetworks.org/viewSubCategory.asp?id=859.

80. http://blogs.telegraph.co.uk/news/jamesdelingpole/100017393/climategate-
the-final-nail-in-the-coffin-of-anthropogenic-global-warming/.

81. http://wattsupwiththat.com/2010/01/27/another-survey-shows-public-
opinion-on-global-warming-is-in-decline/.

82. http://www.nytimes.com/2007/04/09/business/09climate.html.

83. http://philanthropy.com/article/Ford-Commits-85-Million-to/123711/.

84. http://www.discoverthenetworks.org/funderprofile.asp?fndid=5371&
category=79.

85. Christopher C. Horner, *The Politically Incorrect Guide to Global Warming
and Environmentalism* (Regnery Publishing, 2007), p. 30.

86. http://www.washingtonpost.com/wp-dyn/content/article/2009/06/06/
AR2009060601797_pf.html.

87. http://thehill.com/blogs/floor-action/house/159397-obama-floats-plan-to-tax-
cars-by-the-mile.

88. http://www.wnd.com/?pageId=40445.

89. http://www.nytimes.com/2009/11/03/business/energy-environment/03gore
.html.

90. http://ase.org/about-us/our-board-directors.

91. http://173.201.187.68/science-updates/christie-calls-regional-greenhouse-gas-
initiative-a-gimmick-and-failure.

92. http://washingtonexaminer.com/opinion/op-eds/2011/05/epas-green-tyranny-
stifles-america.

93. Ibid.

94. http://www.epa.gov/planandbudget/budget.html.

95. See Appendices IX and X.

Chapter 8. One Nation Under Unions

1. http://host.madison.com/wsj/news/local/govt-and-politics/article_6a42ad28-
2e5e-11e0-9f9e-001cc4c03286.html.

2. http://www.usatoday.com/news/nation/2011-03-01-1Apublicworkers01_ST_N.htm.
3. http://www.jsonline.com/blogs/news/118910229.html.
4. http://www.620wtmj.com/news/local/117732923.html.
5. http://www.nationalreview.com/articles/print/262428.
6. http://www.foxnews.com/politics/2011/03/10/unions-aim-disrupt-wisconsin-vote-today/.
7. http://www.jsonline.com/blogs/news/117340918.html.
8. http://wisconsinwave.org/news/cap-times-walker-acting-not-governor-dictator.
9. http://www.redstate.com/laborunionreport/2011/03/21/wisconsin-judge-maryann-sumi-her-seiu-afl-cio-political-operative-son/.
10. http://www.hks.harvard.edu/news-events/news/articles/rapp-pensions-joshue-rauh-apr11.
11. http://www.washingtonpost.com/wp-dyn/content/article/2011/02/17/AR2011021705494.html.
12. http://blogs.wsj.com/washwire/2009/10/30/seius-stern-tops-white-house-visitor-list/tab/article/.
13. http://en.wikipedia.org/wiki/Patrick_Gaspard.
14. http://www.city-journal.org/2010/20_2_california-unions.html.
15. Ibid.
16. http://www.nationalaffairs.com/publications/detail/the-trouble-with-public-sector-unions.
17. Ibid.
18. Ibid.
19. Ibid.
20. Max Green, *Epitaph for American Labor: How Union Leaders Lost Touch with America* (American Enterprise Institute, 1996) p. 162.
21. http://www.nationalaffairs.com/publications/detail/the-trouble-with-public-sector-unions.
22. http://online.wsj.com/article/SB124227027965718333.html.
23. Martin Halpern, *Unions, Radicals, and Democratic Presidents: Seeking Social Change in the Twentieth Century* (Praeger, 2003), p. 84.
24. Terry Moe, *Special Interest: Teacher's Unions and America's Public Schools* (Brookings Institution Press, 2011), p. 35.
25. http://www.nationalaffairs.com/publications/detail/the-trouble-with-public-sector-unions.
26. http://www.discoverthenetworks.org/printgroupProfile.asp?grpid=7515.
27. http://www.nationalaffairs.com/publications/detail/the-trouble-with-public-sector-unions.
28. http://www.usatoday.com/money/economy/income/2010-08-10-1Afedpay10_ST_N.htm.
29. http://online.wsj.com/article/SB10001424052748704281204575003101210295246.html?KEYWORDS=%22The+Government+Pay+Boom%22.

30. http://www.freedomworks.org/blog/jborowski/top-10-reasons-to-support-wisconsin-governor-walke.
31. Ibid.
32. http://www.nationalaffairs.com/publications/detail/the-trouble-with-public-sector-unions.
33. Ibid.
34. Ibid.
35. Ibid.
36. Ibid.
37. http://online.wsj.com/article/SB10001424052748704281204575003101210295246.html?mod=WSJ_hpp_sections_opinion.
38. http://www.nytimes.com/2011/05/22/us/22bcstevens.html.
39. http://thehill.com/homenews/campaign/99103-unions-100m-to-save-the-dems.
40. http://online.wsj.com/article/SB100014240527023033395045755664817617900288.html.
41. http://www.nationalaffairs.com/publications/detail/the-trouble-with-public-sector-unions.
42. http://washingtonexaminer.com/opinion/special-reports/2011/01/special-report-where-cash-goes-democratic-policy-flows; http://www.cato.org/pubs/journal/cj30n1/cj30n1-2.pdf (p. 40).
43. http://www.nationalaffairs.com/publications/detail/the-trouble-with-public-sector-unions.
44. Max Green, *Epitaph for American Labor*, p. 166.
45. http://www.hoover.org/publications/policy-review/article/43266.
46. Ibid.
47. Ibid.
48. http://www.hoover.org/publications/policy-review/article/43266.
49. Thomas Sowell, *Inside American Education* (Simon and Schuster, 2003).
50. http://hotair.com/archives/2011/04/27/the-national-education-association-and-state-affiliates-a-1-5-billion-annual-enterprise/.
51. http://www.discoverthenetworks.org/printgroupProfile.asp?grpid=7428.
52. SEIU 990 IRS form.
53. http://www.wnd.com/index.php?fa=PAGE.printable&pageId=279141.
54. http://www.whitehouse.gov/the-press-office/president-obama-names-members-bipartisan-national-commission-fiscal-responsibility-.
55. http://www.investors.com/NewsAndAnalysis/ArticlePrint.aspx?id=561404.
56. http://online.wsj.com/article/SB100014240527023045213045764465122840667904.html.
57. http://www.discoverthenetworks.org/printgroupProfile.asp?grpid=7428.

Chapter 9. A Disturbing Prospect

1. David Callahan, *Fortunes of Change: The Rise of the Liberal Rich and the Remaking of America* (John Wiley and Sons, 2010), p. 155.
2. http://www.discoverthenetworks.org/Articles/A%20New%20Alliance%20Of%20Democrats.html.
3. Ibid.
4. http://www.denverpost.com/ci_10623568?source=rss.
5. http://www.weeklystandard.com/Content/Public/Articles/000/000/015/316nfdzw.asp.
6. http://nrd.nationalreview.com/article/?q=ODJmYWRlMDkxMzYxMzM1NTY3YmMwZDc1MzZmMmYzMGU.
7. http://www.weeklystandard.com/Content/Public/Articles/000/000/015/316nfdzw.asp.
8. Rob Witwer and Adam Schrager, *The Blueprint: How Democrats Won Colorado (and Why Republicans Everywhere Should Care)* (Speaker's Corner, 2010).
9. J. Christian Adams, *Injustice: Exposing the Racial Agenda of the Obama Justice Department* (Regnery, 2011).
10. http://www.truethevote.org/.
11. http://www.politifact.com/truth-o-meter/statements/2009/oct/01/michael-moore/michael-moore-claims-majority-favor-single-payer-h/.
12. Martin Morse Wooster, *The Great Philanthropists and the Problem of "Donor Intent"* (Capital Research Center, 2007); Heather Higgins: http://www.philanthropyroundtable.org/fileuploads/ShouldFoundationsExistinPerpetuity1.pdf.

ACKNOWLEDGMENTS

THE authors would like to thank John Perazzo and Mike Bauer, who originally compiled the profiles and data on left-wing funders for the website www.discoverthenetworks.org before updating it for this book. Stanley Kurtz's invaluable *Radical-in-Chief* provided much of the primary information for the chapter on Barack Obama. We would also like to thank Elizabeth Ruiz for her technical help and Mike Finch, without whose support this project would not have been possible.

INDEX